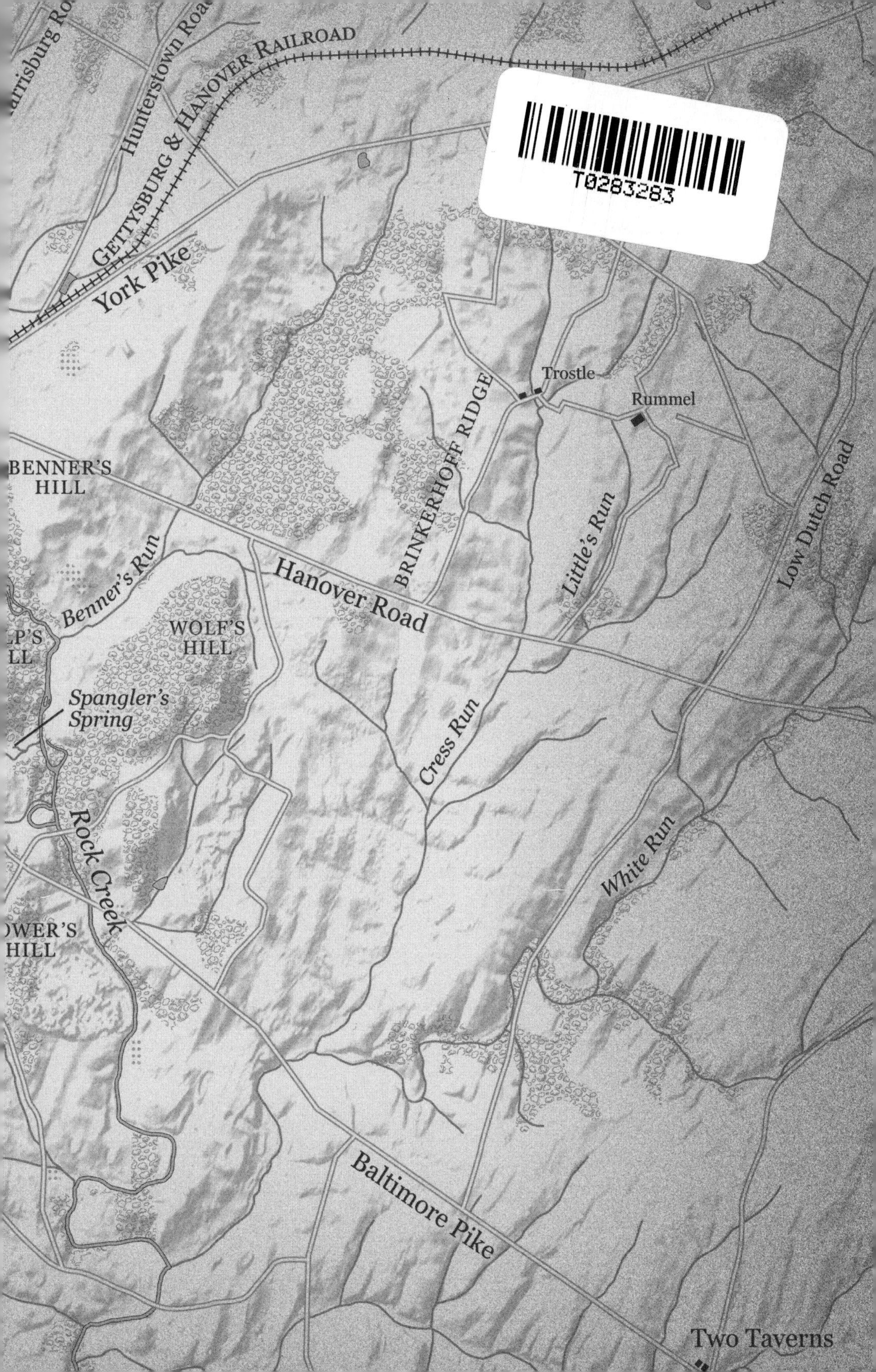

Gettysburg & Hanover Railroad
Hunterstown Road
York Pike
T0283283
Trostle
Rummel
Brinkerhoff Ridge
Benner's Hill
Benner's Run
Hanover Road
Little's Run
Low Dutch Road
Wolf's Hill
Spangler's Spring
Cress Run
Rock Creek
White Run
Baltimore Pike
Two Taverns

Voices from Gettysburg

VOICES FROM GETTYSBURG

LETTERS, PAPERS, AND MEMOIRS FROM THE GREATEST BATTLE OF THE CIVIL WAR

ALLEN C. GUELZO

CITADEL PRESS
KENSINGTON PUBLISHING CORP.
www.kensingtonbooks.com

CITADEL PRESS BOOKS are published by

Kensington Publishing Corp.
900 Third Avenue
New York, NY 10022

All Kensington titles, imprints, and distributed lines are available at special quantity discounts for bulk purchases for sales promotions, premiums, fund-raising, educational, or institutional use. Special book excerpts or customized printings can also be created to fit specific needs. For details, write or phone the office of the Kensington sales manager: Kensington Publishing Corp., 900 Third Avenue, New York, NY 10022, attn Sales Department; phone 1-800-221-2647.

10 9 8 7 6 5 4 3 2 1

First Citadel hardcover printing: June 2024

Printed in the United States of America

ISBN: 978-0-8065-4338-3

ISBN: 978-0-8065-4340-6 (e-book)

Library of Congress Control Number: 2024930264

CONTENTS

AUTHOR'S NOTE

I have been what you might call a "Civil War person" ever since my boyhood, growing up in Pennsylvania in the 1960s. My first comic book was not *Superman*, but *The Red Badge of Courage*; the book I read off its hinges was not Sterling North's *Rascal*, but the *American Heritage Picture History of the Civil War*. Ironically, I was not a history major in college, and it was not until I was a senior undergraduate that I first visited Gettysburg. However, walking out onto the overlook of the old Visitors Center on Cemetery Hill on a balmy spring day in 1975, I was able to recognize, from books I had read in the fifteen years before, every prominent point on the battlefield: The Angle, Seminary Ridge, Little Round Top. It was the beginning of a scholarly romance that propelled me toward fifteen years directing the Civil War Era Studies Program and The Gettysburg Semester at Gettysburg College, and climaxed with me writing *Gettysburg: The Last Invasion* in 2013.

The volume you now hold in your hands grew out of those fifteen years teaching the Civil War and especially the battle of Gettysburg to undergraduates who were fully as enthusiastic as I had been about the Civil War and the great battle. What I learned from that experience, and from writing *Gettysburg: The Last Invasion*, was that there was no substitute for listening to the voices of those who had been at Gettysburg in 1863, whether soldiers or civilians. Americans of the Civil War years enjoyed unprecedented levels of literacy and did not hesitate to record what they had seen, heard, and done in a flood of letters, diaries, and memoirs. This collection is only a sampling of what was written by "they who fought here." But it will allow you to walk from point to point on the battlefield with their words in your hands, to speak to you as you view the places where they gave "the last full measure of devotion." Or it will allow you to read great narratives of the battle with substantial texts of the participants beside you to accompany those narratives. Or it will simply allow the voices of a long-ago moment of tremendous crisis in American history to speak to you whenever you wish.

There will always be a question about how readily historians should rely on reminiscence material. Soldiers in combat can rarely afford to pay much attention to anything beyond what happens a few yards around them, and there are more than a few so-called memoir writers—I think particularly of Augustus Buell, the Union "Cannoneer," and William Swallow, the Confederate staff officer—whose colorful recollections of Gettysburg were, in fact, frauds. Joshua Lawrence Chamberlain's 1913 recounting of the 20th Maine's famous stand on Little Round Top was dismissed by other officers of the regiment as full of "boasting or misrepresentations" due to a "notorious inability to tell the truth." (Chamberlain's account is included here, largely because it became the basis, rightly or wrongly, for John Pullen's famous 1957 regimental history, *The Twentieth Maine*, and Michael Shaara's Pulitzer Prize–winning novel, *The Killer Angels*, in 1974.) On the other hand, reminiscence materials—such as the ones that appear within this text—cannot be totally dismissed, either. Charles Morse, of the 2nd Massachusetts Volunteer Infantry, is represented here by two documents: a letter he wrote shortly after the battle and a lecture he gave decades later. The two documents track with remarkable similarity the events on Culp's Hill in the evening that unites July 2nd and July 3rd, 1863, so it is likely that Morse's lecture was composed with his 1863 letter (or a copy) before him. The same thing can doubtless be said of many other Gettysburg remembrances. Not only were the events experienced in the great battle seared into memories that endured the passage of time, but even the writing of them years later may have been based on letters and diary entries from the battle itself.

There are several other important sources of Gettysburg-related materials, especially in the officers' after-action reports in *The War of the Rebellion: A Compilation of the Official Records of the Union and Confederate Armies*, and in David and Audrey Ladd's edition of *The Bachelder Papers* (the three volumes of John B. Bachelder's correspondence with Gettysburg veterans, published in 1994 by Morningside Press). Since these are both available in a variety of formats (including online), I have been deliberately sparing in any use of them, preferring to rely on previously untouched or less famous sources (in regimental histories or in veterans' newspapers, such as *Confederate Veteran* and the *National Tribune*).

The cover art is from the famous cyclorama painting of the battle of Gettysburg, created by Paul Philippoteaux in 1883. The portion of the painting reproduced here shows an incident at the height of Pickett's Charge, described by Sergeant Frederick Fuger in one of the documents in *Voices from Gettysburg*. The illustrations embedded in the text are taken from the famous *Battles and Leaders of the Civil War* series and from regimental histories of the nineteenth century. The maps were drawn by that veteran Gettysburg mapmaker, Hal Jesperson. A special word of thanks goes to Morgan Silliman Heller and family for permission to use the letters of Capt. James Silliman, and to Ramesh Ponnuru, the editor of *National Review*, for permission to use parts of my 2013 article on Alexander Stewart Webb.

Many people over the years have made Gettysburg a very special place, entirely apart from the remembrance of the battle: teachers such as Linward A. Crowe; students including John, Jess, Brian, Evan, Lauren, Skye, Zachery, Tom, and Dan; colleagues such as Jack, Diane, Ian, Gabor, Alan, Cathy, Tim, and Carol; friends and neighbors Wendy, Elayne, Bill, Fran, Ray, Wayne, Tommy, and Paul; and many, many more. To this roster, I add my co-workers in the James Madison Program in American Ideals and Institutions at Princeton University: Robert P. George, Bradford P. Wilson, Shilo Brooks, Debby Parker, Annika Nordquist, Christine Johnson, and Jonathan Garaffa. My friends Lewis and Louise Lehrman, Thomas Klingenstein, Roger Hertog, Robert Giuffra, Mark O'Brien, Mark Berner, and the Thomas W. Smith Foundation deserve a special word of praise. This book is one small tribute to them and all that they have meant to me and my wife, Debra.

Voices from Gettysburg

INTRODUCTION

"The Waterloo of the Rebellion"

Looking back over twenty years, Alexander Stewart Webb declared that the battle of "Gettysburg . . . was, and is now throughout the world, known to be the Waterloo of the Rebellion." Certainly, Webb had earned the right to speak with authority about Gettysburg. He was twenty-six years old when the American Civil War broke out in 1861, and even though this grandson of a minuteman at Bunker Hill was only six years out of West Point, he rocketed up the ladder of promotion to brigadier general just a week before the Union and Confederate armies collided in a brutal, three-day hammering at the little south-central Pennsylvania town of Gettysburg. It fell to Webb in particular to command the Union brigade which absorbed the spearpoint of the battle's climax, the great charge made by the rebel divisions commanded by George E. Pickett. Webb would survive Gettysburg, and a nearly fatal wound to the head a year after, and eventually go on to become the president of the City College of New York, where a life-size bronze statue of him was installed in 1917 on Convent Avenue at 138th Street. But in his memory, the fattest ring in the tree would always be Gettysburg. "This three days' contest," Webb announced, "was a constant recurrence of scenes of self-sacrifice," especially "on the part of all engaged on the third and last day."

More than a century and a half later, it might be warranted to question if Alexander Webb was suffering from a touch of memory-myopia, inflating the risk—all experiences of his youth under the pressures of peacetime middle age. The name *Gettysburg* is still powerful enough to register in the recognition of even the most reluctant grade-schooler as a big-box event in American history. But we may wonder, does it deserve to stand beside Waterloo?

Except, of course, that it does. Call Gettysburg, if you like, the hinge of fate, or the high-water mark of the Confederacy, or the beginning of the end of the American Civil War. Gettysburg really was what James A. Wright, who fought there in a Minnesota regiment, called "a great battle—not only on account of the numbers engaged and the deadly intensity and determined pertinacity with which it was fought—but also on account of the tremendous issues involved, military and political, at home and abroad." Even more, it was, in practical effect, the last solid chance the breakaway Southern states which made up the Confederate States of America had of winning the war and their independence.

In the first ten months of the Civil War, from April 1861 to February 1862, nearly everything seemed to go the way of the Confederacy: eleven Southern states of the American Union announced their secession from the Union; they wrote a constitution and elected a president, Jefferson Davis; and their hastily assembled army defeated an equally hastily assembled United States army at Bull Run, in Virginia. But in the early spring of 1862, the current began to swerve. Union armies and the Union navy reconquered all but a few stretches of the Mississippi River Valley, and reoccupied western Tennessee. In the east, Confederate fortunes met with more cheering success. But this was largely due to the leadership of Robert E. Lee (and the incompetence of many of his Federal opponents).

Lee had enjoyed a long career in the United States Army, and at the very outset of the year, he had even been offered field command of Union forces. But when his home state of Virginia left the Union to join the Confederacy, Lee went with it. He rose to command Virginia's state forces, then served as a military adviser to Jefferson Davis. Put in charge of the Confederacy's Army of Northern Virginia in June 1862, Lee led his ragtag Confederates to one implausible victory after another over their opposite number, the Union Army of the Potomac.

But the victories were all won on Virginia's soil, and enfeebled the Virginia economy even as they defended it. Lee knew better than any other Southerner that the Confederacy's resources were too limited to keep fending off the Confederacy's enemy indefinitely. Only by carrying the war into the Union states, and only by leveraging the war-weariness of the Union voting public into peace negotiations, could the Confederacy hope to win its independence. Still, this was by no means a far-fetched hope. In the fall of 1862, dissension over President Abraham Lincoln's Emancipation Proclamation had caused unhappy voters in New York and New Jersey to install Democratic governors there; a new round of anti-war Democratic candidates were due to run in the fall 1863 governors' elections in Ohio and Pennsylvania. If those states elected anti-war governors and also turned against the war, they could force Lincoln either to begin peace talks, or to resign.

Lee's army, some 85,000 strong, struck northward in the second week of June, crossing the Potomac River and sweeping in a long arc up the Cumberland Valley until his advance guard was perched on the Susquehanna River, overlooking the Pennsylvania state capital of Harrisburg. Lee's real goal, however, was not Harrisburg; what he really hoped was to lure the Army of the Potomac northward after him, and as soon as the Yankees had strung themselves out on the roads beyond their ability to help each other, to turn and smash the straggling parts of the Union army, piece by piece, as he had planned the year before in Maryland. But even if all Lee did was to let the clock run as his army ravaged central Pennsylvania, he could simply let the politics of disheartenment take their own course in the North thereafter.

It nearly worked. "The . . . *morale* of the army was never more favorable for offensive or defensive operations," wrote one Virginian. "Victory will inevitably attend our arms in any collision with the enemy." True to Lee's expectation, the 95,000 men of the Army of the Potomac, panting and uncertain, set off after him, and as soon as Lee was satisfied that they had frantically marched themselves into disarray, he ordered a concentration of his own army at the south-central Pennsylvania crossroads town and county seat of Gettysburg, only seven miles from the

Maryland-Pennsylvania state line. Lee believed his army would be ready to pounce on the first parts of the Army of the Potomac that obligingly wandered within his reach, but the lead elements of the Army of the Potomac, commanded by Major-General John Fulton Reynolds, got to Gettysburg first, and when Lee's own advance units arrived there on July 1st, they found Union troops holding on for dear life to the ground west of the town. Luckily, there were not many of them—only three of the Army of the Potomac's seven infantry corps—and by day's end on July 1st, Lee's army was able to clear them away from the west of the town and forced them to abandon the town of Gettysburg in a hugely disorganized flight.

But at dusk, the Union soldiers were still holding one strategic height south of the town, known ominously as Cemetery Hill (from the fact that the town burial ground, with its ceremonial arched gateway, was perched on it). Lee assumed that he could wait for daylight to finish the job. However, by the morning of July 2nd, three more infantry corps of the Army of the Potomac had raced up from Maryland to Gettysburg, and Lee was forced to mount a bloody and ambitious assault on a series of Union positions—the Peach Orchard, the Wheatfield, Little Round Top—whose bland and harmless names belied the viciousness of the fighting that raged around them late into the evening.

Lee's attack on July 2nd, organized by his principal lieutenant, James Longstreet, came within an ace of succeeding, so on the next day, Lee

launched Longstreet again in what Lee assumed would be the final blow for a Union army now clearly on the ropes. Lee sent one division of fresh rebel infantry, commanded by George E. Pickett, alongside parts of two other divisions from the earlier days' fights, straight at the vital nape of the Union army's neck, just behind Cemetery Hill. The rebels indeed punched holes in the Union defenses in what would always be known afterward as Pickett's Charge, but they couldn't hold them. Amazed at the failure of his gambit and appalled at the cost in lives, Lee ordered his army to retreat back across the Potomac.

Just on those terms alone, Gettysburg was an unmistakable sign of Confederate disaster. A soldier in Joseph Kershaw's South Carolina brigade complained that "I think we paid dearly for our trip into" Pennsylvania. "We gave 20 thousand mens lives for a few cattle horses & wagons. I think our confederacy is gone up the spout . . . Our men is badly disheartened" and "are beginning to think this war wont end til we are all killed & it wont take long if they make many such mistakes as they have bin making." Across the South, reported the *Southern Literary Messenger*, "there is great depression, and in many States positive disaffection." (It did not brighten Southern hopes that one day after the close of Gettysburg, the last Confederate outpost on the Mississippi River, Vicksburg, surrendered to Ulysses S. Grant, thus giving the Union—and Abraham Lincoln—the happiest weekend they had yet enjoyed in the war.)

Lee would never regain the military initiative in the war. Although fighting would go on for another twenty-one months, the Confederates were confined to the sort of defensive warfare they could least afford. "The ebbing of that sea of blood and flame was still slow and sullen," wrote one Maine veteran, but "its waves were never again to dash so high against the sturdy barriers that withstood the shock of its tide of destruction. And no more should it threaten to overleap the living walls that restrained it, and to break across the broad North in a resistless flood of desolation."

There were other, more immediate, costs for the Confederacy imposed by Gettysburg. The Army of Northern Virginia reported 2,592 killed, 12,709 wounded, and 5,150 "captured or missing" after Gettysburg—20,451 casualties in all, based on data collected by the army's chief medical officer, Lafayette Guild. Given the inadequacy of military record-keeping in the Civil War—there were no identifying dog tags, no graves registration units in the nineteenth-century armies—these losses may have been even higher.

But even beyond the simple numerical shock of the casualty lists, Lee's army suffered a body blow to its command infrastructure from which it never adequately recovered. This will give some idea of the damage done to chains of command in the Army of Northern Virginia: Of Lee's fifty-two generals at Gettysburg, a third of them became casualties of some sort, including major-generals (Isaac Trimble, Dorsey Pender, Harry Heth, John Bell Hood) and brigadier-generals (Lewis Armistead, William Barksdale, Richard Garnett, Paul Semmes, George "Tige" Anderson, Alfred Scales, James Kemper, James Johnston Pettigrew, Jerome Bonaparte Robertson, John M. Jones, Albert Jenkins, Wade Hampton, James J. Archer). As individuals, all of these officer casualties could be replaced, but their months and years of experience, familiarity, networking, and confidence could not.

Of course, if we want to measure Gettysburg purely by the numbers, then the battle imposed even higher costs on the Union army. George Gordon Meade, who commanded the Army of the Potomac at Gettysburg, cited 2,834 of his own men killed, 13,713 wounded, and 6,643 missing; two months later, he adjusted those numbers slightly, and then submitted final figures that set the totals at 3,155 killed, 14,529 wounded, and 5,365 "captured or missing." In testimony before a joint congressional committee in 1864, Meade rounded his estimate upward to "24,000 men killed, wounded and missing." In 1900, Thomas Livermore scanned the unit reports for the Army of the Potomac and recalculated the bill at 3,903 dead, 18,735 wounded, and 5,425 "missing," meaning that the overall cost to the Union army at Gettysburg edged up to 28,063. And, like the Confederates, there was damage to the Union's upper command echelon: One major-general commanding a corps was killed—John Fulton Reynolds, of the 1st Corps—and another was mangled and put out of action—Daniel Sickles, of the 3rd Corps.

Michael Jacobs, a mathematics professor at Pennsylvania College (which was located on the northern outskirts of Gettysburg), estimated in the book he hurriedly published in the fall of 1863, *Notes on the Rebel Invasion of Maryland and Pennsylvania*, that there were in total "9000 dead" in and around Gettysburg after the two armies moved on. If we grant Jacobs his high-end estimate and accept a ratio (based on the official statistics) of five wounded for every man killed, then we have to reckon on each army suffering something like 4,500 killed and 22,500 wounded—which translates into approximately a third of each army dead or maimed in some way. In other words, three times the bloodletting suffered, in percentages, by the British and allied forces at Waterloo.

But even with those costs, Gettysburg meant something entirely different for the Union. "What do the people of the North think now of the Old Army of the Potomac?" exulted a soldier in the 28th Pennsylvania. John White Geary, who commanded a division in the 12th Corps, wrote to his wife that "the result of the war seems no longer doubtful, and . . . the beginning of the end appears." "The victory at Gettysburg gave proof that our days of pupilage in the art of war were over," rejoiced a contributor to the *New Englander and Yale Review*, "and that at last we could develop and direct our forces."

The success at Gettysburg, coming hand in hand with the capture of Vicksburg, prompted Lincoln's chief of staff, John Nicolay, to remark that "public feeling has been wonderfully improved and buoyed up by our recent successes at Gettysburg and Vicksburg." Lincoln himself was delighted. He addressed a noisy demonstration of well-wishers at the White House on July 7th by drawing a symbolic bright line between Independence Day and the Gettysburg victory: "How long ago is it?—eighty odd years—since on the Fourth of July for the first time in the history of the world a nation by its representatives, assembled and declared as a self-evident truth that 'all men are created equal.'"

The victories of Gettysburg and Vicksburg, coming on the anniversary of that self-evident truth, had now put "the cohorts of those who opposed the declaration that all men are created equal" on the run. Even the newspapers crowed that any "escape from our army will be a matter of great difficulty," and predicted that if Lee was pursued and brought to bay, a "great, if not, indeed, a decisive victory over the insurgents" would follow.

But perhaps a better way to measure the importance of Gettysburg for granting the Union a second wind would be to consider what the alternative might have been. Richard Henry Dana, the prominent Boston lawyer and literary lion, believed that Gettysburg "was the turning-point in our history," not so much for winning a victory as for avoiding a defeat that would have proven to be the Army of the Potomac's—and the Union's—*last* defeat. "Had Lee gained that battle, the Democrats would have risen and stopped the war," Dana asserted. "With the city of New York and Governor [Horatio] Seymour, and Governor [Joel] Parker in New Jersey, and a majority in Pennsylvania, as they then would have had, they would so have crippled us as to end the contest. That they would have attempted it we at home know."

That would only have been the best scenario. "I do not hesitate to express the conviction," wrote one observer of the battle, "that, had the Army of the Potomac been whipped at Gettysburg . . . it would have dissolved." Doubtless "some of the other volunteer regiments would have held together and made some sort of retreat toward the Susquehanna," but the others would simply have melted away just as Napoleon's army disintegrated after Waterloo, leaving "the rebel chieftain . . . at liberty to go where and do what he pleased."

Other veterans of the battle nodded vigorously in agreement. Vermonter George Benedict wrote six months after the battle that if Lee had been successful, it "would doubtless have been the signal for organized outbreaks of the Northern allies of the Confederacy in Baltimore, Philadelphia and New York." It would even "have assured the fall of the National capital." Captain Alfred Lee, an Ohioan who fought at Gettysburg in a regiment that saw twenty of its twenty-two officers killed or wounded, dreaded the prospect of "the Northern sympathizers with secession" rising up in anti-war resistance that "would have established mob rule over the whole chain of Atlantic cities, torn up the railroads, destroyed supplies, cut off reinforcements, and thus paralyzed the whole machinery of our Government."

Even the Confederates thought so. Theodore Dodge, a Union officer who was seriously wounded and captured at Gettysburg, remembered that his rebel captors were "confident . . . that it would result in a peace favorable to the Confederacy; their usual argument being that the Northern Democrats would soon see an end put to the war, and an honorable peace secured to their brother politicians South."

As it was, New York City blew up in draft riots ten days after the battle. If Robert E. Lee had been crossing the Susquehanna at that time, it might conceivably have been the Army of Northern Virginia that was called in to restore order, rather than Union veterans and New York state militia fresh from the Gettysburg campaign. Gettysburg did not end the war in one stroke, but it was decisive enough to restore the sinking morale of the Union, decisive enough to keep at bay the forces that hoped Lincoln could be persuaded to revoke emancipation, decisive enough to make people look back and understand that the Confederacy would never be able to mount a serious invasion again.

Abraham Lincoln, however, was not satisfied with just a "decisive enough" result. After a desultory ten-day pursuit that ended with the Army of the Potomac chasing Lee's army into a pocket with its back to a rain-flooded Potomac River, nothing was done by Meade's infantry to strike at the rebels. During the night of July 13-14th, Lee's damaged army was able to slip across the Potomac on improvised bridges and barely usable fords to re-recruit, resupply, and carry the war onward, and with little more than brief rear-guard clash. "We had them in our grasp," Lincoln wailed. "We had only to stretch forth our hands & they were ours."

A great deal of the blame for Lee's escape was laid by Lincoln, and by others, at the feet of George Meade. "I do not believe you appreciate the magnitude of the misfortune involved in Lee's escape," Lincoln wrote to Meade, and again, the image of the unclosed hand came to him. "He was within your easy grasp, and to have closed upon him would, in connection with our other late successes, have ended the war." Deciding instead to be grateful for what Meade actually had won at Gettysburg, Lincoln filed the letter away, scribbling on the envelope, "To Gen. Meade, never sent, or signed." But the failure to make Gettysburg the complete victory Lincoln had been hoping for always hung like a cloud over the unhappy George Meade.

There is an element of injustice in this. Meade had only been shoved into command of the Army of the Potomac three days before the battle, and he was compelled by circumstances to pick up the army where he found it, using a staff he had no time to replace, and under the unappreciative gaze of other major-generals who saw no reason to yield their freshly promoted equal any automatic deference. That Meade did as well as he did in the face of a confident and aggressive opponent in Robert E. Lee rightly earns him one of the principal military laurels of the Civil War.

On those grounds, there have been serious efforts, from time to time, to refashion Meade in glowing and sympathetic colors, as the unsung genius who bettered the Confederacy's best. Few of them have been entirely successful, and a large part of the reason lies with Meade himself. At first meeting, the nearsighted Philadelphia aristocrat "might have been taken for a Presbyterian clergyman"—that is, "unless one approached him when he was mad," for Meade possessed a volcanic temper, which did not require much to trigger, and his "irritability of temper, and over-sensitiveness to implied censure or criticism on the part of the newspapers" were notorious.

No one questioned Meade's personal courage or competence. But he was not a lovable or dashing commander. In September 1862, Meade chased down a private who had pinched "two large bundles" of straw from a farmer's field in Maryland and demanded that the soldier take them back. "General, I suppose I will have to obey your order, but if you were not wearing shoulder straps, I'll be d—— if I would." Enraged, Meade dismounted, "pulled off his coat," and "struck him aside of the head and almost knocked him over." Meade was just as hard on his superiors. "I am tired of this playing war without risks," Meade declared angrily. "We must encounter risks if we fight, and we cannot carry on war without fighting."

Yet, the real flaw in George Meade was not his fiery temper, but, ironically, the same aversion to taking risks that he complained about in other generals. Once in command of the Army of the Potomac, he saw his task as purely defensive: shadow Lee's army as it moved in its great swift arc into Pennsylvania, but keep between the rebels and Washington and Baltimore. "I can only now say that it appears to me I must move toward the Susquehanna," Meade wrote, "keeping Washington and Baltimore well covered." Only if "the enemy is checked in his attempt to cross the Susquehanna, or if he turns toward Baltimore" would Meade try "to give him battle."

Once Lee's army turned away from the Susquehanna to concentrate near Gettysburg, Meade considered his work done, and his first impulse thereafter was to pull his own army back, dig it in behind Pipe Creek, twenty-five miles southeast, and thus keep a shield in place between the Confederates and the capital—not to go hunting for a high-noon encounter with Lee. Having "relieved Harrisburg and Philadelphia," Meade concluded that it was now time "to look to his own army, and assume position for offensive or defensive, as occasion requires, or rest to the troops." And that meant "the collecting of our troops behind Pipe Creek . . ."

If Meade's plan had been obeyed, moaned one 1st Corps staffer, "General Lee in all probability would have simply left one Corps [of the rebel army] in observation, while he would have ravaged the whole country with the other two Corps and have taken Harrisburg." But the order was not obeyed, or at least not uniformly by Meade's seven corps commanders, and especially not by John Reynolds, who directed the three army corps that made up the Army of the Potomac's left wing. Much more than Meade, it was Reynolds who precipitated an encounter at Gettysburg. Reynolds complained that if Meade gave the rebels "time by dilatory measures or by taking up defensive positions they would strip" Pennsylvania "of everything." Reynolds was eager "to attack the enemy at once, to prevent his plundering the whole State." We must, Reynolds announced, "get at the enemy as soon as possible and fight them at once as they were plundering the richest part of the State of Pennsylvania and gaining immense supplies of all kind for their army." Reynolds knew south-central Pennsylvania as his home, and Gettysburg "as the place where he intended to make a final stand." In his last message to Meade on July 1st—*last,* because a few minutes later, Reynolds would be shot dead by a Confederate skirmisher as the battle opened west of Gettysburg—Reynolds said, "While I am aware that it is not your desire to force an engagement at that point, still I feel at liberty to advance and develop the strength of the enemy."

Even after Reynolds's death, Meade still tried to recall his prematurely committed troops from Gettysburg. (Reynolds's successor in command of the left wing, Oliver Otis Howard, was rumored to have "received five distinct orders from Gen. Meade to withdraw his forces and not attempt to hold the position he had chosen" on Cemetery Hill.) Not until he had sent off his own eyes and ears to Gettysburg in the form of Major-General Winfield Scott Hancock did Meade finally relent and order a concentration at Gettysburg. Even then, after the battering given the Army of the Potomac on July 2nd—which rivaled Antietam as the single bloodiest day of the Civil War—Meade was still debating whether to fall back to Pipe Creek, and called a war council of his corps commanders to consider it. They refused, but not without expressing an element of surprise that Meade even wanted to talk about it. "Good God," exclaimed a division commander in the 2nd Corps, "Gen. Meade is not going to retreat, is he?"

No, he was not, but the credit may have to be shared by Meade with a hefty list of lower-ranking officers in the Army of the Potomac, who, time and again during the three days of the battle, seized the initiative on their own and kept the Army of the Potomac from falling apart. Names that most of us have never heard before—George Sears Greene, Samuel Sprigg Carroll, Francis Heath, Patrick Henry O'Rorke, Strong Vincent, Gouverneur Warren, Norman Hall, George Stannard, Joshua Lawrence Chamberlain, who actually became the centerpiece of a Pulitzer Prize–winning novel and a full-length movie about the battle—introduce Union men who, over and over again, with miraculous spontaneity, took responsibility on themselves to act, and somehow to act in just the right fashion.

These unheralded performances became almost routine for junior Union officers at Gettysburg. By comparison, Meade's command behavior at Gettysburg was almost entirely reactive. Many of his soldiers never forgave him. "Whatever Gen. Meade's intentions were," wrote a Wisconsin officer in 1902, "his action was not only a terrible mistake, but a piece of gross injustice and inhumanity," while one of Meade's staffers complained that "Meade's was an accidental victory, and he would not risk his fame." Taking a little of his own advice about risks might have made George Meade the most famous general in American history. What he accomplished was a magnificent gift to the Union; what has always tarnished the edges of that gift, fairly or unfairly, was the lost opportunity to have ended the war entirely. "Oh! How I wished at that time that we had an officer like Napoleon at the head of the Army of the Potomac," wrote another headquarters staffer, "instead of the vascillating and timid General who then commanded it!"

It remained for Abraham Lincoln to illumine the ultimate significance of Gettysburg, in the address given at the dedication of the national cemetery laid out on Cemetery Hill in the months after the battle. The words of the Gettysburg Address have been worn so familiar with usage that it may be hard now to realize the depths of meaning in Lincoln's "few, brief remarks"—all of 272 words—at that dedication in November 1863.

In Lincoln's mind, the fundamental significance of Gettysburg—and the Civil War—was the survival of democracy itself and whether "any nation so conceived and so dedicated can long endure." Remember that in 1863, democracy was by no means a given, and by no means what contemporary American political scientist Francis Fukuyama called "the end of history." Far from it: Every experiment in democracy launched in the heyday of popular revolutions had gone up in smoke, with the most smoke emerging from the French Revolution. Everywhere in 1863, monarchy and privilege seemed to be on the march while the last outpost of democracy was obligingly shooting itself through the head in a civil war and thereby demonstrating that democracies were inherently unstable.

How, argued the aristocrats, could they help but be so? Democracies are run by the consent of the governed—by the ordinary people of a nation themselves—and as aristocrats well know, ordinary people can be ordinary in very mean, very selfish, very cowardly, and very dull ways. The American democracy had been exhibiting signs of dysfunction ever since its founding by tolerating the abomination of slavery. How could anyone speak realistically of all men being created equal when some of those equal men were allowed to own others in the same way one might own a horse or a pig?

Lincoln, however, saw in the battle of Gettysburg a shaft of sunlight in the storm. The war was testing, as the great historian Allan Nevins once put it, "whether a democracy of continental dimensions and idealistic commitments could triumphantly survive, or must ignobly perish." Gettysburg, with its dead, was proof that there were a great many of those supposedly dull and ordinary people who were willing to make the ultimate sacrifice to preserve the solidarity of their nation and the right to self-government and the propositions around which it was built. Lincoln could not look out across the semicircular avenues of the dead in that cemetery—where fully a quarter of the 3,900 men buried there were unknowns—and not feel confirmed in the longevity of democracy, and in calling on living Americans to dedicate themselves "to that cause for which they gave the last full measure of devotion," and ensure that "government of the people, by the people, for the people, shall not perish from the earth."

That brings us the final answer to the question of Gettysburg's importance. Yes, it had great military significance, as the victory that cracked the image and power of Robert E. Lee and his army and gave the Union armies their second wind. The sheer scale of the carnage and death the battle visited—not only on the soldiers, but on every family and household linked to those soldiers—is past any calculating that numbers can do. But even more, Gettysburg still sings for us because of how Abraham Lincoln translated the raw experience of the seething chasm of battle into an anthem of democracy.

"The battle of Gettysburg is the most important battle of this century," said Union brigadier-general James Clay Rice in November 1863, "a battle which resolved the greatest political problem of this age and of all ages to come . . . whether the United States should be all free or all slave—whether the flag of oppression should flaunt in every banner, or the banner of freedom . . . be set up, forever, throughout the land."

So, was Alex Webb right after all? Was Gettysburg really "the Waterloo of the Rebellion"? The answer to that question, in the words of those who fought there, is spread before you in this book.

THE SITUATION

1863

After its initial season of victories in the summer and fall of 1861, the tide of the American Civil War turned abruptly against the Southern Confederacy. In February 1862, Union forces in Tennessee, under the unlikely command of a former U.S. Army officer named Ulysses Grant, struck suddenly at the two principal barrier fortifications of the upper Confederacy, at Fort Henry on the Tennessee River and Fort Donelson on the Cumberland River. Both surrendered after little more than token resistance, which opened a river pathway straight into the heart of the western parts of the Confederacy. An attempt by a hastily gathered Confederate army to plug the hole blown in the Confederacy's defenses at the battle of Shiloh failed, and within weeks, the Confederacy's greatest seaport, New Orleans, was captured by the U.S. Navy. At the same time, an immense Union army—Major-General George B. McClellan's Army of the Potomac—landed on Virginia's James River peninsula in a daring army-navy combined operation and began slowly steamrolling its way to the outer suburbs of the Confederacy's capital in Richmond.

It was at this moment that Confederate president Jefferson Davis turned to Robert E. Lee, and in a dramatic reversal of Confederate fortunes, Lee and his Army of Northern Virginia not only drove McClellan away from Richmond, but bounded northward to defeat another Federal army at the second battle of Bull Run, and then leaped across the Potomac River to invade Maryland. Confederate leaders began the Civil War believing that all they would need to secure their independence was a defensive strategy that would simply fend off Union invasions or, at worst, "decoy the enemy into the interior, and then to cut them off as were Braddock, and Burgoyne." Lee, who had served two tours of duty in New

York in the old U.S. Army and knew the power the Northern economy could bring to bear, understood that the Confederacy could not sit on its haunches. "I think it all important that we should assume the aggressive," he advised the Confederate leaders, urging a campaign north of the Potomac. A Confederate invasion of the North would trigger "a great change in public opinion in the North." Lincoln's "Republicans will be destroyed," and Northern Democrats acting as "the friends of peace will become so strong as that the next administration will go in on that basis." Otherwise, if Confederate armies merely tried to protect their territory, Union armies would simply clamp sieges around their cities and that would be the end. Follow that course, Lee scolded one of his subordinates, and the result "would be but a work of time."

Lee's calculated aggressiveness was reinforced by his chief lieutenant, Thomas Jonathan "Stonewall" Jackson, who had been badgering Confederate politicians like Alexander R. Boteler to launch Confederate forces northward to the Susquehanna River as early as his celebrated campaign against Union forces in the Shenandoah Valley in the spring of 1862. But when Lee and Jackson invaded Maryland that fall, the results were disappointing, especially after a copy of Lee's campaign orders fell into Union hands, revealing the details of his invasion plans. Cornered by McClellan and the Army of the Potomac at the Antietam Creek in western Maryland, Lee's Army of Northern Virginia survived an all-day hammering and escaped across the Potomac River back into Virginia. But it had been an exceedingly close call. It was almost a relief when the Army of the Potomac launched two new offensives of its own in Virginia, under two new commanders, Ambrose Burnside and Joseph Hooker. Lee handily turned them back, first at Fredericksburg, in December 1862, and then at Chancellorsville, in May 1863.

Those months became the winter of the Union's discontent. In the West, Grant's early victories lost their momentum, especially after a failed attempt by Grant and his principal subordinate, William T. Sherman, to strike at the Confederate citadel of Vicksburg on the Mississippi River that December. Horace Greeley, the longtime anti-slavery editor of America's most widely read newspaper, the *New-York Tribune*, lamented that these were "the darkest hours of the National cause," and discouraged Northerners turned in increasing numbers to Abraham Lincoln's opponents to bring peace. In state election after state election in the fall of 1862, the majorities won by Lincoln's Republican Party in the election of 1860 were whittled dangerously thin. Lincoln's Emancipation Proclamation, freeing three million slaves in the Confederacy, was announced on September 22, 1862 (and signed into law by him on January 1, 1863). But that, together with a new military draft, only strengthened Northern disenchantment with the Lincoln administration's war effort. The Republican Party lost more than thirty seats in Congress in the November 1862 off-year elections, and they were staring at more opposition in 1863 after the defeats at Fredericksburg and Chancellorsville as voters went to the polls in Pennsylvania and Ohio to elect governors there.

The Confederacy was jubilant at the news of Lee's victories, but Lee was not. Chancellorsville had cost him the life of Jackson, and the terrible losses he had inflicted on the Army of the Potomac could be made up by fresh Northern enlistments. They would be back, with new recruits, new equipment, and new generals, while the South would be slowly ground to powder. "We had really accomplished nothing," Lee complained. "We had not gained a foot of ground, and I knew the enemy could easily replace the men he had lost." Instead, Lee proposed a fresh invasion north of the Potomac. He remained convinced that the Confederacy's best hope lay in stoking Union war weariness to the point where voters would rebel against further support for the Lincoln administration. A successful Confederate invasion of Pennsylvania in the summer of 1863 might win more governors' races for anti-Lincoln candidates and create a solid bloc of opposition states whose weight would force Lincoln to the negotiating table. A strategy of "dividing and weakening our enemies" and giving encouragement to "the rising peace party of the North" would likely bring the war to an end, and the Confederacy its independence.

Horace Greeley, *The American Conflict: A History of the Great Rebellion in the United States of America, 1860–'65* (Hartford, CT, 1866), Vol. 2

Unquestionably the darkest hours of the National cause were those which separated [Major-General Ambrose E.] Burnside's and [Major-General William T.] Sherman's bloody repulses, at Fredericksburg [on December 13, 1862] and Vicksburg [at Chickasaw Bayou, December 26-29, 1862] respectively from the triumphs of Meade at Gettysburg, Grant in the fall of Vicksburg, and [Major-General Nathaniel P.] Banks in the surrender of Port Hudson. Our intermediate and subordinate reverses at Galveston, and at Chancellorsville, also tended strongly to sicken the hearts of Unionists and strengthen into confidence the hopes of the Rebels and those who, whether in the loyal States or in foreign lands, were in sympathy, if not also in act, their virtual allies. No one in Europe but those who ardently desired our success spoke of disunion otherwise than as an accomplished fact, which only purblind obstinacy and the invincible lust of power constrained us for a time to ignore. Hence, when the French Emperor [Napoleon III] made, during the dark Winter of 1862-3, a formal, diplomatic proffer of his good offices as a mediator between the American belligerents, he was regarded and treated on all hands as proposing to arrange the terms of a just, satisfactory, and conclusive separation between the North and the South . . .

The State elections of 1863 opened in New Hampshire; where the Republican party barely escaped defeat; losing one of the three Representatives in Congress for the first time in some years, and saving their Governor [Joseph A. Gilmore] through his election by the Legislature; he not having even a plurality of the popular vote. The regular Democratic poll was larger than at any former election.

The next State to hold her Election was Rhode Island; where the Republicans triumphed, electing both Representatives in Congress as well as their State ticket; but by a majority considerably reduced from that exhibited on any clear trial of party strength for some years.

Connecticut had, by common consent, been chosen as the arena of a determined trial of strength, at her State Election this Spring, between the supporters and opponents respectively of the War for the Union. The nomination for Governor by the Republicans of William A. Buckingham, the incumbent, who had, both officially and personally, been a strenuous and prominent champion of "coercion," was fairly countered by the presentation, as his competitor, of Col. Thomas H. Seymour, an ex-Governor of decided personal popularity, but an early, consistent, outspoken condemner of the War—or rather, of the National side of it. His nomination was made by a very large Convention, and with a degree of unanimity and genuine enthusiasm rarely manifested; while the canvass that ensued thereon was one of the most animated and energetic ever witnessed even in that closely balanced State: its result being the triumph of the Republicans by a much reduced but still decisive majority. It is quite probable that a candidate less decidedly and conspicuously hostile to the War than Col. Seymour might, while polling fewer votes, have come much nearer an election; since Seymour's nomination was a challenge to the War party which incited it to the most vehement exertions.

No other general Election was held in any of the loyal States during the earlier half of 1863; yet the result in these three—though maintaining the Republican ascendency in each—left no room for reasonable doubt that, apart from the soldiers in the field, a majority of the voters in the loyal States were still . . . opposed to a further prosecution of the War, and certainly opposed to its prosecution on the anti-Slavery basis established by the action of Congress and by the President's two [Emancipation] Proclamations of Sept. 22, 1862, and Jan. 1, 1863. If called to vote directly on the question of making peace on the basis of a recognition of the Southern Confederacy, some of those who voted the Opposition tickets . . . might have shrunk from an open committal to such a peace; but it is none the less certain that their attitude and action tended directly to insure a result which their bolder or more candid compatriots frankly proclaimed inevitable. Many who adhered to the Democratic organization asserted, what some, at least, must have believed, that the Confederates . . . might yet, by conciliatory overtures and proper concessions, be reconciled to a restoration of the Union; but very few who still adhered to that body, out of the army, averred if all proffers and guaranties should be rejected, they would favor a prosecution of the War for their subjugation.

The Rebel Congress having long since passed a conscription act, whereby all the White males in the Confederacy between the ages of 18 and 35 were placed at the disposal of their Executive, while all those already in the service, though they had enlisted and been accepted for specific terms of one or two years, were held to serve through the War, our Congress was constrained to follow afar off in the footsteps of the enemy . . . The passage and execution of this act inevitably intensified and made active the spirit of opposition to the War. Those who detested every form of coercion save the coercion of the Republic by the Rebels, with those who especially detested the National effort under its present aspects as "a war not for the Union, but for the Negro," were aroused by it to a more determined and active opposition . . .

Gen. Lee . . . was aware that our army had been depleted, directly after its sanguinary experience of Chancellorsville, of the mustering out of some 20,000 nine months' and two years' men; while his own had been largely swelled by . . . drafts on every quarter whence a regiment could be gleaned; so that it is probable that the superiority in numbers was temporarily on his side . . . In fact, Lee's invasion of Maryland and Pennsylvania at that juncture was justifiable on political grounds alone. The Confederate chiefs must have acted on the strength of trusted assurances that the Northern Peace Democracy, detesting the Emancipation policy now steadfastly ascendant at Washington, and weary of high taxes, dear [expensive] fabrics, a disordered currency, and an enormous yet swelling National Debt, were ripe for revolt: so that a Rebel victory on Northern soil would enable the devotees of Slavery in the loyal States to seize upon the pending Conscription and wield it as an engine of revolution.

Alexander Robinson Boteler, "Stonewall Jackson in the Campaign of 1862," *Southern Historical Society Papers* 40 (September 1915)

It will be remembered by those who are familiar with the history of military operations in the Valley of Virginia during the late Civil War that the Battle of Winchester [Virginia], which was so successfully fought by Stonewall Jackson, on Sunday, the 25th of May, 1862, not only forced the Federal general, [Nathaniel] Banks, to seek safety for himself and followers beyond the Potomac and, in his precipitate flight, to abandon an immense amount of valuable stores of every description, but that it, likewise, caused such uneasiness among the authorities at Washington as to lead them to countermand their orders to [Major-General Irvin] McDowell, who at that time had an army of 40,000 men at Fredericksburg, with which to reinforce McClellan in front of Richmond, but, who, instead of doing that, was required to detach a portion of his command to the defense of the Federal capital, and with another part of it, consisting of 20,000 men, to march across the Blue Ridge to Front Royal for the purpose of intercepting the victorious Confederates. So that Jackson, by one and the same blow, effectually disposed of the force under Banks, furnished his own command with a superabundance of much-needed supplies, practically neutralized the fine army of McDowell and indefinitely postponed the plans of McClellan for the reduction of Richmond. But in securing these advantages, while he had diminished the dangers that threatened the Confederate capital, he had at the same time increased the perils of his own position, for the Federal government, as already intimated, being thoroughly frightened by his successes and supposing that his purpose was to advance on Washington, promptly put in motion all the available means in its power to check his progress . . .

With this preliminary explanation it will be seen what was the state of affairs with Jackson on Friday, the fifth day after the battle of Winchester . . . Early in the afternoon of the Friday above mentioned, May 30th, the general and his staff—of which I was then a member—were on a hill near Halltown, to the right of the turnpike, where one of our batteries was engaged in an artillery duel with some heavy guns of the enemy that were posted on an eminence in the direction of Bolivar Heights . . . On placing myself by his side, he said: "I want you to go to Richmond for me. I must have reinforcements. You can explain to them down there what the situation is here. Get as many men as can be spared, and I'd like you, if you please, to go as soon as you can." After expressing to him my readiness to go at once and to do what I could to have his force increased.

I said: "But you must first tell me, general, what is the situation here." Whereupon he informed me of McDowell's movement, how he was transferring a large portion of his army from Fredericksburg to the Valley, by way of Manassas Gap, to cut him off . . . Said he . . . "You may tell them, too, that if my command can be gotten up to 40,000 men a movement may be made beyond the Potomac, which will soon raise the siege of Richmond and transfer this campaign from the banks of the James to those of the Susquehanna."

James Longstreet, "Lee in Pennsylvania," *Annals of the War Written by Leading Participants North and South* (Philadelphia, 1879)

After the defeat of Burnside at Fredericksburg, in December, it was believed that active operations were over for the winter, and I was sent with two divisions of my corps to the eastern shore of Virginia, where I could find food for my men during the winter, and send supplies to the Army of Northern Virginia. I spent several months in this department, keeping the enemy close within his fortifications, and foraging with little trouble and great success. On May 1st, I received orders to report to General Lee at Fredericksburg. General Hooker had begun to throw his army across the Rappahannock, and the active campaign was opening. I left Suffolk as soon as possible, and hurried my troops forward. Passing through Richmond, I called to pay my respects to Mr. [James] Seddon, the Secretary of War. Mr. Seddon was, at the time of my visit, deeply considering the critical condition of [Major-General John C.] Pemberton's army at Vicksburg, around which General Grant was then decisively drawing his lines. He informed me that he had in contemplation a plan for concentrating a succoring army at Jackson, Mississippi, under the command of [Major-General Joseph E.] Johnston, with a view of driving Grant from before Vicksburg by a direct issue-at-arms. He suggested that possibly my corps might be needed to make the army strong enough to handle Grant, and asked me my views. I replied that there was a better plan, in my judgment, for relieving Vicksburg than by a direct assault upon Grant. I proposed that the army then concentrating at Jackson, Mississippi, be moved swiftly to Tullahoma, where General [Braxton] Bragg was then located with a fine army, confronting an army of about equal strength under General [William Starke] Rosecrans, and that at the same time the two divisions of my corps be hurried forward to the same point. The simultaneous arrival of these reinforcements would give us a grand army at Tullahoma. With this army General Johnston might speedily crush Rosecrans, and that he should then turn his force toward the north, and with his splendid army march through Tennessee and Kentucky, and threaten the invasion of Ohio. My idea was that, in the march through those States, the army would meet no organized obstruction; would be supplied with provisions and even reinforcements by those friendly to our cause, and would inevitably result in drawing Grant's army from Vicksburg to look after and protect his own territory. Mr. Seddon adhered to his original views; not so much, I think, from his great confidence in them, as from the difficulty of withdrawing the force suggested from General Lee's army. I was very thoroughly impressed with the practicability of the plan, however, and when I reached General Lee I laid it before him with the freedom justified by our close personal and official relations. The idea seemed to be a new one to him, but he was evidently seriously impressed with it. We discussed it over and over, and I discovered that his main objection to it was that it would, if adopted, force him to divide his army. He left no room to doubt, however, that he believed the idea of an offensive campaign was not only important, but necessary.

At length, while we were discussing the idea of a western forward movement, he asked me if I did not think an invasion of Maryland and Pennsylvania by his own army would accomplish the same result, and I replied that I did not see that it would, because this movement would be too hazardous, and the campaign in thoroughly Union States would require more time and greater preparation than one through Tennessee and Kentucky. I soon discovered that he had determined that he would make some forward movement, and I finally assented that the Pennsylvania campaign might be brought to a successful issue if he could make it offensive in strategy, but defensive in tactics. This point was urged with great persistency. I suggested that, after piercing Pennsylvania and menacing Washington, we should choose a strong position, and force the Federals to attack us, observing that the popular clamor throughout the North would speedily force the Federal general to attempt to drive us out. I recalled to him the battle of Fredericksburg as an instance of a defensive battle, when, with a few thousand men, we hurled the whole Federal army back, crippling and demoralizing it, with trifling loss to our own troops; and Chancellorsville as an instance of an offensive battle, where we dislodged the Federals, it is true, but at such a terrible sacrifice that half a dozen such victories would have ruined us. It will be remembered that Stonewall Jackson once said that "we sometimes fail to drive the enemy from a position. They always fail to drive us." I reminded him, too, of Napoleon's advice to [Marshal Auguste de] Marmont, to whom he said, when putting him at the head of an invading army, "Select your ground, and make your enemy attack you." I recall these points, simply because I desire to have it distinctly understood that, while I first suggested to General Lee the idea of an offensive campaign, I was never persuaded to yield my argument against the Gettysburg campaign, except with the understanding that we were not to deliver an offensive battle, but to so maneuvre that the enemy should be forced to attack us—or, to repeat, that our campaign should be one of offensive strategy, but defensive tactics. Upon this understanding my assent was given, and General Lee, who had been kind enough to discuss the matter with me patiently, gave the order of march . . .

"Letter from Major-General Henry Heth, of A.P. Hill's Corps, A.N.V.," *Southern Historical Society Papers* 4 (September 1877)

Just here let us take a retrospective view, and consider what the Army of Northern Virginia had in one year accomplished. In 1862, eighty thousand strong, it attacked the Federal army, one hundred thousand strong, and after seven days' fighting drove that army to shelter under its gunboats. Following up this success, after a series of engagements, [Major-General John] Pope was driven across the Potomac. Then followed the battle of Sharpsburg (Antietam), when possibly the fighting capacity of the Army of Northern Virginia never shone brighter. Its numbers reduced by fighting, fatigue, and hard marching to less than forty thousand strong, it gained a drawn battle against its adversary, who numbered nearly, if not quite one hundred thousand men. Then came Fredericksburg, where, with its ranks recuperated to seventy-eight thousand, it hurled across the Rappahannock river an adversary who had crossed with one hundred and ten thousand men. Then follows that most daring and wonderful battle, Chancellorsville, where it again triumphed, fifty thousand strong, against its adversary, numbering one hundred and thirty-two thousand, compelling him again to seek shelter behind the Rappahannock. After such a series of successes, with such disparity of numbers, is it wonderful that the Army of Northern Virginia and its great leader should have believed it capable of accomplishing anything in the power of an army to accomplish?

[Louis-Philippe-Albert d'Orléans, the Comte de Paris, who wrote a *History of the Civil War in America* in 1875] says "it was a mistake to invade the Northern States at all," and then gives very clearly and concisely his reasons for entertaining this opinion. Some of the reasons substantiating this view I shall answer hereafter. I think from [his] standpoint, and especially looking at the sequel of the invasion of Pennsylvania in 1863, he is correct, and I have no doubt that by far the greater number of historians who may follow him will entertain like opinions. It is, possibly, very natural for myself and other officers who served in the Army of Northern Virginia to permit our judgments to be biased by the opinions of one whom we loved, admired and trusted in, as much as we did, in any opinion entertained by our great Commander. I will state General Lee's views in regard to the invasion of Pennsylvania, as given by him to me and to another. A short time before General Grant crossed the Rapidan, in the spring of 1864, General Lee said to me: "If I could do so—unfortunately I cannot—I would again cross the Potomac and invade Pennsylvania. I believe it to be our true policy, notwithstanding the failure of last year. An invasion of the enemy's country breaks up all of his preconceived plans, relieves our country of his presence, and we subsist while there on his resources. The question of food for this army gives me more trouble and uneasiness than everything else combined; the absence of the army from Virginia gives our people an opportunity to collect supplies ahead. The legitimate fruits of a victory, if gained in Pennsylvania, could be more readily reaped than on our own soil. We would have been in a few days' march of Philadelphia, and the occupation of that city would have given us peace." It is very difficult for anyone not connected with the Army of Northern Virginia to realize how straitened we were for supplies of all kinds, especially food. The ration of a general officer was double that of a private, and so meagre was that double supply that frequently to appease my hunger I robbed my horse of a handful of corn, which, parched in the fire, served to allay the cravings of nature. What must have been the condition of the private?

After the battle of Gettysburg the President of the Confederate States, desiring to communicate with General Lee, sent Major [John] Seddon, a brother of the Secretary of War, to General Lee's headquarters, when the following conversation took place: General Lee said, "Major Seddon, from what you have observed, are the people as much depressed at the battle of Gettysburg as the newspapers appear to indicate?" Upon Major Seddon's reply that he thought they were, General Lee continued: "To show you how little value is to be attached to popular sentiment in such matters, I beg to call your attention to the popular feeling after the battles of Fredericksburg and Chancellorsville. At Fredericksburg we gained a battle, inflicting very serious loss on the enemy in men and material; our people were greatly elated—I was much depressed. We had really accomplished nothing; we had not gained a foot of ground, and I knew the enemy could easily replace the men he had lost, and the loss of material was, if anything, rather beneficial to him, as it gave an opportunity to contractors to make money. At Chancellorsville we gained another victory; our people were wild with delight—I, on the contrary, was more depressed than after Fredericksburg; our loss was severe, and again we had gained not an inch of ground and the enemy could not be pursued. After the battle of Chancellorsville matters stood thus: Hooker in my front, with an army more than a hundred thousand strong; [Major-General John Gray] Foster preparing to advance into North Carolina; [Major-General John Adams] Dix preparing to advance on Richmond from Fortress Monroe; [Brigadier-General Erastus Bernard] Tyler in the Kanawha Valley preparing to unite with [Major-General Robert Huston] Milroy, who was in the Valley of Virginia, collecting men and material for an advance on Staunton. To oppose these movements I had sixty thousand men. It would have been folly to have divided my army; the armies of the enemy were too far apart for me to attempt to fall upon them in detail. I considered the problem in every possible phase, and to my mind it resolved itself into the choice of one of two things: either to retire on Richmond and stand a siege, which must ultimately have ended in surrender, or to invade Pennsylvania. I chose the latter . . ."

Robert E. Lee to Jefferson Davis (June 10, 1863), in *The War of the Rebellion: A Compilation of the Official Records of the Union and Confederate Armies* (Washington, DC, 1881-1901), Series 1, Vol. 27 (pt 3)

Mr. President:

I beg leave to bring to your attention a subject with reference to which I have thought that the course pursued by writers and speakers among us has had a tendency to interfere with our success. I refer to the manner in which the demonstration of a desire for peace at the North has been received in our country.

I think there can be no doubt that journalists and others at the South, to whom the Northern people naturally look for a reflection of our opinions, have met these indications in such wise as to weaken the hands of the advocates of a pacific policy on the part of the Federal Government, and give much encouragement to those who urge a continuance of the war.

Recent political movements in the United States, and the comments of influential newspapers upon them, have attracted my attention particularly to this subject, which I deem not unworthy of the consideration of Your Excellency, nor inappropriate to be adverted to by me, in view of its connection with the situation of military affairs.

Conceding to our enemies the superiority claimed by them in numbers, resources, and all the means and appliances for carrying on the war, we have no right to look for exemptions from the military consequences of a vigorous use of these advantages, excepting by such deliverance as the mercy of Heaven may accord to the courage of our soldiers, the justice of our cause, and the constancy and prayers of our people. While making the most we can of the means of resistance we possess, and gratefully accepting the measure of success with which God has blessed our efforts as an earnest of His approval and favor, it is nevertheless the part of wisdom to carefully measure and husband our strength, and not to expect from it more than in the ordinary course of affairs it is capable of accomplishing. We should not, therefore, conceal from ourselves that our resources in men are constantly diminishing, and the disproportion in this respect between us and our enemies, if they continue united in their efforts to subjugate us, is steadily augmenting.

The decrease of the aggregate of this army, as disclosed by the returns, affords an illustration of this fact. Its effective strength varies from time to time, but the falling off in its aggregate shows that its ranks are growing weaker and that its losses are not supplied by recruits.

Under these circumstances, we should neglect no honorable means of dividing and weakening our enemies, that they may feel some of the difficulties experienced by ourselves. It seems to me that the most effectual mode of accomplishing this object, now within our reach, is to give all the encouragement we can, consistently with truth, to the rising peace party of the North.

Nor do I think we should, in this connection, make nice distinction between those who declare for peace unconditionally and those who advocate it as a means of restoring the Union, however much we may prefer the former.

We should bear in mind that the friends of peace at the North must make concessions to the earnest desire that exists in the minds of their countrymen for a restoration of the Union, and that to hold out such a result as an inducement is essential to the success of their party.

Should the belief that peace will bring back the Union become general, the war would no longer be supported, and that, after all, is what we are interested in bringing about. When peace is proposed to us, it will be time enough to discuss its terms, and it is not the part of prudence to spurn the proposition in advance, merely because those who wish to make it believe, or affect to believe, that it will result in bringing us back to the Union. We entertain no such apprehensions, nor doubt that the desire of our people for a distinct and independent national existence will prove as steadfast under the influence of peaceful measures as it has shown itself in the midst of war.

If the views I have indicated meet the approval of Your Excellency, you will best know how to give effect to them. Should you deem them inexpedient or impracticable, I think you will nevertheless agree with me that we should at least carefully abstain from measures or expressions that tend to discourage any party whose purpose is peace.

With the statement of my own opinion on the subject, the length of which you will excuse, I leave to your better judgment to determine the proper course to be pursued.

THE ARMIES

The two armies that became the principal players in the Gettysburg campaign—the Confederate Army of Northern Virginia and the Union Army of the Potomac—were both alike and unalike in significant ways. They were overwhelmingly male, although a few women managed to disguise themselves and slip past recruitment inspectors and into the ranks. A few women secured noncombatant positions (like Mary Tepe, a French-style *vivandière* who supported soldiers of the equally French-style Federal unit, the 114th Pennsylvania, on the firing lines with canteens and rudimentary first aid), but otherwise, the armies were a world populated by men. Especially *young* men. The average age of Civil War soldiers was between twenty-five and twenty-six, although the men in the ranks included a dismaying number of mid-teenagers whose enlistments were winked at by recruiters. In an age of limited nutritional resources, their average height and weight was surprisingly slight: 5 feet 8 inches in height, 143 pounds. Their officers were often not much older than the men themselves. There was only a sprinkling of greybeard generals: George Sears "Old Pappy" Greene (age sixty-two) and James Barnes (age sixty-one) in the Army of the Potomac; "Extra Billy" Smith (age sixty-five) and Isaac Trimble (age sixty-one) in the Army of Northern Virginia. Even the general officers were young men. The youngest in the Army of the Potomac was the wild cavalryman George Armstrong Custer (a brigadier-general at twenty-three); in the Army of Northern Virginia, the prize for youngest general is shared by Stephen Dodson Ramseur and Evander McIvor Law, at age twenty-six.

The Confederacy began drafting young men in the spring of 1862, and the Union was about to begin its own draft in the summer of the Gettysburg battle, but at Gettysburg the fighting would be done, at least on the Union side, entirely by citizen-soldier volunteers who had willingly signed up for it. They were, for that reason, utterly unprepared for either the demands of military life or for the shock of combat. Soldiers wrote in dismay that "no words can depict the ghastly picture" of battle. "You have asked to give a description of a field after the Angel of Death has passed over it," wrote a surgeon in the 121st New York, "but I can no more do so than I can give you an idea of anything indescribable." "Oh, my God, if war ain't the terriblest thing that I ever come across yet," wrote one appalled Confederate conscript. "There was the most people shot that ever I saw. Some with their arms off, some their legs off, and some shot about the head, and some lying dead."

The term *volunteer* was also a technical description, distinguishing units of soldiers who had been recruited for two- or three-year terms of service in the war from *regulars* (long-service professional soldiers) and from state *militia* (roughly the equivalent of our modern National Guard). Volunteer units were recruited by the state authorities, and their officers, up to the rank of colonel, were appointed by state governors, but they were mustered into national service, and fed, paid, clothed, and equipped by the national government.

The basic unit of military organization—the one that soldiers were usually likely to use as a way of identifying themselves—was the *regiment*. The regiment was known by a numerical and state designation, as in *1st Minnesota Volunteer Regiment*. Regiments were organized into a brigade (of three to five regiments, and commanded by a brigadier-general), brigades into a division (of two to five brigades, commanded by a junior major-general), and divisions into a corps (usually three or four divisions, commanded by a senior major-general). At Gettysburg, the Army of Northern Virginia was organized into three corps, usually numbering roughly 21,000 to 26,000 men; the Union forces were organized into seven smaller-size corps of about 11,000 to 13,000 men.

The soldiers of these armies were largely native-born, but both included sizeable proportions of immigrants—German and Irish immigrants composing up to a third of all Federal volunteer forces. In fact, immigrants sometimes composed entire regiments: the 39th New York (the "Garibaldi Guard") and the five regiments of the "Irish Brigade" (63rd, 68th, 88th New York, 28th Massachusetts, and 116th Pennsylvania), for example. The Army of the Potomac's 11th Corps contained so many German immigrants that in some regiments, officers gave orders in German.

For the native-born, the war was often their first experience away from home, and lacking the kind of immunities that might come from exposure to large numbers of strangers, they suffered from diseases at a shockingly high rate (one in eight Union soldiers died of disease during the war, as well as one of every five Confederates). But a large part of that mortality also arose from lack of camp hygiene—in the nineteenth century, there were only the most primitive notions of what constituted sanitation, and little idea as yet of how germs communicated disease—and from how poorly fed and badly clothed they were. Union uniforms consisted of an ill-fitting navy-blue frock coat or shorter sack coat, with sky-blue or robin's-egg-blue trousers, and either a black felt slouch hat or a baggy-looking, flat-topped forage cap sometimes called (after its French pattern) a *kepi.* Confederate uniforms were even less well-defined, with "rusty slough hats, sandy beards, sallow skins, butternut coats, and pantaloons down to their mud-stained shoes."

Yet, these armies were surprisingly literate and pervasively religious, and they did not hesitate to organize evangelical revival meetings and pray, "Oh God pardon my many sins Consecrate my heart to do thy will protect my dear wife & let the day come soon that I may be with her . . ." In the 116th Pennsylvania, "meetings for prayer were of almost daily occurence, and the groups of men sitting on the ground or gathered on the hill side listening to the Gospel were strong reminders of the mounds of Galilee when the people sat upon the ground to hear the Savior teach." They were not the poor, beaten-down "scum" whom the Duke of Wellington once described as the fabric of the European armies, who had been driven into the ranks by an indifferent class of aristocrats. In the Union armies, 47 percent were farmers (as opposed to 43 percent in the overall Northern male population), 25 percent were skilled laborers (compared to 24.9 percent in the Union states), and 3 percent were professional (which tallies favorably with the 3.5 percent then comprising the professional class in the North). The statistics were similar in the Confederate armies: 61 percent were farmers (compared to 57.5 percent in the South), 14 percent skilled laborers (almost the same as the 15.7 percent of the Southern population), and 5.2 percent were professionals (which matches the 5 percent of professionals in the

Confederacy). In the 2nd South Carolina, there were actually forty-nine men who owned more than $1,000 in property.

These volunteer regiments were usually recruited company-by-company from specific locales, so there would be a high concentration of neighbors and relatives (fifty-three sets of brothers would fight in the armies at Gettysburg) in any given unit. But there would also be some scapegraces as well: Ira Thomas Turner, a twenty-three-year-old carpenter from Edgefield, South Carolina, enlisted as a private in 1861 and was wounded and captured at Gettysburg on July 2nd. He was paroled, took the oath of loyalty to the United States, married a nurse whom he met in an army hospital, and never went back to South Carolina. Instead, Turner took up farming in New Jersey, where he died and was buried in in the Cold Spring Cemetery, near Cape May, in 1916.

They were not in love with war. A soldier in the 155th Pennsylvania Volunteers wrote that "the anxiety for battle and thirst for gore and terms so freely used by descriptive writers, belongs to the domain of fiction, and describes a sentiment far from the truth." Yet, in both armies, whether volunteers or conscripts, they were remarkably determined to stick with their duty if that was what was necessary. Spencer Cavendish, the Marquess of Hartington, toured the Confederacy in 1862 and 1863, and afterward wrote that he had met in Lee's army "men who have spent their whole lives in affluent circumstances and in rural pursuits, men who have led quiet and peaceable lives. I have seen them serving as privates in regiments of their States, serving badly clothed, badly fed, perhaps hardly with shoes upon their feet . . . I have seen men who have lived all their lives in poverty, who you would say have nothing to lose and nothing to gain, who had no interest in slavery, but who have joined with as much readiness as those who had the ranks of the army—I have seen these men in their camps as cheerful as possible, and asking for nothing but again to be led to battle with the enemy . . . I say surely a people animated with such a feeling . . . [are] not a people who are going to give in."

For all their similarities and all their virtues, there were also great points of difference between the Army of the Potomac and the Army of Northern Virginia, starting with how many of the Confederates were either draftees or men who enlisted one step ahead of conscription. Much more telling, however, is the simple percentage—some 47 percent, by the estimate of military historian Joseph Glatthaar—who were slaveholders or came from households which owned slaves. And they were not shy about affirming their determination to defend slavery, either. "Our homes, our firesides, our land and negroes and even the virtue of our fair ones are at stake," explained a soldier in the 13th Georgia. The great irony of this determination lies in how a large portion of the Army of Northern Virginia *was* black—not black soldiers, but slaves (or, euphemistically, "servants") amounting to anywhere between ten thousand and thirty thousand, who provided the logistical underpinnings of Lee's army.

The Union soldiers, by contrast, were not of one mind about fighting a war to free African Americans. Still, they were clearly hostile to the institution of slavery: They sheltered fugitive slaves and employed many of them as wageworkers in their own camps. Even for those who swore that "we were fighting for the union and constitution," and not one thing more, understood that restoring the Union was bound up with emancipation, and they could not see any hope for a meaningful restoration of the Union without the cause of the Union's disruption being eliminated. The Army of the Potomac was not necessarily the slaves' best friends, but it was definitely slavery's worst enemy.

Their weapons were collections of domestic manufactures and foreign imports, with the basic infantry firearm being the "rifle musket" (mostly either the American-made Springfield or the British-import Enfield). The rifle was a major improvement in nineteenth-century weapons technology, although the scale of that improvement has been often overstated. The grooved rifling in the barrel increased the range and accuracy of the old-fashioned smoothbore musket, but the gains were usually seen under perfect target-range circumstances. Both rifles and smoothbores remained single-shot, black-powder muzzleloaders that kicked out substantial clouds of whitish-gray smoke; used in large formations, the powder smoke could easily obscure the sight of an enemy and reduce the new range and accuracy of the rifle to zero. On a battlefield, recalled one Confederate, powder smoke "hung pall-like over the fields and woods all day along the battle lines," often becoming "so thick and dense sometimes during the day that it was impossible to discern anything fifty paces away." The Civil War remains, in practice, more the last

Napoleonic war than the harbinger of the new ways of war which arrived on the Western Front in 1914.

Civil War cavalry were the dramatic arm of each service, but they were also the most expensive to maintain. The pre-war U.S. Army had never employed more than five regiments of horse-mounted soldiers, and even those were technically "light cavalry"—armed with saber and carbine—and limited both in size and scope compared to the mounted divisions of European armies. Cavalry in the Civil War served largely as scouts and screens, rather than actual combatants on the battlefields against infantry. At Gettysburg, the opening of the fighting on July 1st would see Union cavalry facing Confederate infantry, but only for the purpose of slowing the Confederates' progress toward Gettysburg until Union infantry could reach the town.

Much more deadly than cavalry in Civil War combat was the artillery. At Gettysburg, the Army of the Potomac would bring 360 cannon to the battle, organized into sixty-eight batteries of four to six guns each, while the Army of Northern Virginia would employ 272 guns in seventy batteries. These were not, however, long-range weapons; they relied on direct sight to their targets, and the most common artillery piece was the short-range smoothbore "Napoleon" bronze gun-howitzer (whose effective reach petered out at 1,620 yards). The Union army possessed more longer-range pieces at Gettysburg: the three-inch Ordnance rifle (which could hit targets at 1,830 yards) and the big ten-pound and twenty-pound (from the weight of their shot) Parrott rifled guns. But the Confederates possessed two of the strangest artillery pieces used in the entire war: two Whitworth breech-loading rifled cannons (that could reach out to 2,800 yards), which had been purchased in England and run through the U.S. Navy's blockade of the Confederacy. All of these cannon were drawn by teams of four to six horses, which (together with wagon teams and officers' mounts) translated into the use of over 8,400 horses at Gettysburg for the Army of the Potomac, and another 4,100 for the Army of Northern Virginia.

The staffs that managed the two armies at Gettysburg—the aides, military secretaries, quartermasters, inspectors, medical directors, and so forth—were primitive in size and function. The pre-war U.S. Army had no staff college to train officers in various administrative roles, and the U.S. Military Academy at West Point (where Robert E. Lee had served as superintendent in the 1850s) concentrated on instruction in engineering and fortification-building. But even if there had been better staff training, the actual numbers of officers with professional experience would have been overwhelmed by the sheer volume of volunteer officers whose total knowledge of tactics, combat, and war in general could have been squeezed onto a calling card without difficulty. Without skilled staff management, both the Army of the Potomac and the Army of Northern Virginia had a much harder time being herded from point to point than their European counterparts. As it was, Civil War staffs generally turned into placement services for senior generals' relatives or protégés.

It sounds neither heroic nor romantic to admit that, compared with their European counterparts in the Crimean War of 1854 to 1856, the North Italian War of 1859, and the Wars of German Unification from 1864 to 1871, the armies at Gettysburg displayed dismaying levels of amateurism, poor discipline, and even poorer training at every level. Even Robert E. Lee admitted to the Prussian military observer Captain Justus Scheibert, "Our people are so little liable to control that it is difficult to get them to follow any course not in accordance with their inclination." Yet, these same soldiers impressed a British observer with their "indomitable perseverance, cheerfulness under fatigue and hardship, diligence in entrenching, and stubbornness in defending these entrenchments." It was often a courage of the moment, and sometimes of fear, and occasionally of principle. But it was also the courage of people who had not learned that it was impossible for them to do extraordinary things, and who therefore went and did them.

Richard Taylor, *Destruction and Reconstruction: Personal Experiences of the Late War in the United States* (New York, 1879)

A high opinion has been expressed of the strategy of Lee, by which Jackson's forces from the [Shenandoah] Valley were suddenly thrust between M'Dowell and M'Clellan's right, and it deserves all praise; but the tactics on the field were vastly inferior to the strategy. Indeed it may be confidently asserted that from Cold Harbour to Malvern Hill

inclusive, there was nothing but a series of blunders, one after another, and all huge. The Confederate commanders knew no more about the topography of the country than they did about Central Africa. Here was a limited district, the whole of it within a day's march of the city of Richmond, capital of Virginia and the Confederacy, almost the first spot on the continent occupied by the British race, the Chickahominy [River] itself classic by legends of Captain John Smith and Pocahontas; and yet we were profoundly ignorant of the country, were without maps, sketches, or proper guides, and nearly as helpless as if we had been suddenly transferred to the banks of the Lualaba. The day before the battle of Malvern Hill, President Davis could not find a guide with intelligence enough to show him the way from one of our columns to another; and this fact I have from him . . . For two days we lost M'Clellan's great army in a few miles of woodland, and never had any definite knowledge of its movements. Let it be remembered, too, that M'Clellan had opened the peninsular campaign weeks before, indicating this very region to be the necessary theatre of conflict; that the Confederate commander (up to the time of his wound at Fair Oaks), General [Joseph E.] Johnston, had been a topographical engineer in the United States army; while his successor, General Lee—another engineer—had been on duty at the War Office in Richmond and in constant intercourse with President Davis, who was educated at West Point and served seven years; and then think of our ignorance in a military sense of the ground over which we were called to fight. Everyone must agree that it was amazing. Even now I can scarcely realise it. M'Clellan was as superior to us in knowledge of our own land as were the Germans to the French in their late war [the

Franco-Prussian War of 1870-71], and owed the success of his retreat to it, although credit must be given to his ability. We had much praying at various headquarters, and large reliance on special providences; but none were vouchsafed, by pillar of cloud or fire, to supplement our ignorance; so we blundered on, like people trying to read without knowledge of their letters.

John S. Robson, *How a One-Legged Rebel Lives: Reminiscences of the Civil War* (Durham, NC, 1898)

We used to notice one curious difference between the Northern and Southern generals during the war. Their commanding generals of armies and army corps on battle-days kept at their headquarters, long distance from the field, and using their well-appointed staff officers and couriers exclusively in communicating their orders to the troops, while the Southern generals were up among their men, directing and leading their movements, and encouraging them at the critical points.

I am sure that if the Northern soldiers had been thus led and handled, so they could have had the same confidence in their generals the Southern men had, they would have ended the war in less than four years. Everything else being equal, one man is as good as another, but one soldier, having confidence in his commander, is worth ten half-hearted fellows, who have little faith in their general and only see him at review. We did not have the same discipline—in regard to our generals

anyhow—that the Northern army had, and ours did not make the same display of "fuss and feathers" with brilliant staff officers, nor require the same flourishing of caps and saluting with arms presented whenever they met us. Ours met spontaneous salutes of cheers right from the hearts of their admiring soldiers, and I have seen Jackson, [Richard S.] Ewell and others do some very hard riding, bareheaded, along the columns to escape the noisy homage of their devoted followers.

George H. Washburn, *A Complete Military History and Record of the 108th Regiment N.Y. Vols., from 1862 to 1894* (Rochester, NY, 1894)

Washed or unwashed the "gray back" [lice] would insidiously invade men's clothing, and as they multiplied rapidly and as thickly as grass seed, soldiers garments became a medium for mass conventions of livestock of a maddening, aggravated character . . . We have noticed officers and men's limbs raw from the parasites feasting on them, and unless strenuous efforts were made to check their revelry, the afflicted subjects would become emaciated, disheartened and fall victims thereto . . . They did not invade the hair on the head; their race-course seemed to be men's spinal columns, and their lunching resort was mostly on the woof of men's stockings about the ankles. On a hot day, marching, they were very aggravating . . . Another parasite that would engraft itself upon and in men's flesh was the coy "wood tick," and they were of such dimensions that no magnifying lens was required to see them. Camping in woods and lying upon wet leaves would yield a full quota of the torment to the men, with their heads embedded in the flesh; and the task of pulling them off, generally leaving the heads in the flesh, which caused an irritating pea-like swelling, was not of a nature . . . to check the profanity which waxed strong.

Thomas W. Hyde, *Following the Greek Cross, or Memories of the Sixth Army Corps* (Boston, 1894)

[At the time of the recruitment of the 7th Maine in Augusta, ME] They insisted on making me major in spite of my extreme youth, as I was the only man in the regiment who could drill a company. Even now I can recall the thrill of joy and dread and gratified pride that the unexpected vote gave me; but the responsibilities were too huge and I promptly declined, and would probably have persisted in declining, had not Mr. John B. Swanton and Colonel [Ephraim K.] Harding, by their encouragement and insistence, almost forced me into it. I did not know then that the principal duties of a major were to ride on the flank of the rear division, say nothing, look as well as possible, and long for promotion. The two lieutenants soon heard of my unexpected exaltation, and promptly took the train for their homes, neither being willing to take the captaincy; and it was only on my promising to be captain, too, till I could find a substitute, that I was able to get them back to camp.

It was intended that the 7th Maine should stay long enough in camp at Augusta to get some cohesion and be able to march together; but long before they did it happened that orders came to send us to the front. Imagine my consternation on receiving them, when I reflected that the colonel had not yet been allowed by the war department to accept, that the lieutenant-colonel had not come, and that I, the newly fledged major, had to take this mob of one thousand men to Washington. To make it worse, when the order to break camp came, it was a literal copy of the one used by Colonel Oliver Otis Howard, a West Pointer, to take the 3d Maine out of Augusta. He had taken one used at West Point for some grand function by the corps of cadets, and it was longer than one of Grant's orders moving the army toward Richmond. I remember the tent pegs were to be pulled in order at tap of drum, and the operation of taking care of them would take a week to learn.

Spencer Glasgow Welch to Cordelia Strother Welch (August 18, 1862), in *A Confederate Surgeon's Letters to His Wife* (New York, 1911)

I have often read of how armies are disposed to pillage and plunder, but could never conceive of it before. Whenever we stop for twenty-four hours every corn field and orchard within two or three miles is completely stripped. The troops not only rob the fields, but they go to the houses and insist on being fed, until they eat up everything about a man's premises which can be eaten. Most of them pay for what they get at the houses, and are charged exorbitant prices, but a hungry soldier will give all he has for something to eat, and will then steal when hunger again harasses him. When in health and tormented by hunger he thinks of little else besides home and something to eat. He does not seem to dread the fatiguing marches and arduous duties.

A wounded soldier who has been in Jackson's army for a long time told me his men had but one suit of clothes each, and whenever a suit became very dirty the man would pull it off and wash it and then wait until it dried. I believe this to be a fact . . .

Abner Ralph Small, *The Road to Richmond: Civil War Memoirs of Major Abner R. Small of the Sixteenth Maine Volunteers,* ed. H.A. Small (Berkeley, CA, 1939)

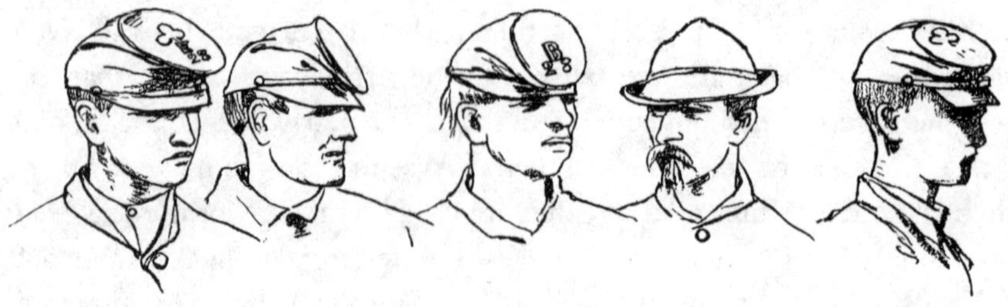

[The new recruit's] suit is a model one, cut after the regulation pattern, fifty thousand at a time, and of just two sizes. If he is a small man, God pity him; if he is a big man, God pity him still more . . . His forage cap, with its leather visor, when dry curls up, when wet hangs down, and usually covers one or both ears. His army brogans [large, square-toed shoes], nothing can ever make shine, or even black . . . and he doesn't crease trousers . . . The knapsack . . . is an unwieldy burden with its rough, coarse contents of flannel and sole leather and sometimes twenty rounds of ammunition extra . . . All this is crowned with a double wool blanket and half a shelter tent rolled in a rubber blanket. One shoulder and the hips support the "commissary department"—an odorous haversack, which often stinks with its mixture of bacon, pork, salt junk, sugar, coffee, tea, desiccated vegetable, rice, bits of yesterday's dinner, and old scraps husbanded with miserly care against a day of want . . .

Mrs. Arabella M. Willson, *Disaster, Struggle, Triumph: The Adventures of 1000 "Boys in Blue," from August, 1862, until June, 1865* (Albany, NY, 1870)

As *skirmishing* is a most important feature in war, and as few unmilitary people have a correct idea of it, we will insert some descriptive notices of this peculiar mode of warfare. So important is it, that *skirmish drill* is part of the training in every well drilled organization. The men are trained to use every wile and manoeuvre to conceal their own persons, while they watch every opportunity to pick off their antagonists. To run with a dodging, irregular, zigzag motion, so as to foil the eye of a marksman; to crawl like a reptile among vines and bushes; to hide behind trees, or rocks and stones, or in rifle-pits; to keep the eye stealthily but steadily fixed upon the foe; in short, to imitate in every possible manner the cunning of the savage or the beast of prey, these are the accomplishments of the skirmisher. No trick is thought disgraceful; no stratagem to throw the enemy off his guard is thought unmilitary, if only successful; and, when he takes his murderous aim, the skirmisher is fully aware that, at the same moment, an unseen foe may be taking equally fatal aim at him.

John H. Rhodes, *The History of Battery B, First Regiment Rhode Island Light Artillery, in the War to Preserve the Union* (Providence, RI, 1894)

Previous to the fall of 1861 the field artillery was in an unsatisfactory condition. The high reputation which it had gained in Mexico was lost by the active and persistent hostility of the war department, which almost immediately dismounted three fourths of its authorized batteries . . . Again in 1861 Congress amply provided for the proper organization and command of the artillery in the field, but as there was no chief nor special administration for that arm, and no regulation for its government, its organization, control and direction were left to the fancies of the various army commanders . . . No adequate measures were taken for the supply of recruits, and the batteries were frequently dependent on the infantry of the divisions to which they were attached for men enough to work their guns in battle. For battery-draft they were often glad to get the refuse horses after the ambulance and quarter-masters' trains were supplied . . . On taking command of the army General [Joseph] Hooker had transferred the military command of the artillery to his own headquarters . . . which resulted in such mismanagement and confusion at Chancellorsville that he consented to organize the artillery into brigades. This was a decided improvement and would have been greater if the brigade commanders had held adequate rank. Of the fourteen brigades organized four were commanded by field officers, nine by captains, and one by a lieutenant taken from their batteries for the purpose. The number of field batteries was sixty-five of 370 guns, 212 with the infantry, fifty with the cavalry, and 108 in the reserve.

A Gallant Captain of the Civil War: Being the Record of the Extraordinary Adventures of Frederick Otto Baron von Fritsch [68th New York], ed. Joseph Tyler Butts (New York, 1902)

General Alexander von Schimmelpfennig was, in spite of his long name, a man of small stature, and slender build. His health was not good, and he suffered from dyspepsia, as a consequence of the eighteen months of hard life in the field. He was highly educated, and, after having left the

Prussian service as a captain, he became by profession an engineer and splendid draughtsman. He was not sociable, and liked to be left alone, except before retiring at night. In the day time, when not feeling well, he was generally cross, and his orders were given in a sharp and very commanding voice. He was a strict disciplinarian and an excellent officer, but somewhat soured, and with no inclination to meet superior officers. He dressed in very old uniforms, and thought nothing of appearances . . . "The great misfortune and worst feature in this army is that the Generals lack experience," he said once. "They provide remarkably well, and at times most extravagantly, for the troops; they plan good campaigns; but when firing commences, or the enemy does not act as they had calculated, they lose their heads and are unable to control, assist or manoeuvre their corps. We always lack support in case of need, and reserves are never placed in the right positions. I have seen no generalship shown on the battlefield as yet. The selection of staff officers is very bad with most Generals. They detail relations, sons of old friends, or men recommended by Congressmen, and most of these latter are not scientific soldiers, have no maps, no knowledge of the country, no eyes

to see where help is needed, and brigades, or regiments are left in the lurch after the attacks. But things will get better and better, and may God inspire our great President soon to pick out a commander who possesses some of Napoleon's or [Helmut von] Moltke's genius. There is much jealousy among the Generals, and each one is anxious for personal glory and not over-anxious to assist his fellow commanders, particularly if the latter be German-Americans. So, my dear Aid, in any battle we may fight together, let us look out for ourselves, and never expect outside help. Do not even trust other German Generals. They have caught the spirit, and wish success for themselves only. Very selfish, but almost excusable in the general circumstances. I have given up all hopes of further promotion, but intend to do my duty at all times, and if possible gain some reputation for my brigade, small as it is."

Robert K. Beecham, *Gettysburg: The Pivotal Battle of the Civil War* (Chicago, 1911)

The unit of both armies was the regiment, and in that respect the Confederate army had a decided advantage over the Union army. The regimental formation was the same, but the Confederacy adopted a different method of adding recruits.

The Confederacy, while it lasted, was a military organization, pure and complete; and at the very start their military leaders determined that everything else should bow to the efficiency of their army. Therefore, after the second year of the war they added very few new regiments. Instead, they almost robbed the cradle and the grave for recruits to fill up their armies, but instead of making up full regiments entirely of raw and unseasoned men, they divided them up among the old regiments long in the field, wherein every private soldier was as good or better than an officer of a new regiment. Usually, an old regiment of three hundred experienced men is worth more in battle than a new regiment of nine hundred. Take a regiment reduced by hard service to two hundred men, or twenty to the company; increase it to three hundred by adding ten recruits to each company; within a week or ten days the whole three hundred are veterans, and the recruits are about as good as the best of them. In that way five hundred recruits are better for an army than two full regiments of a thousand men each, fresh from civil life with no military experience . . .

It is doubtful if any of our military authorities ever learned the superiority of the system of sending recruits to old regiments in the field, over adding entirely new regiments; and if they did they could not, or at least did not, put it into practice to any extent. Up to the last year and last month of the war, the State authorities recruited full regiments of green troops and sent them to the front in great unwieldy bodies to fill up the armies, while the old and experienced regiments dwindled into nothingness.

That plan furnished official positions for political pets, most of whom were worthless as soldiers in any position, but it did not do the best that could be done for the army. If one of these full regiments was added to a brigade, it outnumbered the old four regiments combined; but in the first battle any one of the first regiments with a hundred men or less, was usually worth the most. The new regiment would soon become a power in the brigade, but at a terrible sacrifice of life. When reduced to about five hundred men, that regiment was at its best, and became the backbone of the brigade. By their system of filling up their old regiments, the Confederates kept them at all times at very nearly their fighting weight, which, as we have stated, was about five hundred men to the regiment; and as each brigade in both armies contained four or five regiments, it is easy to understand how even a slight difference in the numerical strength of the units created a difference in all the organizations above the unit.

"The Rifle and the Soldier," *Journal of the Royal United Service Institution* (1861)

We must not exaggerate the efficiency of the rifle, and fancy that because the range has been tripled, and the probability of hitting a target has been equally increased, we are going to mow down an army in a few hours, as the reapers manage a field of wheat . . . In its utmost perfection the range of the rifle is 1,000 yards and upwards . . . [But] there is scarcely a rifle in which allowance has not to be made for incorrect sighting. Who can do that in the crash of battle?

It may be affirmed that at great distances firing on isolated men or deployed lines is tantamount to firing at random. It is seldom that the ground presents a sufficiently even surface to permit cannon to fire further than the rifle when firing effectively at 750 yards—at this distance slopes and obstacles often conceal from sight not only a single man but entire bodies of troops—or we are unable to get that inclination of the axis of the piece which is so essential to ensure good results. Of course we can show boards riddled with bullets at 500 and 600 yards or paces, and from this fact the annihilation of cavalry has been predicted; but such practice, in cold blood, with a cool head, at measured distances, lacks the experience of the battle-field . . .

To train a body of men to act essentially and exclusively as skirmishers, is of the utmost importance; since every future battle is sure to be an affair of companies or battalions rather than brigades or divisions, as of old. In a word, much more will depend upon individual officers and men.

Without yielding to anyone in the *adequate* estimate of the rifle, I do not hesitate to share the opinion that it has given no advantage whatever to the fire of the line . . . On the target-ground we strictly prohibit talking—the least disturbance that may distract the attention of the candidate for harmless distinction in complete security. How will it be in the ranks at volley-firing or file-firing: the soldiers excited to the highest degree, cannon-balls decimating the ranks, shells and bullets whistling their infernal tune overhead (which no one forgets, having once heard it), surrounded by smoke, amid the groans of the dying and the shrieks of the wounded? Do what you like beforehand—as we *now* do it—it will matter little; the soldier will simply raise his rifle to the horizontal, and fire without aiming. All will depend upon how much the rifle's horizontal can do, and with regard to the rifles now in use, that is decidedly very little.

At the supreme crisis alluded to the soldier cannot think of aiming at an enemy's feet, belly, or head, nor calculate distance. He directs his muzzle to the breast of the enemy in a word, right before him horizontally . . . In fact, when surrounded by dust and smoke, how is it possible for the soldier to do more than fire horizontally? We may rest assured that between 50 and 250 paces, with our present rifles, there will be more ammunition wasted than ever.

George F. Noyes, *The Bivouac and the Battle-Field; Or, Campaign Sketches in Virginia and Maryland* (New York, 1863)

One trouble is that our men, in going into battle, are weighed down, overloaded with ammunition, having to stuff their pockets as well as their cartridge-boxes with the sixty or eighty rounds ordered. Of course very much of this is thrown away and wasted; but this is only a trifling evil compared with the encouragement thus given to the too prevalent idea among the men that he who fires the greatest number of rounds in battle is the best soldier. I have heard men boasting of their achievements in this regard, and the result of such an idea is a hurried loading and discharge without any regard to aim; a wasting upon trees and foliage of ammunition which, if used at all, should be used so as to defeat the enemy. I was struck with a remark made by a rebel prisoner to his captors, "We never carry more than forty rounds into action, and usually expend about ten."

There is altogether too much of this wild, reckless firing, the men discharging their pieces before bringing them fairly down to a level, and utterly regardless of taking aim. Of course there are periods when heavy, rapid, and continuous volleys are necessary; still it would be well if every man could be drilled as a sharpshooter, taught to shoot slowly, and always take aim, either at the enemy or his supposed locality. This, and the more frequent trust in cold steel alone, the latter being especially necessary in operations against a fortified and sheltered foe, have seemed desirable for our volunteers. How gallantly they can charge, and how fatal have been their volleys, has been too often illustrated on many a bloody field to require any praise of mine; my only suggestion being that if they discharged fewer cartridges, and still more frequently depended on the bayonet alone, it might be better for our cause . . .

I have seen troops in battle discharging their pieces at an angle of forty-five degrees, and the instances of their firing into each other are by no means rare. An appeal may safely be made to many of our officers whether the first duty to be taught an inexperienced soldier should not be this—to fire slowly and composedly, or not at all. I would rather have five hundred men who fired thus, once in two minutes, than a thousand who should be anxious only to discharge their muskets . . . The proportion between the killed and the wounded is about as 1 to 5, and of the wounded about 1 in 10 never recovers. If this be even approximative to the truth, it certainly robs war of some of its presumed fatality. As I have before remarked, the escape of so large a majority of the men, amid such storms of bullets sweeping and yelling around their ears, has always been the great mystery of war.

THE COMMANDERS

In the story of Gettysburg, no two figures bulk larger as commanders than Robert E. Lee and George Brinton McClellan—which is surprising, since McClellan had not been in command of the Army of the Potomac since the previous November. Nevertheless, it was McClellan who created the Army of the Potomac in the fall and winter of 1861 and 1862, who led it into its first great campaign against the Confederate capital of Richmond, on the James River peninsula, who reconstituted it in September 1862 and fought Lee to a standstill at Antietam later that month, and who still commanded the imaginations and loyalties of its soldiers. But it was also McClellan, an 1846 graduate of West Point and one of the shining military intellects of the U.S. Army, who had failed to capture Richmond, who had also failed to pursue Lee's mauled army after Antietam, and who had dared to dictate political policy to his civilian commander in chief, Abraham Lincoln. McClellan had been appointed, shelved, reappointed, reshelved; and on the eve of Gettysburg, there was more than a little expectation that he would be reappointed to command the Army of the Potomac once again.

Not, however, if Abraham Lincoln could help it. When Lincoln first put McClellan in charge of the disorganized troops who had straggled back from defeat at Bull Run, in the summer of 1861, the choice seemed like a stroke of good fortune. McClellan was the child of an elite Philadelphia family, served in the Mexican War, wrote the U.S. Army's assessment of the European armies after the Crimean War, and commanded the Ohio volunteers who crossed into western Virginia and won the first small-scale Union victories of the war. His reorganization of what he named the Army of the Potomac set up brigade, divisional, and eventually corps structures, and promoted new officers to command them. But

McClellan was also a Democrat who regarded Lincoln's Republicans and their anti-slavery enthusiasm as the real cause of the conflict. In July 1862, amid rumors that Lincoln was contemplating an emancipation proclamation, McClellan directly warned Lincoln that he must abandon any thought of emancipating Southern slaves lest the Army of the Potomac disintegrate—as though McClellan himself would bear no responsibility for such disintegration.

Lincoln might have cashiered McClellan on the spot, but he knew that "McClellan has the army with him," and there were whispers that McClellan might stage a coup d'etat. But when McClellan failed to undertake more than a perfunctory pursuit of Lee after Antietam, Lincoln dismissed McClellan, once and for all. It almost backfired. At a farewell review of the Army of the Potomac, "whole regiments broke and flocked" around McClellan, "and with tears and entreaties besought him not to leave them, but to say the word and they would soon settle matters in Washington." McClellan's two successors, Ambrose Burnside and Joseph Hooker, only blundered into fresh defeats and further depressed the army's confidence. Finally, at the end of June 1863, with Lee sweeping rapidly into Pennsylvania, Lincoln ordered the commander of the Army of the Potomac's 5th Corps, George Meade, to take over. Three days later, the fighting at Gettysburg began, and stories that "McClellan was again in command" brought cheers from the Union columns.

And there were still a good many in the Army of the Potomac who would have welcomed that. It is possible to plot the political loyalties of the Army's seven infantry corps along a spectrum that begins with the 2nd Corps, under a veteran Democratic officer from Pennsylvania, Major-General Winfield Scott Hancock, Meade's old 5th Corps, now commanded by Major-General George Sykes, and the 6th Corps under John Sedgwick (who wrote in 1862, "I mean to stand or fall with McClellan"). Meade himself was a Pennsylvania Democrat whose commission in the volunteer service had been delayed in 1861 because of doubts about his political credentials, and one of his division commanders, Abner Doubleday, accused Meade of seeking out McClellan supporters in the Army "to promote these men over the heads of others equally deserving" and "change the army of the Union into a partisan force." At the other end of the Army's political spectrum, the 11th Corps had been fashioned from elements of Union forces in the Shenandoah with a strong anti-slavery flavor, and their commander was Major-General Oliver Otis Howard, one of the staunchest abolitionists and Republicans in the Army of the Potomac. The 3rd Corps was in the hands of Daniel Sickles, a raffish and unscrupulous New York politician who had been a Democratic congressman, but who now threw all his energies and opinions behind Lincoln. Somewhere in the middle was the 1st Corps, commanded by yet another Pennsylvania Democrat, John Reynolds, but with three abolitionist division commanders (Abner Doubleday, James Wadsworth, and John Cleveland Robinson) and the 12th Corps, under Henry Warner Slocum. If the nation had been a "house divided," so were the politics of the Army of the Potomac.

At least, by the time they were on the roads to Gettysburg, all seven of these generals had acquired important combat experience—all except Sickles, in fact, were graduates of West Point and had seen substantial service in the war—and the seven corps had settled into community-like identities of their own. The same could not be said of the Army of Northern Virginia. Its title had been the gift of its first commander, Joseph E. Johnston, during the Peninsula campaign of 1862. But after a serious wound had removed Johnston from action and paved the way for Lee to step into his place, Lee re-created the Army of Northern Virginia as a formidable fighting machine. Lee relied principally on two officers, Thomas Jonathan "Stonewall" Jackson and James Longstreet, with whom he could communicate his intentions almost intuitively, and divided the Army of Northern Virginia between them as commanders of two large-scale infantry corps. Together, Lee, Jackson, and Longstreet forced McClellan away from Richmond and inflicted humiliating defeats on the Army of the Potomac at the second battle of Bull Run, at Fredericksburg and at Chancellorsville.

Unhappily for Lee, his supply of reliable subordinates ran dry after Jackson and Longstreet, and when Jackson died after being wounded at Chancellorsville in May 1863, Lee had to undertake another restructuring of the Army of Northern Virginia. Longstreet would remain his chief lieutenant and command one corps, but the rest of the army's divisions would be rearranged to create two more infantry corps, with command bestowed on two of Jackson's subordinates, Ambrose Powell Hill and

Richard Stoddert Ewell. Both had performed well at division level. But making the jump to corps command, which would require a large measure of independent initiative, would prove beyond both of them and contribute in fatal ways to Confederate defeat at Gettysburg.

This reorganization did nothing to heal a political divide within this Army, too—not over slavery, but over state identities. To the Georgians, Mississippians, and especially the North Carolinians in his army, Lee bestowed entirely too much favor on Virginia officers and gave too much credit to Virginia brigades (not to mention the army being *named* for Virginia, or at least its northern part). An officer in the 52nd North Carolina particularly complained that the Confederate leadership was "rough and harsh with North Carolina troops . . . since the war commenced" because North Carolina had not been considered "well affected to the cause" (or "did not secede quite soon enough to suit some other slave states") and was a persistent "source of Unionism."

Some of the disaffection surrounded James Longstreet, born in South Carolina and raised in Georgia—not Virginia. Unlike Jackson, who was almost deferential in his relation to Lee, Longstreet had ambitions for independent command. Perhaps in pursuit of that, Longstreet made direct suggestions to the Confederate War Department in 1863 that the Confederacy should consider putting its operations in Virginia on hold and diverting troops to the west to shake loose the Union choke hold on Vicksburg. Lee successfully persuaded both the War Department and Longstreet that Confederate resources would be better spent that summer in an invasion of Pennsylvania. But Longstreet conditioned his agreement on his insistence that, once on Northern soil, Lee should adopt defensive tactics rather than seeking to attack the Army of the Potomac. In the years after the battle, Longstreet would amplify these recommendations into a full-dress dissent, extending it even as far as the claim that he had actively discouraged Lee from launching the final attack at Gettysburg under George Pickett on July 3rd.

What is at least true in the case of both armies is that the Union and Confederate generals approached Gettysburg each with a measure of uncertainty dogging their march. Lee would exhibit the most confidence, predicting, as the Army of Northern Virginia moved up into Pennsylvania, that the Army of the Potomac would chase after him in disarray, and allow him to turn and deliver a concentrated blow to the Union army on a piece-by-piece basis. But Lee would himself suffer from a certain measure of uncertainty, since the jovial and spirited commander of his cavalry, James Ewell Brown Stuart (who was routinely referred to, by collapsing his numerous initials together, as "Jeb Stuart"), not only failed to provide sufficient scouting and screening, but unintentionally allowed himself and most of Lee's cavalry to become completely separated from the rest of the Army of Northern Virginia. Two great armies were moving across the landscape of Maryland and Pennsylvania, formidable in appearance, but unsteady and unsure at their heads of what they expected to accomplish.

Peter Wellington Alexander, "Robert E. Lee," *Southern Literary Messenger* (January 1863)

The Confederacy is fortunate in having such a man as General Lee in its service. He is still in the prime and vigor of physical and intellectual manhood, being about fifty-five years of age. He is six feet in height, weighs about one hundred and ninety pounds; is erect, well-formed, and of imposing appearance; has clear, bright, benignant eyes, dark gray hair, and a heavy gray beard. He is exceedingly plain in his dress, and one looks at his costume in vain for those insignia of rank for which most officers show such a weakness. He wears an unassuming black felt hat, with a narrow strip of gold lace around it, and a plain Brigadier's coat, with three stars on the collar, but without the usual braiding on the sleeves. He travels and sleeps in an ambulance, where the army is in motion, and occupies a tent when it is stationary, and not the largest and best house in the neighbourhood, as is the custom of some officers. In a few words, he cares but little for appearances, though one of the handsomest men in the Confederacy, and is content to take the same fare his soldiers get.

On character and personal deportment, he is all that the most ardent patriot can desire. Grave and dignified, he is yet modest and painfully distrustful of his own abilities. The descendant of a gallant officer of the elder revolution [Henry "Light-Horse Harry" Lee] the husband of the grand daughter (by adoption) of Gen. Washington [Mary Custis Lee], the inheritor of a large estate [Arlington], and the trusted leader of a great and victorious army, he is nevertheless accessible to the humblest and most ragged soldier in the ranks, courteous to his officers, just and kind to citizens, and withal, and above all, a meek and humble christian.

During the time the army was in Maryland, an officer of high position in the country suggested a number of reasons to Gen. Lee in support of a grave measure then under discussion. Among others, he remarked to him, that he was trusted by his Government, had the hearts of his soldiers, and possessed the entire confidence of his country, and that the army, the Government and the people relied upon his patriotism and genius. Tears rushed to his eyes, and he exclaimed, "Do not say that—do not say that. I am sensible of my weakness, and such a responsibility as your remark implies would crush me to the earth." He said, in the course of the same conversation, that there was nothing he so much desired as peace and independence. All he had and all he hoped for—all that ambition would suggest or glory give—he would freely give them all to stop the flow of blood and secure freedom to the country. He did not doubt that these blessings would come in due season; but he wanted them now, and would readily sacrifice every thought of personal aggrandizement to save the life of even one soldier.

Gen. Lee, though not possessing the first order of intellect, is endowed with rare judgment and equanimity, unerring sagacity, great self-control, and extraordinary powers of combination. Like Washington, he is a wise man and a good man, and possesses in an eminent degree those qualities which are indispensable in the great leader and champion upon whom the country rests its hope of present success and future independence. In simple intellect, there are other officers in the service who are his equals, and perhaps his superiors; and as a mere fighter, there are some who may excel him. But in the qualities of a commander entrusted with the duty of planning and executing a campaign upon a large scale, and with the direction and government of a large army, whether scattered over a broad extent of territory or massed together as at Richmond, he surpasses them all, and is the peer of any living chieftain on the new World or the Old. The country should feel grateful that Heaven has raised up one in our midst so worthy of our confidence and so capable to lead. The grandson of Washington, so to speak, let us hope that the mantle of the ascending hero has fallen upon the wise and modest chief who now commands the army of Northern Virginia.

J. William Jones, *Personal Reminiscences, Anecdotes, and Letters of Gen. Robert E. Lee* (New York, 1874)

In his address at a memorial meeting in Baltimore, Hon. Reverdy Johnson [U.S. Attorney-General, U.S. senator and U.S. minister to Great Britain] bore the following testimony: "It was his good fortune to know him many years since, before the Mexican War, immediately preceding the great struggle, and after it. The conduct of General Lee at every period was everything that could command the respect, admiration, and love of man. He (Mr. Johnson) had been intimate with the late General [Winfield] Scott, commander of the Army of Mexico . . . and he had heard General Scott more than once say that his success was largely due to the skill, valor, and undaunted energy of Robert E. Lee. It was a theme upon which he (General Scott) liked to converse, and he stated his purpose to recommend him as his successor in the chief command of the army.

"He (Mr. Johnson) was with General Scott in April, 1861, when he received the resignation of General Lee, and witnessed the pain it caused him. It was a sad blow to the success of that war, in which his own sword had as yet been unsheathed. Much as General Scott regretted it, he never failed to say that he was convinced that Lee had taken that step from an imperative sense of duty. General Scott was consoled in a great measure by the reflection that he would have as his opponent a soldier worthy of every man's esteem, and one who would conduct the war upon the strictest rules of civilized warfare. There would be no outrages committed upon private persons or private property which he could prevent . . ."

Robert E. Lee is worthy of all praise. As a man, he was peerless among men. As a soldier, he had no superior and no equal. As a humane and Christian soldier, he towers high in the political horizon. He remembered with what delight, while he was the representative of the country at the court of Great Britain, he heard the praises of General Lee's character and fame from eminent soldiers and statesmen of that country. The occasion does not require any comparisons that were made between the generals of the North and Lee by the public opinion of England. There was not one of them who was the superior of Robert E. Lee. It was not only the skill with which he planned his campaigns, it was the humane manner in which he carried them out.

Jefferson Davis, "Robert E. Lee," *North American Review* 150 (January 1890)

ROBERT EDWARD LEE, gentleman, scholar, gallant soldier, great general, and true Christian, was born in Westmoreland County, Virginia, on January 19, 1807. He was the youngest son of General Henry Lee, who was familiarly known as Light-Horse Harry in the traditions of the war of the Revolution, and who possessed the marked confidence and personal regard of General Washington. R.E. Lee entered the United States Military Academy in the summer of 1825, after which my acquaintance with him commenced. He was, as I remember him, larger and looked more mature than the average "pleb," but less so than [Charles] Mason, who was destined to be the head of his class. His soldierly bearing and excellent conduct caused him in due succession to rise through the several grades and to be the adjutant of the corps of cadets when he was graduated. It is stated that he had not then a demerits mark standing against him, which is quite credible if all reports against him had been cancelled, because they were not for wanton or intentional delinquency.

Though numerically rated second in his class, his proficiency was such that he was assigned to the engineer corps, which for many years he adorned both as a military and civil engineer. He was of the highest type of manly beauty, yet seemingly unconscious of it, and so respectful and unassuming as to make him a general favorite before his great powers had an opportunity for manifestation. His mind led him to analytic rather than perceptive methods for obtaining results. From the date of his graduation in 1829 until 1846 he was engaged in various professional duties, and had by regular promotion attained to the grade of captain of engineers. As such he offered for that which is the crowning glory of man: he offered himself for the welfare of others. He went to Mexico with the rank of captain of engineers, and by gallantry and meritorious conduct rose to the rank of colonel in the army, commission by brevet. After his return he resumed his duties as an officer of the Engineer Corps. While employed in the construction of Fort Carroll, near Baltimore, an event occurred which illustrates his nice sentiment of honor. Some members of the Cuban Junta called upon him and offered him the command of an expedition to over-throw the Spanish control of the island. A very large sum of money was to be paid immediately upon his acceptance of their proposition, and a large sum thenceforward was to be paid monthly. Lee came to Washington to converse with me upon the subject. After a brief discussion of the military problem, he said it was not that he had come to consult me about; the question he was considering was whether, while an officer in the United States Army and because of any reputation he might have acquired as such, he could accept a proposition for foreign service against a government with which the United States were at peace. The conclusion was his decision to decline any further correspondence with the Junta. In 1852 Colonel Lee was made superintendent of the United States Military Academy; a position for which he seemed to be peculiarly fitted as well by his attainments as by his fondness for young people, his fine personal appearance, and impressive manners. When, a year or two thereafter, I visited the academy, and was surprised to see so many gray hairs on his head, he confessed that the cadets did exceedingly worry him, and then it was perceptible that his sympathy with young people was rather an impediment than a qualification for the superintendency. In 1855 four new regiments were added to the army, two of cavalry and two of infantry. Captain Lee, of the engineers, brevet-colonel of the army, was offered the position of lieutenant-colonel of the Second Regiment of cavalry, which he accepted. He was a bold, graceful horseman, and the son of Light-Horse Harry now seemed to be in his proper element; but the chief of engineers endeavored to persuade him that it was a descent to go from the Engineer Corps into the cavalry. Soon after the regiment was organized and assigned to duty in Texas, the colonel, Albert Sidney Johnston, was selected to command an expedition to Utah, and the command of the regiment and the protection of the frontier of Texas against Indian marauders devolved upon Colonel Lee. There, as in every position he had occupied, diligence, sound judgment, and soldierly endowment made his service successful. In 1859, being on leave of absence in Virginia, he was made available for the suppression of the John Brown raid. As soon as relieved from that special assignment he returned to his command in Texas, and on April 25, 1861, resigned from the United States Army. Then was his devotion to principle subjected to a crucial test, the severity of which can only be fully realized by a West-Pointer whose life has been spent in the army. That it was to sever the friendships of youth, to break up the habits of intercourse, of manners, and of thought, others may comprehend and estimate; but the sentiment most profound in the heart of the war-worn cadet, and which made the change most painful to Lee, he has partially expressed in the letters he wrote at the time to his beloved sister [Ann Kinloch Lee Marshall] and to his venerated friend and commander, General Winfield Scott.

Partisan malignants have not failed to misrepresent the conduct of Lee, even to the extent of charging him with treason and desertion; and, unable to appreciate his sacrifice to the allegiance due to Virginia, they have blindly ascribed his action to selfish ambition. It has been erroneously asserted that he was educated at the expense of the general government, and an attempt has been made thence to deduce a special obligation to adhere to it. The cadets of the United States Military Academy are apportioned among the States in proportion to the number of representatives they severally have in the Congress; that is, one for each congressional district, with ten additional for the country at large. The annual appropriations for the support of the army and navy include the commissioned, warrant, and non-commissioned officers, privates, seamen, etc., etc. The cadets and midshipmen are warrant officers, and while at the academies are receiving elementary instruction in and for the public service. At whose expense are they taught and supported? Surely at that of the people, they who pay the taxes and imposts to supply the treasury with means to meet appropriations as well to pay generals and admirals as cadets and midshipmen. The cadet's obligation for his place and support was to the State, by virtue of whose distributive share he was appointed, and whose contributions supplied the United States treasury; through the State, as a member of the Union, allegiance was due to it, and most usefully and nobly did Lee pay the debt both at home and abroad.

No proposition could be more absurd than that he was prompted by selfish ambition to join the Confederacy. With a small part of his knowledge of the relative amount of material of war possessed by the North and South, any one must have seen that the chances of war were against us; but if thrice-armed Justice should enable the South to maintain her independence, as our fathers had done, notwithstanding the unequal contest, what selfish advantage could it bring to Lee? If, as some among us yet expected, many hoped, and all wished, there should be a peaceful separation, he would have left behind him all he had gained by long and brilliant service, and could not have in our small army greater rank than was proffered to him in the larger one he had left. If active hostilities were prosecuted, his large property would be so exposed as to incur serious injury, if not destruction. His mother, Virginia, had revoked the grants she had voluntarily made to the Federal Government, and asserted the state sovereignty and independence she had won from the mother-country by the war of the Revolution; and thus, it was regarded, the allegiance of her sons became wholly her own. Above the voice of his friends at Washington, advising and entreating him to stay with them, rose the cry of Virginia calling her sons to defend her against threatened invasion. Lee heeded this cry only; alone he rode forth . . . his guiding star being duty, and offered his sword to Virginia. His offer was accepted, and he was appointed to the chief command of the forces of the State. Though his reception was most flattering and the confidence manifested in him unlimited, his conduct was conspicuous for the modesty and moderation which had always been characteristic of him. The South had been involved in war without having made due preparation for it. She was without a navy, without even a merchant marine commensurate with her wants during peace; without arsenals, armories, foundries, manufactories, or stores on hand to supply those wants. Lee exerted himself to the utmost to raise and organize troops in Virginia, and when the State joined the Confederacy he was invited to come to Montgomery and explain the condition of his command; but his engagements were so pressing that he sent his second officer, General J.E. Johnston, to furnish the desired information. When the capital of the Confederacy was removed from Montgomery to Richmond, Lee, under the orders of the President, was charged with the general direction of army affairs. In this position the same pleasant relations which had always existed between them continued, and Lee's indefatigable attention to the details of the various commands was of much benefit to the public service.

In the meantime disasters, confusion, and disagreement among the commands in western Virginia made it necessary to send there an officer of higher rank than any then on duty in that section. The service was disagreeable, toilsome, and in no wise promising to give distinction to a commander. Passing by all reference to others, suffice it to say that at last Lee was asked to go, and, not counting the cost, he unhesitatingly prepared to start. By concentrating the troops, and by a judicious selection of the position, he compelled the enemy finally to retreat. There is an incident in this campaign which has never been reported, save as it was orally given to me by General Lee, with a request that I should take no official notice of it. A strong division of the enemy was reported to be encamped in a valley which, one of the colonels said he had found by reconnoissance, could readily be approached on one side, and he proposed, with his regiment, to surprise and attack. General Lee accepted his proposition, but told him that he himself would, in the meantime, with several regiments, ascend the mountain that over-looked the valley on the other side; and at dawn of day on a morning fixed the colonel was to make his assault. His firing was to be the signal for a joint attack from three directions. During the night Lee made a toilsome ascent of the mountain and was in position at the time agreed upon. The valley was covered by a dense fog. Not hearing the signal, he went by a winding path down the side of the mountain and saw the enemy preparing breakfast and otherwise so engaged as to indicate that they were entirely ignorant of any danger. Lee returned to his own command, told them what he had seen, and, though the expected signal had not been given by which the attacking regiment and another detachment were to engage in the assault, he proposed that the regiments then with him should surprise the camp, which he believed, under the circumstances, might successfully be done. The colonels went to consult their men and returned to inform him that they were so cold, wet, and hungry as to be unfit for the enterprise. The fog was then lifting, and it was necessary to attack immediately or to withdraw before being discovered by the much larger force in the valley. Lee therefore withdrew his small command and safely conducted them to his encampment. The colonel who was to give the signal for the joint attack, misapprehending the purpose, reported that when he arrived upon the ground he found the encampment protected by a heavy *abatis* [a barricade of felled trees or branches with sharpened ends facing toward the enemy], which prevented him from making a sudden charge, as he had expected, not understanding that if he had fired his guns at any distance he would have secured the joint attack of the other detachments, and probably brought about an entire victory. Lee generously forbore to exonerate himself when the newspapers in Richmond criticised him severely, one denying him any other consideration except that which he enjoyed as "the President's pet." It was an embarrassment to the Executive to be deprived of the advice of General Lee, but it was deemed necessary again to detach him to look after affairs on the coast of Carolina and Georgia, and so violent had been the unmerited attacks upon him by the Richmond press that it was thought proper to give him a letter to the Governor of South Carolina, stating what manner of man had been sent to him. There his skill as an engineer was manifested in the defences he constructed and devised.

On his return to Richmond he resumed his functions of general supervisor of military affairs. In the spring of 1862 [Episcopal] Bishop [William] Meade lay dangerously ill. This venerable ecclesiastic had taught General Lee his catechism when a boy, and when he was announced to the bishop the latter asked to have him shown in immediately. He answered Lee's inquiry as to how he felt by saying, "Nearly gone, but I wished to see you once more," and then in a feeble voice added: "God bless you, Robert, and fit you for your high and responsible duties . . ."

After the battle of Seven Pines Lee was assigned to the command of the army of Virginia. Thus far his duties had been of a kind to confer a great benefit, but to be unseen and unappreciated by the public. Now he had an opportunity for the employment of his remarkable power of generalization while attending to the minutest details. The public saw manifestation of the first, but could not estimate the extent to which the great results achieved were due to the exact order, systematic economy, and regularity begotten of his personal attention to the proper adjustment of even the smallest part of that mighty machine, a well-organized, disciplined army. His early instructor, in a published letter, seemed to regard the boy's labor of finishing a drawing on a slate as an excess of care. Was it so? No doubt, so far as the particular task was concerned; but this seedling is to be judged by the fruit the tree bore. That little drawing on the slate was the prototype of the exact investigations which crowned with success his labors as a civil and military engineer as well as a commander of armies. May it not have been, not only by endowment but also from these early efforts, that his mind became so rounded, systematic, and complete that his notes written on the battlefield and in the saddle had the precision of form and lucidity of expression found in those written in the quiet of his tent? These incidents are related, not because of their intrinsic importance, but as presenting an example for the emulation of youths whose admiration of Lee may induce them to follow the toilsome methods by which he attained to true greatness and enduring fame.

In the early days of June, 1862, General McClellan threatened the capital, Richmond, with an army numerically much superior to that to the command of which Lee had been assigned. A day or two after he had joined the army, I was riding to the front and saw a number of horses hitched in front of a house, and among them recognized General Lee's. Upon dismounting and going in, I found some general officers engaged in consultation with him as to how McClellan's advance could be checked, and one of them commenced to explain the disparity of force and with pencil and paper to show how the enemy could . . . by successive parallels make his approach irresistible. "Stop, stop," said Lee; "if you go to ciphering we are whipped before-hand . . ."

I have had occasion to remonstrate with General Lee for exposing himself, as I thought, unnecessarily in reconnoissance, but he justified himself by saying he "could not understand things so well unless he saw them." In the excitement of battle his natural combativeness would sometimes overcome his habitual self-control; thus it twice occurred in the campaign against Grant that the men seized his bridle to restrain him from his purpose to lead them in a charge.

He was always careful not to wound the sensibilities of any one, and sometimes, with an exterior jest or compliment, would give what, if properly appreciated, was instruction for the better performance of some duty; for example, if he thought a general officer was not visiting his command as early and as often as was desirable, he might admire his horse and suggest that the animal would be improved by more exercise.

He was not of the grave, formal nature that he seemed to some who only knew him when sad realities cast dark shadows upon him; but even then the humor natural to him would occasionally break out. For instance, General Lee called at my office for a ride to the defences of Richmond, then under construction. He was mounted on a stallion which some kind friend had recently sent him. As I mounted my horse, his was restive and kicked at mine. We rode on quietly together, though Lee was watchful to keep his horse in order. Passing by an encampment, we saw near a tent two stallions tied at a safe distance from one another. "There," said he, "is a man worse off than I am." When asked to explain, he said: "Don't you see he has two stallions? I have but one." His habits had always been rigidly temperate, and his fare in camp was of the simplest. I remember on one battle-field riding past where he and his staff were taking their luncheon. He invited me to share it, and when I dismounted for the purpose it proved to have consisted only of bacon and cornbread. The bacon had all been eaten, and there were only some crusts of cornbread left, which, however, having been saturated with the bacon gravy, were in those hard times altogether acceptable, as General Lee was assured in order to silence his regrets. While he was on duty in South Carolina and Georgia, Lee's youngest son, Robert, then a mere boy, left school and came down to Richmond, announcing his purpose to go into the army. His older brother, Custis, was a member of my staff, and, after a conference, we agreed that it was useless to send the boy back to school, and that he probably would not wait in Richmond for the return of his father; so we selected a battery which had been organized in Richmond and sent Robert to join it. General Lee told me that at the battle of Sharpsburg this battery suffered so much that it had to be withdrawn for repairs and some fresh horses; but, as he had no troops even to form a reserve, as soon as the battery could be made useful it was ordered forward. He said that as it passed him a boy mounted as a driver of one of the guns, much stained with powder, said, "Are you going to put us in again, general?" After replying to him in the affirmative, he was struck by the voice of the boy and asked him, "Whose son are you?" to which he answered, "I am Robbie," whereupon his father said, "God bless you, my son, you must go in."

When General Lee was in camp near Richmond his friends frequently sent him something to improve his mess-table. A lady noted for the very good bread she made had frequently favored him with some. One day, as we were riding through the street, she was standing in her front door and bowed to us. The salutation was, of course, returned. After we had passed he asked me who she was. I told him she was the lady who sent him such good bread. He was very sorry he had not known it, but to go back would prove that he had not recognized her as he should have done. His habitual avoidance of any seeming harshness, which caused him sometimes, instead of giving a command, to make a suggestion, was probably a defect. I believe that he had in this manner indicated that supplies were to be deposited for him at Amelia Court-House, but the testimony of General [John C.] Breckenridge, Secretary of War, of General [Isaac Monroe] St. John, Commissary General, and Louis Harvey, president of the Richmond and Danville Railroad, conclusively proves that no such requisition was made upon either of the persons who should have received it; and, further, that there were supplies both at Danville and Richmond which could have been sent to Amelia Court-House if information had been received that they were wanted there. Much has been written in regard to the failure to occupy the

Round Top at Gettysburg early in the morning of the second day's battle, to which failure the best judgment attributes our want of entire success in that battle. Whether this was due to the order not being sufficiently positive or not, I will leave to the historians who are discussing that important event.

I have said that Lee's natural temper was combative, and to this may be ascribed his attack on the third day at Gettysburg, when the opportunity had not been seized which his genius saw was the gate to victory. It was this last attack to which I have thought he referred when he said it was all his fault, thereby sparing others from whatever blame was due for what had previously occurred . . . Arbitrary power might pervert justice and trample on right, but could not turn the knightly Lee from the path of honor and truth. Descended from a long line of illustrious warriors and statesmen, Robert Edward Lee added new glory to the name he bore, and, whether measured by a martial or an intellectual standard, will compare favorably with those whose reputation it devolved upon him to sustain and emulate.

"Letter From Maj. Scheibert, of the Prussian Royal Engineers," *Southern Historical Society Papers* 5 (January-February 1878)

I cannot remember, notwithstanding my earnest studies in military history, one case where the history of a battle has been so fully illustrated and illuminated by individual reports given by all of the prominent leaders—not immediately after the battle, when personal impressions are conflicting, but after a lapse of more than ten years, when time and matured judgment have ripened the fresh sketch into a splendid picture. The result is so impressive that if I were professor of military science, I would choose the battle of Gettysburg for the special study of my students. My personal impressions about the poor result of the battle of Gettysburg have been exactly expressed by Gen'l Heth, whose letter I fully endorse. But he, as well as the other writers, has omitted one element which seems to me to be of the highest importance. I refer to the individual character of Gen'l Lee. I have made the military character of this General, who has never had an admirer of such fervour as myself, my peculiar study, and have written a biographical sketch of him, which appeared in a German paper.

Lee was, in my opinion, one of the ablest leaders of this century in two great qualities. He weighed everything, even the smallest detail, in making his general plan of battle, and he made the boldest dispositions with heroic courage and the most stubborn energy. He gave to every link the right place in the construction of a chain which became a masterpiece of military workmanship.

He did not reach his conclusions . . . by an instinctive, sudden impulse; his plans did not come upon him like the lightning's flash followed by the thunder's crash: but he painfully and studiously labored in order to arrange those splendid dispositions fraught with the keenest and most hardy enterprises, and well worthy of the troops which were ordered to execute them. General Lee, in speaking to me of his dispositions, said: "Captain, I do everything in my power to make my plans as perfect as possible, and to bring the troops upon the field of battle; the rest must be done by my generals and their troops, trusting to Providence for the victory." . . .

But in all these cases General Jackson (who had his special information coupled with his natural instincts, his sudden impulses, and his peculiar ideas) came or was ordered to headquarters to give his personal opinions to the Commanding General, who linked the genial thoughts of Jackson to his own beautiful chain: *e.g.*, before the battle of Chancellorsville these famous leaders met on a hill near the Aldrich house to mature those plans which resulted in the unequaled battles of the Wilderness and Chancellorsville. Each of these generals was the supplement to the other; just as in the family, both man and wife are necessary to keep up the household.

When Jackson fell, Lee, as he himself said, lost his right arm, the army lost the other, and thus the void which had been made was too great to be so soon closed, the wound which the army received too deep to be healed in four weeks. Thus the carefully-planning general encountered the fearful odds at Gettysburg without . . . his ready counsellor, General Jackson. He himself felt this great loss in making his dispositions . . .

All who saw him on these two occasions, Chancellorsville and Gettysburg, will remember that Lee at Chancellorsville (where I had the honor of being at his side in the brunt of the struggle) was full of calm, quiet, self-possession, feeling that he had done his duty to the utmost, and had brought the army into the most favorable position to defeat the hostile host. In the days at Gettysburg this quiet self-possessed calmness was wanting. Lee was not at his ease, but was riding to and fro, frequently changing his position, making anxious inquiries here and there, and looking care worn. After the shock of battle was over he resumed his accustomed calmness, for then he saw clearly and handled the army with that masterly ability which was peculiar to him. This uneasiness during the days of the battle was contagious to the army, as will appear from the reports of Longstreet, [John Bell] Hood, Heth, and others, and as appeared also to me from the peep I had of the battlefield. What a difference from the systematic advance of the army from the Wilderness to the assault of the breastworks at Chancellorsville, where a unity of disposition and a feeling of security reigned in all the ranks. At Gettysburg there was cannonading without real effect, desultory efforts without combination, and lastly, the single attack which closed the drama, and which I, from my outlook in the top of the tree, believed to be only a reconnaissance in heavy force. Want of confidence, misapprehensions, and mistakes were the consequences, less of [Major-General Jeb] Stuart's absence than of the absence of Jackson, whose place up to this time had not been filled.

After this it was filled by Lee himself, who, like a father when the mother dies, seeks to fill both her place and his own in the house . . .

The battle of Gettysburg would have been won by Lee's army if it could have advanced at any time and on any part of the field to one concentrated and combined attack on the enemy's position . . .

Isaac R. Trimble, "The Battle and Campaign of Gettysburg," *Southern Historical Society Papers* 26 (January-December 1898)

June 26th [1863]

General Lee entered Maryland. I met him in Hagerstown and suggested sending at once a brigade to Baltimore to take that city, rouse Maryland, and thus embarrass the enemy. He so far considered the plan as to write to General A.P. Hill, the only corps commander near, to ask if he could spare a brigade for that purpose, who told me he had sent a reply to General Lee, that it would reduce his force too much, so it was not done.

June 27th

In the afternoon I met General Lee again at his tent pitched near the road, for a night halt. He called me to where he was seated, and unfolding a map of Pennsylvania, asked me about the topography of the country east of the South Mountain in Adams county and around Gettysburg. He said with a smile, "as a civil engineer you may know more about it than any of us." After my description of the country and saying that "almost every square mile contained good positions for battle or skillful maneuvering," he remarked (and I think I repeat his words nearly verbatim) "Our army is in good spirits, not over fatigued, and can be concentrated on any one point in twenty-four hours or less. I have not yet heard that the enemy have crossed the Potomac, and am waiting to hear from General [Jeb] Stuart. When they hear where we are they will make forced marches to interpose their forces between us and Baltimore and Philadelphia. They will come up, probably through Frederick; broken down with hunger and hard marching, strung out on a long line and much demoralized, when they come into Pennsylvania. I shall throw an overwhelming force on their advance, crush it, follow up the success, drive one corps back on another, and by successive repulses and surprises before they can concentrate; create a panic and virtually destroy the army."

When asked my opinion, I said the plan ought to be successful, as I never knew our men to be in finer spirits in any campaign. He said: "That is, I hear, the general impression."

At the conclusion of our interview, he laid his hand on the map, over Gettysburg, and said hereabout we shall probably meet the enemy and fight a great battle, and if God gives us the victory, the war will be over and we shall achieve the recognition of our independence. He concluded by saying General Ewell's forces are by this time in Harrisburg; if not, go and join him, and help to take the place.

Moxley Sorrel, *Recollections of a Confederate Staff Officer* (New York, 1905)

I was a volunteer aide with the rank by courtesy, but no pay. When I saw my messmates taking theirs in very comfortably . . . I wrote my application to the Secretary of War asking to be appointed a second lieutenant,

C.S.A., and assigned as might be thought proper. Blushing like a girl, I asked General Longstreet if he could endorse it favorably. Glancing hastily at the paper, he said, "Certainly," and then added carelessly, "but it isn't necessary." The words made no impression at the time, but they came to mind later . . . This had been going on for some time until the official mail one fine morning brought me a commission as captain in the Adjutant-General's Department, with orders to report to Longstreet . . . I had had no military training except some drill and tactics at school, but it seemed he thought I took to the work handily. He instructed me to . . . take over all the duties of the office. I rose with Longstreet to be major and lieutenant-colonel in that department, and brigadier-general commanding in Hill's corps, and my affection for him is unfailing. Such efficiency on the field as I may have displayed came from association with him and the example of that undismayed warrior. He was like a rock in steadiness when sometimes in battle the world seemed flying to pieces . . .

It was while we were about Centerville [Virginia] that a great change came over Longstreet. He was rather gay in disposition with his chums, fond of a glass, and very skilful at poker. He, [Major-General Earl] Van Dorn, and G[ustavus] W. Smith were accustomed to play almost every night with T. J. [Thomas Grimke] Rhett, General [Albert Sidney] Johnston's adjutant-general, and we sometimes heard of rather wild scenes amid these old army chums—all from West Point, all having served in Mexico and against the Indians. Longstreet's wife and children were at Richmond. He was devoted to them. Suddenly scarlet fever broke out and three of the children died within one week. He was with them, and some weeks after resumed his command a changed man. He had become very serious and reserved and a consistent member of the Episcopal Church. His grief was very deep and he had all our sympathies; later years lightened the memory of his sorrow and he became rather more like his old cheerful self, but with no dissipation of any kind . . .

Longstreet's conduct [at the battle of Antietam] was magnificent. He seemed everywhere along his extended lines, and his tenacity and deep-set resolution, his inmost courage, which appeared to swell with the growing peril to the army, undoubtedly stimulated the troops to greater action, and held them in place despite all weakness. My staff comrades described to me later his appearance and reception by Lee when they met at night after firing ceased. Longstreet, big, heavy, and red, grimly stern after this long day's work, that called for all we could stomach, rolled in . . . Lee immediately welcomed him with unconcealed joy. "Here comes my war horse just from the field he has done so much to save!"

James Longstreet, "The Mistakes of Gettysburg," *Annals of the War Written by Leading Participants North and South* (Philadelphia, 1879)

The invasion of Pennsylvania was a movement that General Lee and his council agreed should be defensive in tactics, while, of course, it was offensive in strategy; that the campaign was conducted on this plan until we had left Chambersburg, when, owing to the absence of our cavalry, and our consequent ignorance of the enemy's whereabouts, we collided with them unexpectedly, and that General Lee had lost the matchless equipoise that usually characterized him, and, through excitement and the doubt that enveloped the enemy's movements, changed the whole plan of the campaign, and delivered a battle under ominous circumstances . . . At this late day the official relations of General Lee and myself are brought into question. He is credited with having used uncomely remarks concerning me, in the presence of a number of subordinate officers, just on the eve of battle. It is hardly possible that any one acquainted with General Lee's exalted character will accept such statements as true. It is hardly possible that any general could have been so indiscreet as to have used such expressions under such circumstances. There certainly never was, in the relations between General Lee and myself, anything to admit the possibility of his having used the expression attributed. Our relations were affectionate, intimate, and tender during the whole war. That his confidence in me was never shaken, there is the most abundant proof; but I cannot be tempted, even by direct misrepresentations, into a discussion of this subject . . . I regret most deeply that this discussion was not opened before the death of General Lee. If the charges so vehemently urged against me after his death had been preferred, or even suggested, in his lifetime, I do not believe they would have needed any reply from me. General Lee would have answered them himself, and have set history right. But, even as the matter is, I do not fear the verdict of history on Gettysburg. Time sets all things right. Error lives but a day—truth is eternal.

Heros von Borcke, *Memoirs of the Confederate War for Independence* (Philadelphia, 1867)

General [James Ewell Brown] Stuart was a stoutly-built man, rather above the middle height, of a most frank and winning expression, the lower part of his fine face covered with a thick brown beard, which flowed over his breast. His eye was quick and piercing, of a light blue in repose, but changing to a darker tinge under high excitement. His whole person seemed instinct with vitality, his movements were alert, his observation keen and rapid, and altogether he was to me the model of a dashing cavalry leader. Before the breaking out of hostilities between the North and South, he had served in the 1st United States Cavalry, of which regiment General Joseph E. Johnston was the Lieut.-Colonel, against the Indians of the Far West, and was severely wounded in an encounter with the Cheyennes on the Solomon's Fork of the Kansas river, in July 1857. In that wild life of the prairie . . . Stuart had passed nearly all his waking hours in the saddle, and thus became one of the most fearless and dexterous horsemen in America, and he had acquired a love of adventure which made activity a necessity of his being. He delighted in the neighing of the charger and the clangour of the bugle, and he had something of [Joachim] Murat's weakness for the vanities of military parade. He betrayed this latter quality in his jaunty uniform, which consisted of a small grey jacket, trousers of the same stuff, and over them high military boots, a yellow silk sash, and a grey slouch hat, surmounted by a sweeping black ostrich plume. Thus attired, sitting gracefully on his fine horse, he did not fail to attract the notice and admiration of all who saw him ride along.

Richard Taylor, *Destruction and Reconstruction: Personal Experiences of the Late War in the United States* (New York, 1879)

I had abundant opportunities for studying the original character of "Dick Ewell." We had known each other for many years, but now our friendship and intercourse became close and constant. Graduated from West Point in 1840, Ewell joined the 1st Regiment of United States Dragoons, and, saving the Mexican war, in which he served with such distinction as a young cavalryman could gain, his whole military life had been passed

on the plains, where, as he often asserted, he had learned all about commanding fifty United States dragoons, and forgotten everything else. In this he did himself injustice, as his career proves; but he was of a singular modesty. Bright, prominent eyes, a bomb-shaped, bald head, and a nose like that of Francis of Valois, gave him a striking resemblance to a woodcock; and this was increased by a bird-like habit of putting his head on one side to utter his quaint speeches. He fancied that he had some mysterious internal malady, and would eat nothing but frumenty, a preparation of wheat; and his plaintive way of talking of his disease, as if he were someone else, was droll in the extreme. His nervousness prevented him from taking regular sleep, and he passed nights curled around a camp-stool, in positions to dislocate an ordinary person's joints . . . On such occasions, after long silence, he would suddenly direct his eyes and nose toward me with, "General Taylor, what do you suppose President Davis made me a major-general for?"— beginning with a sharp accent and ending with a gentle lisp. Superbly mounted, he was the boldest of horsemen, invariably leaving the roads to take timber and water . . . With a fine tactical eye on the battlefield, he was never content with his own plan until he had secured the approval of another's judgment, and chafed under the restraint of command, preparing to fight with the skirmish line. On two occasions in the Valley, during the temporary absence of Jackson from the front, Ewell summoned me to his side, and immediately rushed forward among the skirmishers, where some sharp work was going on. Having refreshed himself, he returned with the hope that "old Jackson would not catch him at it." He always spoke of Jackson, several years his junior, as "old," and told me in confidence that he admired his genius, but was certain of his lunacy, and that he never saw one of Jackson's couriers approach without expecting an order to assault the North Pole.

Later, after he had heard Jackson seriously declare that he never ate pepper because it produced a weakness in his left leg, he was confirmed in this opinion. With all his oddities, perhaps in some measure because of them, Ewell was adored by officers and men.

Horace Porter, *Campaigning With Grant* (New York, 1907)

General Meade was a most accomplished officer. He had been thoroughly educated in his profession, and had a complete knowledge of both the science and the art of war in all its branches. He was well read, possessed of a vast amount of interesting information, had cultivated his mind as a linguist, and spoke French with fluency. When foreign officers visited the front they were invariably charmed by their interviews with the commander of the Army of the Potomac. He was a disciplinarian to the point of severity, was entirely subordinate to his superiors, and no one was more prompt than he to obey orders to the letter. In his intercourse with his officers the bluntness of the soldier was always conspicuous, and he never took pains to smooth any one's ruffled feelings.

There was an officer serving in the Army of the Potomac who had formerly been a surgeon. One day he appeared at Meade's headquarters in a high state of indignation, and said: "General, as I was riding over here some of the men in the adjoining camps shouted after me and called me 'Old Pills,' and I would like to have it stopped." Meade just at that moment was not in the best possible frame of mind to be approached with such a complaint. He seized hold of the eye-glasses, conspicuously large in size, which he always wore, clapped them astride of his nose with both hands, glared through them at the officer, and exclaimed: "Well, what of that! How can I prevent it! Why, I hear that, when I rode out the other day, some of the men called me a 'd——d old goggle-eyed snapping-turtle,' and I can't even stop that!" The officer had to content himself with this explosive expression of a sympathetic fellow-feeling, and to take his chances thereafter as to obnoxious epithets.

George G. Meade, jnr., *The Life and Letters of George Gordon Meade, Major-General United States Army* (New York, 1913), Vol. 2

General Meade lay quietly asleep in his tent at three o'clock of the morning of June 28, when he was aroused by hearing on the outside an inquiry for his tent, by a person who claimed to be the bearer of important despatches to him. This proved to be Colonel James A. Hardie, of General [Henry Wager] Halleck's staff, who entered General Meade's tent and executed his mission.

What this mission might have been was the occasion of agitated comment among several of General Meade's aides, who, their tents being in the immediate vicinity, were awakened by the stir in camp at that hour. That it had been executed in the dead of night, by an officer direct from the general-in-chief at the War Department, proved it to be of the last importance; but that was the only thing evident. What it portended, whether good or ill, to their general, no one could pretend to say. Enough, however, of the misunderstandings and difficulties with which he lately had had to contend was known to that little band to make some apprehensive that all was not well. The details of the interview between General Meade and Colonel Hardie will be left for the general himself to relate in the next letter to his wife.

General Meade soon appeared from his tent, and designating one of his aides [George G. Meade, jnr.] as the only officer, besides Colonel Hardie, to accompany him, just as the day was faintly dawning he mounted and set out with his two companions for the head-quarters of the army. The little party rode silently along, the conversation almost restricted to a few questions asked by General Meade, who seemed deeply absorbed in his own thoughts, until, head-quarters being reached just after daylight, he was ushered into the tent of General Hooker, who was apparently ready to receive him. The interview between Generals Hooker and Meade lasted for some time, when the latter issued from the tent and called to his aide, who had been patiently waiting outside, still uninformed as to what was taking place, but with a vague impression that the fate of his general was not to be that predicted by his brother aides-de-camp. Although, as he answered the general's summons, he could not fail to observe that the general continued very grave, he also perceived a familiar twinkle of the eye, denoting the anticipation of surprise at information to be imparted, the effect of which he was curious to see; and so, when he at last quietly said, "Well, George, I am in command of the Army of the Potomac," his hearer was not, after all, very much surprised.

Giving immediate directions for his other aides-de-camp to join him at head-quarters, and for having personal effects brought over from the head-quarters of the Fifth Corps, the general retired into one of the tents, and in his consummate manner, in which all his powers were at his disposal at a moment's notice, at once bent his mind and energies to the task before him. The magnitude of this task may be faintly imagined but cannot be realized. It must be remembered that a change of commanders had been made in an army, not when, the preliminary manoeuvres having been executed, it awaited or was engaged in battle, where, in either case, a change of commanders is an ordinary incident of war, but that the change had been made in an army on the march, with its corps necessarily distributed over a great extent of territory, advancing to intercept and concentrate against an army of supposably equal or superior numbers, the whereabouts of which was not accurately known, led by the ablest general of the enemy.

George G. Meade Papers, Historical Society of Pennsylvania

(To 'Dear Doct.,' August 5, 1861) I have great confidence personally in McClellan—know him well—know he is one of the best men we have to handle large armies, but I fear the means at his disposal will not be [equal] to the task assigned him.

(To Margaretta Meade, October 12, 1861) They do not any of them officers or men seem to have the least idea of the solemn duty they have imposed upon themselves in becoming soldiers. Soldiers they are not in any sense of the word.

(To Margaretta Meade, November 24, 1861) The men are good material, and with good officers might readily be molded into soldiers—but the officers, as a rule with but few exceptions are ignorant, inefficient, & worthless. They have no control or command over the men . . . Let the ultras on both sides be repudiated, & the masses of conservative & moderate men may compromise & settle the difficulty.

(To John Sergeant Meade, March 29, 1862) Conquering the South is no child's play, and will involve an immense expenditure of money . . . If it should please God to give us a decisive victory in *Va. Kentucky* & *Missouri* the South will conclude it is useless to contend any longer—on the other hand should our forces meet with disaster, in the three fields . . . I think the people of the North will be prepared, to yield the independency of the South on the ground that it does not pay to resist them. This is the conviction without doubt, that makes McClellan so cautious & determined not to risk a battle until he has every reason to believe the chances of success are in our favor . . .

(To Margaretta Meade, June 22, 1862) [McClellan] was very civil & kind to me . . . He talked very freely of the way in which he had been treated, and said positively that had not McDowell's corps been withdrawn, he would long before now have been in Richmond.

(To John Sergeant Meade, October 23, 1862) I must confess I do not mourn the results of the election in Pa Ohio & Indiana. A proper & loyal opposition to the administration will effect much good, in requiring those in power to be careful their acts cannot be subjected to legitimate criticism.

(To John Sergeant Meade, March 31, 1863) Gen. Biddle . . . who is I believe a regular abolitionist . . . is expansive, but in a little discussion we had at breakfast this morning, I gave him to understand that we eschew politics in the army . . .

There is much talk of a forthcoming letter from the President to a convention in Illinois which is to precede a Proclamation to the South offering amnesty to the masses, if they will give up their leaders—I don't believe much in this story . . . The leaders at the South have too strong a hold on the people to permit themselves to be sacrificed. I believe Peace could be made but not on the terms that the rulers of the North would require . . .

(To Margaretta Meade, August 9, 1863) [If] the draft is not heartily responded to the Govt had better wake up their minds to letting the South go unless they avail themselves of the present opportunity to attempt a reconstruction on some terms the South can accede to . . . I am nothing of a copperhead. I am for a vigorous prosecution of the war. But unless more troops volunteer or are drafted, then I say make terms of some kind or other with the South . . .

(To Margaretta Meade, January 30, 1865, on meeting with the Confederate peace commissioners bound for Hampton Roads) I called this morning with Genl Grant on them & remained after Genl Grant left, and talked very freely with them. I told them very plainly what I thought was the basis on which the people of the North would be glad to have peace—by the emphatic restoration of the Union, and such a settlement of the slavery question, as should be final, removing it forever as a subject of strife . . . They found the difficulty would be to obtain such modification of the old Constitution as would protect the states, in case of other questions arising to produce strife. I said if you mean to propose a reorganization & change in our government—I don't think you will meet with success . . . Mr. [Robert M.T.] Hunter then asked me, what we proposed to do with the slaves after freeing them, as it was well known they would not work unless compelled—I replied this was understandably a grave question but not insurmountable—they must have labor & the negroes must have support—between the two necessities I thought some system could be found accommodating both interests, which would not be as obnoxious as slavery . . . All thus I have written you, must be confidential, as it would not do to let it be known I have been talking with them, or what I have said.

"Testimony of Major-General Abner Doubleday" (March 1, 1864), in *Report of the Joint Committee on the Conduct of the War at the Second Session, Thirty-Eighth Congress* (Washington, DC, 1865)

There has always been a great deal of favoritism in the army of the Potomac. No man who is an anti-slavery man or an anti-McClellan man can expect decent treatment in that army as at present constituted.

QUESTION. Has that, in your judgment, led to great disasters, from time to time, in the army of the Potomac?

ANSWER. Yes, I think it has.

QUESTION. You speak of political favoritism. Explain what you mean by that.

ANSWER. I think there have been pro-slavery cliques controlling that army, composed of men who, in my opinion, would not have been unwilling to make a compromise in favor of slavery, and who desired to have nobody put in authority except those who agreed with them on that subject.

QUESTION. Do you believe that this feeling of rivalry and jealousy, that seems to have actuated the high corps commanders of that army, has been detrimental to the public service, and led to checks and defeats?

ANSWER. Undoubtedly. I cannot but think that there has been an indifference, to say the least, on the part of certain officers, to the success of our army . . .

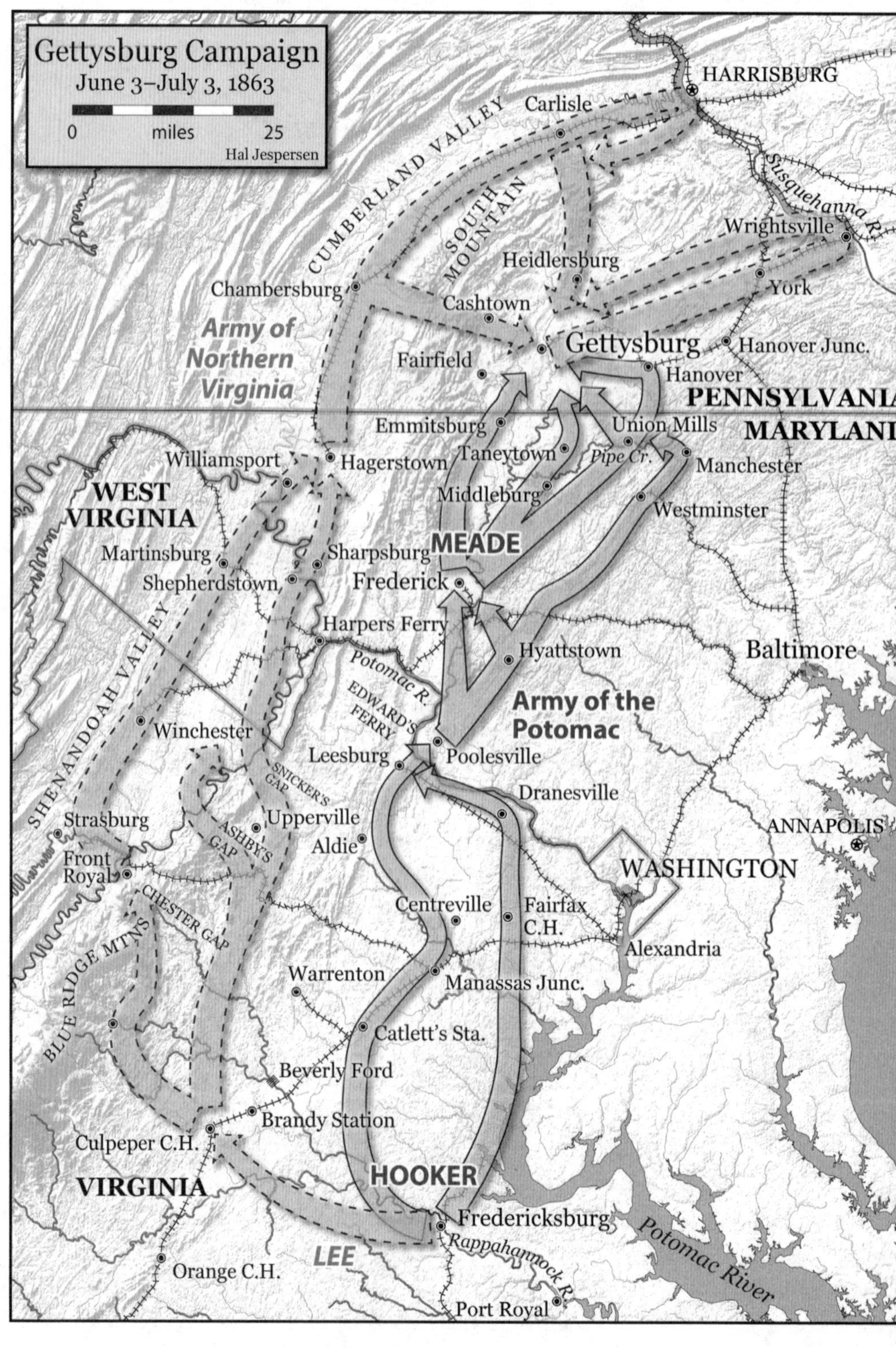

Gettysburg Campaign
June 3–July 3, 1863
0 miles 25
Hal Jespersen
HARRISBURG
Carlisle
CUMBERLAND VALLEY
SOUTH MOUNTAIN
Susquehanna R.
Wrightsville
Heidlersburg
York
Chambersburg
Cashtown
Army of Northern Virginia
Gettysburg
Hanover Junc.
Fairfield
Hanover
PENNSYLVANIA
MARYLAND
Emmitsburg
Union Mills
Taneytown
Pipe Cr.
Manchester
Williamsport
Hagerstown
Middleburg
Westminster
WEST VIRGINIA
MEADE
Martinsburg
Sharpsburg
Shepherdstown
Frederick
Harpers Ferry
Hyattstown
Baltimore
Potomac R.
SHENANDOAH VALLEY
EDWARD'S FERRY
Army of the Potomac
Winchester
Leesburg
Poolesville
SNICKER'S GAP
Dranesville
Strasburg
Upperville
ASHBY'S GAP
ANNAPOLIS
Aldie
Front Royal
WASHINGTON
CHESTER GAP
Centreville
Fairfax C.H.
Alexandria
BLUE RIDGE MTNS
Warrenton
Manassas Junc.
Catlett's Sta.
Beverly Ford
Brandy Station
Culpeper C.H.
HOOKER
VIRGINIA
Fredericksburg
Potomac River
Rappahannock R.
LEE
Orange C.H.
Port Royal

THE FIRST MOVES

Brandy Station and Winchester

The battle of Gettysburg was the climax of a campaign that began nearly a month before, on June 3rd, when Robert E. Lee began pulling the first elements of the Army of Northern Virginia away from their positions behind the Rappahannock River and sliding them westward toward Culpeper Court House, and then pivoting northward and entering the Shenandoah Valley. The Valley would serve as their highway to the Potomac. Once across that barrier, they would continue northward across the narrow neck of western Maryland and into central Pennsylvania. There, they divided, with various parts of the Army heading northeastward toward the Pennsylvania state capital of Harrisburg, while others moved on a direct line east from the railroad center at Chambersburg toward York and the Susquehanna River.

This plan was carefully constructed. A year before, Lee had lunged across the Potomac into Maryland, aiming to march into central Pennsylvania, just as he was doing now. He then chose to cross the Potomac much closer to Washington, DC, which left the Federal garrison at Harpers Ferry in his rear. At that time, to prevent any mishap and to open the way for establishing a new supply line, Lee sent off "Stonewall" Jackson and almost half of the Army of Northern Virginia to capture Harpers Ferry. But, in the most famous intelligence mishap of the war, Lee's campaign orders fell into the hands of George McClellan, then commanding the Army of the Potomac; and just as bad, Harpers Ferry held out longer than Lee had predicted. This nearly allowed McClellan to fall on the separated pieces of Lee's army, and it was only by the narrowest of margins that Lee was able to reassemble his forces and stand McClellan off at Antietam before retreating into Virginia. Lee was not going to make that mistake again. This time he would bypass Harpers Ferry to the west.

That didn't mean Lee wouldn't meet Federal resistance as he began to move. Joseph Hooker picked up reports of large-scale Confederate movement by June 6th. He was convinced, however, that this was only a cover for a cavalry raid northward by Jeb Stuart, one of several Stuart had conducted over the previous year, and he ordered the cavalry of the Army of the Potomac, under Major-General Alfred Pleasonton, to intercept the rebels in a freewheeling cavalry fight at Brandy Station. Stuart was embarrassed at being caught napping, and even more by having to be rescued by the arrival of Lee's infantry. But Hooker failed to realize that Stuart's cavalry was not, in fact, the real substance of the Confederate movement, and he made no significant move to prevent Lee's movement into the Valley until rebel infantry showed up outside the Valley's Federal garrison at Winchester, Virginia.

Winchester had already changed hands several times in the war and was about to change hands again. Richard Ewell's corps led the way down the Valley, and it was Ewell's corps which overran Winchester's Union defenders (under Robert H. Milroy) on June 14th. Milroy was a political general—which is to say that he had only marginal experience in war, but perfect Republican credentials, and he had made himself roundly hated in the environs of Winchester. Ewell's divisions under Jubal Early and Edward Johnson easily squeezed Milroy's troops out of Winchester and gave them a highly profitable chase down the Valley toward the Potomac. As many as six to seven thousand Union prisoners were captured, along with artillery, supplies, and 2,800 horses. By June 18th, Ewell's men were fording the Potomac and crossing into Maryland.

Ewell's victory at Winchester seemed to confirm the wisdom of Lee's choice of Ewell to command most of "Stonewall" Jackson's old corps. But those advantages were soon squandered. After the fall of Winchester, Lee began to worry about where Hooker and the Army of the Potomac might be, since no useful news had come his way about either. Jeb Stuart, still smarting from the humiliation of Brandy Station, fought three sharp little cavalry actions at Aldie, Middleburg, and Upperville between June 17th and June 22nd. His confidence restored, Stuart proposed taking three of the Army of Northern Virginia's seven cavalry brigades in a wide sweep eastward to the Potomac, covering the flank of Lee's infantry as it moved northward, but also contacting and observing the Army of the Potomac as it moved to the river in pursuit. Stuart, with just under five thousand Confederate cavalrymen, began his sweep on June 25th. Almost at once, he encountered large masses of Federal infantry in motion near Haymarket, Virginia; and in an ill-considered effort to get around them, Stuart moved even farther eastward, and soon found himself entirely on the far side of the Union army and completely out of communication with Lee.

Rather than attempt retracing his steps, Stuart struck north, hoping to move entirely around the Army of the Potomac, then across its front, and regain his position between Lee and the Federals. Instead, Stuart was barely able to keep pace with the Union army, crossing the Potomac, capturing a Federal wagon train outside Washington, DC, and finally reaching Westminster, Maryland, with only the dimmest idea of where Lee's army could be found. Feeling his way toward Pennsylvania, Stuart's three brigades tangled with increasing numbers of Federal cavalry at Westminster, Maryland, on June 29th and then at Hanover, Pennsylvania, the next day. Stuart actually rode as far north as Carlisle, Pennsylvania, where he staged a minor raid on the town. Finally, on the evening of July 1st, one of Stuart's couriers returned from Lee with directions to "march to Gettysburg at once." Stuart at last rejoined Lee at Gettysburg late on July 2nd.

After Gettysburg, fingers would increasingly be pointed at Stuart for what happened to the Army of Northern Virginia. By galloping-off on what his critics would characterize as a joyride intended to refurbish his reputation after Brandy Station, Stuart foolishly rode himself almost entirely out of the campaign. In the process, Stuart was accused of depriving Lee of badly needed information on the movements of the Army of the Potomac, rendering Lee blind in Union territory and setting up an unlooked-for collision with the Federals at Gettysburg.

Stuart's defenders, and especially his chief of staff (and later, biographer) Henry McClellan, insisted that vainglory had nothing to do with Stuart's ride. Lee had authorized Stuart to use his discretion in making his ride, and Stuart had merely done the best that could be done under the circumstances. Stuart probably deserves more sympathy than he has gotten, although not quite for the reasons Henry McClellan offered. First, the importance of Civil War cavalry, especially for intelligence gathering, should not be overestimated. Cavalry were, after all, soldiers in uniform; no one in an opposing army was going to allow a trooper to slip into a camp and overhear important discussions, the way a spy might. Civil War cavalry were light cavalry (as opposed to *heavy* cavalry of the sort used in the Napoleonic wars to break up enemy infantry formations), and light cavalry was mostly effective at raiding in an enemy's rear and screening one's own infantry from prying observation by an enemy. Second, Lee did not actually lack for cavalry after Stuart's departure (Stuart left four brigades—under Albert Jenkins, John Imboden, William Jones, and Beverly Robertson—at Lee's disposal), nor did he lack for intelligence gathering, which came to his hands from "scouts" (military spies who risked capture and immediate execution if caught) and, even more obligingly, from Northern newspapers. Lee's orders to concentrate his army at Gettysburg on June 29th were, in fact, prompted by the report of a "scout," Henry T. Harrison, who also informed Lee of a change of command at the top of the Army of the Potomac, replacing Joe Hooker with George Meade.

Still, Stuart had unnecessarily endangered half the cavalry force of Lee's army by riding without real direction north of the Potomac and giving the Federals an opportunity to surround and annihilate half of that force. That Stuart survived his predicament with as few consequences as he did may be the best thing that can be said for him.

"Fight at Brandy Station" (June 10, 1863), *The Rebellion Record: A Diary of American Events, with Documents*, ed. Frank Moore (New York, 1864), Vol. 7

Yesterday introduced and ended the most terrific and desperate cavalry fight that ever occurred on this continent—a fight which commenced at sunrise and closed at the setting of the same.

We had learned that Stuart, with a heavy force of cavalry and artillery, was encamped at Brandy Station. It was determined to give him fight for two reasons: to find out the whereabouts of the enemy, and to disturb his plan of a contemplated raid into Pennsylvania. Our success was complete. We found out the whereabouts of the enemy emphatically. We interfered with his purposed raid, for we captured his plan and letters of instruction, which we have now at headquarters, Second brigade, Third cavalry division. General [John] Buford was to cross Beverly Ford and attack the enemy in front, while General [David McMurtrie] Gregg's and Colonel

[Alfred Napoleon] Duffie's divisions crossed at Kelly's Ford, and passing around his rear attacked him there . . .

Your correspondent was with General Gregg's division. At sunrise we heard the cannonading of Buford's command. At half-past seven a.m., we commenced to cross; at ten, we nabbed the enemy's picket; at half-past ten, the Second brigade, Third division, commanded by Colonel [Percy] Wyndham, struck his main body, and the play began. A section of artillery, supported by the First Maryland cavalry, was instantly thrown to the front and placed in position. As soon as his regiment was formed Major [Charles H.] Russell, First Maryland cavalry, led his second squadron to the charge. He routed the enemy's advance, sent it flying over fields and roads, captured an ambulance—which was afterward found to contain a major and all General Stuart's plans and letters of instruction from General Lee—drove the enemy before him down the Culpeper road, and, alas! charged too far. Before he could rally his men and bring them back, the enemy had brought up two regiments and cut him off, with fifteen of his command. The artillery now opened on both sides. Captain [John K.] Buckley and Lieutenant Apple [Henry Appel] led the third squadron First Maryland cavalry into the charge to meet the advancing foe. The Captain was taken prisoner, then rescued by his boys. The Lieutenant was wounded; his men faltered and shivered before an overwhelming force. Lieutenant Erick [Henry C. Erich] rallied them and led them to the charge again. He, too, was wounded. Then brave, fearless Captain Creager [Francis M. Kreager] led on his brave boys of company I. Three times they charged the foe. Twice they were driven back; but in the third charge

Captain Creager fell from his horse, wounded in the left breast. Then Lieutenant [Roger J.] Kimble took command of company I, rallied the men behind a hill and led them back to the charge. Eight times did that fearless officer and those brave boys charge with shrieks and yells against fearful odds. Lieutenant-Colonel [James M.] Deems was conspicuous on the field, rallying and cheering on his men.

On our left stood a house around which a body of rebel cavalry had gathered. Lieutenant-Colonel [Virgil] Broderick led his brave New-Jersey boys in a charge by battalions against them. As they closed up, the rebels fell back, when the whole house full of infantry poured a murderous fire from the hundreds of loop holes which pierced the walls of the house. The Lieutenant-Colonel and the Major were wounded, and the boys fell back.

The scene now became terrific, grand, and ludicrous. The choking dust was so thick that we could not tell "t'other from which." Horses, wild beyond the control of their riders, were charging away through the lines of the enemy and back again. Many of our men were captured, and escaped because their clothes were so covered with dust that they looked like gray-backs. Captain Buckley was three times a prisoner, and finally escaped. Sergeant [Charles W.] Embrey, of company I, was taken prisoner. He wore a brown blouse. He played secesh orderly to a secesh colonel for a while, and then escaped. Sergeant Hiteshem [Philip L. Hiteshaw], same company, was captured, and escaped because he wore a gray pair of trowsers.

Our men fought well and lost heavily. But the enemy met every charge with overwhelming numbers. He had both wings supported by infantry; had three batteries against our three guns.

I was in the fight, and have only mentioned, therefore, what passed under my own eye, and in the dust one man could not see far.

I must not forget to mention that Major Russell, after he found that he was cut off, lost none of his usual coolness, courage, and sagacity. His wit sharpened with the emergency; he reached the rear of the enemy's army. He rallied his fifteen men, and set immediately to work. The enemy moved out of the woods and tried to turn our left flank. The Major had most of his men partly concealed, partly exposed. Every time the enemy moved out of the woods the Major would dash at them with three or four men, and when close upon them would turn upon his horse and call upon some imaginary officer to bring up those imaginary squadrons out of those woods. Then he would retire, always bringing some prisoners with him. When they (the enemy) moved out again he would repeat the joke. At one time he had between forty and fifty prisoners whom he had thus captured. He thus perplexed and checked them until our division had retired.

At length the rebels charged upon him and retook all the prisoners excepting fourteen. The Major turned, fired his pistol into their faces, and again called upon that imaginary officer to bring up those imaginary squadrons. The charging squadron of rebels halted to reform for the charge, and while they were forming he slid his men and prisoners between two divisions of the rebel cavalry and rejoined his regiment.

Two things probably saved the Major. He lost his hat and took a secesh cap from a prisoner. He looked like a reb. When he returned through thc two divisions of rebel cavalry he had so many prisoners and so few men that they doubtless mistook him and his party for their own men moving out to reconnoitre.

This may sound extravagant, but I have the word of the prisoners he brought in (fourteen) and of his own men for its fidelity, and the ambulance he captured, with General Stuart's trunk, papers, letters, and plans, are at headquarters.

The battle soon became a fight for Beverly Ford. We drove the enemy back, secured the ford, and recrossed about sundown.

We accomplished our great design, that is, found out that the enemy was there . . .

Randolph H. McKim, *A Soldier's Recollections: Leaves from the Diary of a Young Confederate* (New York, 1911)

Three weeks after the battle of Chancellorsville I received . . . orders to report for duty at Fredericksburg, and on Wednesday, the 27th of May, I set out from Staunton for the army. On Thursday, after a ride of twenty-seven miles, I reached General Lee's headquarters at 1.45 p.m. The general received me graciously and asked me to dine with him, which I was, of course, glad to do. The highest officer in the army would have esteemed it a great honor—what, then, were the feelings of a young "first lieutenant and A.D.C." in sitting down at the board of the great soldier who was the idol of the armies and the people of the South? The simple courtesy and genial hospitality of General Lee would have put me at ease, if I had been a stranger; but he had several times been a guest at my father's house in Baltimore, when he was in charge of the construction of Fort Sollers [Carroll] in the Patapsco River, so that I felt at home in his presence. Our families were on very friendly and familiar terms. Indeed the general was a cousin of my mother, both being descended from the famous "King" Carter.

As I talked with him after dinner, he cast his eyes across the Rappahannock to the camps of General Hooker's army and said to me, "I wish I could get at those people over there." That was the expression by which he uniformly designated the Federal Army. He was very friendly, talked of the days when he used to visit Belvidere, and inquired after my father and mother and my sisters. I spent that night, or the next, at the headquarters of Gen. Edward Johnson, who was to be such a familiar figure to me in battle in the approaching campaign . . .

On Saturday, the 20th, General Ewell arrived in camp with his wife a new acquisition—and with one leg less than when I saw him last. From a military point of view the addition of the wife did not compensate for the loss of the leg. We were of the opinion that Ewell was not the same soldier he had been when he was a whole man and a single one . . . It was on the evening of June 3d that we received orders to break camp at Hamilton's Crossing, cook three days rations, and take up the line of march northward. That day may be said to mark the opening of the Gettysburg campaign . . .

Tuesday, June 9th, was an eventful day. As we marched toward Sperryville, cannonading was heard in the direction of Culpeper Court House. We halted instantly and soon orders came to march back. This was about three in the afternoon. General Pleasanton after a night march had crossed the Rappahannock at two points with the intention of destroying General Stuart's cavalry, which was massed in Culpeper County. In a very severe fight, characterized by great gallantry on both sides, our superb J.E.B. Stuart had routed both of Pleasanton's brigades and captured a good deal of his artillery and hundreds of his troopers. Again, as at Chancellorsville, General Stuart showed a very high degree of skill in handling his brigades. Owing to the thick fog on the river, the Federal cavalry were able to cross without being discovered, and the Confederates were taken by surprise; but by the valor of the officers and men, both of the cavalry and artillery, and by the brilliant leadership of their chief, the tide of battle was turned, and both Gregg and Buford driven back over the river, Stuart having beaten them in detail . . .

June 11th we again had an early reveille and marched at 4.30 a.m., passing through Sperryville and Little Washington, and making camp at 1.30 p.m., having made sixteen miles.

Friday, June 12th, we had reveille at three, and at 4.30 a.m. took up our march via Flint Hill for Front Royal . . . At four we crossed the Shenandoah on Confederate pontoons—that is, by wading straight through in column of fours. Forded both branches, the men cheering and in fine spirits. I never saw a ford so well made . . . Many of the men took off shoes and stockings, but some regiments marched straight through without breaking ranks. The water was nearly waist deep, but the men pushed on with shouts, in fine spirits. It was one of the most picturesque scenes I have ever witnessed, and the second of the kind in which I have borne a part since the war began. It was Sunday, but the air was fresh and cool, the roads in splendid order, and I enjoyed the march very much . . . The orders about [the fence] rails have been very strict and the general ordered me to go through every regiment in the brigade and see if there was a single rail taken, and if so, to make the men carry it back to the fence. It was a very disagreeable duty, and, I felt, put me in the light of a spy before the men. Still, I made no complaint, but rode up and down our five regiments, among the poor weary fellows, and executed his order faithfully. When I returned, and had unsaddled and unbridled, I reported to the general, and he ordered me to saddle up again and ride through the wagon yard and search for rails . . . I exchanged a pound of sugar for more than half a pound of fresh butter and a quart and a half of buttermilk. Then we had some bread toasted and some black-eyed peas boiled and some ham fried, and though we ate with our pen-knives, we enjoyed it very much.

Ruth Hairston Early, ed., *Lieutenant General Jubal Anderson Early, C.S.A.: Autobiographical Sketch and Narrative of the War Between the States* (Philadelphia, 1912)

Very early in the morning of the 13th . . . my division crossed over the Shenandoah, and I received orders from General Ewell to move to the Valley pike at Newtown, and along that road against the enemy then occupying Winchester, while Johnson moved along the direct road from Front Royal to the town, Rodes being sent to the right to Berryville, where there was also a force. Milroy occupied the town of Winchester with a considerable force in strong fortifications, and my orders were to move along the pike to Kernstown, and then to the left, so as to get a position on the northwest of Winchester from which the main work of the enemy could be attacked with advantage . . .

The enemy had strong position on Bower's Hill, held by infantry and artillery, and it was difficult of access, from the nature of Abraham's Creek, a boggy stream, running at its base, and the steep ascent to the hill on the other side. [Brigadier-General John Brown] Gordon formed his brigade in line across the Valley pike. [Brigadier-General Harry Thompson] Hays was posted on his left along a ridge between Cedar Creek pike and Abraham's Creek, and [Brigadier-General Robert Frederick] Hoke's and [Brigadier-General William] Smith's brigades were brought up and the latter placed on Hays' left, with a view to further operations against the enemy, in order to drive him from Bower's Hill; Hoke's brigade, under Colonel [Isaac Erwin] Avery of the 6th North Carolina being held in reserve. During these arrangements the enemy shelled my brigades heavily from his guns on Bower's Hill; and by the time they were made it became too dark to proceed farther . . . Very early on the morning of the 14th, I ordered Hays and Gordon to advance each a regiment across the creek to drive the enemy's skirmishers from Bower's Hill, which was done after some sharp skirmishing. At the same time Smith's skirmishers were advanced across the creek on the left, and we got possession of the works on the hill . . .

After that the only person we saw was a young girl of about thirteen years of age whom we met on horseback with her young brother behind her. She was carrying before her a large bundle of clothes tied up in a sheet, and when she unexpectedly came upon us she was at first very much frightened, but soon discovering that we were Confederates, she pulled off her bonnet, waved it over her head and "hurrahed," and then burst into tears. She told us that the enemy had been shelling the woods all around, firing occasionally into her father's house, and that she had been sent from home by her father and mother to get out of the way. She said that they had not been able to imagine what the shelling meant, as they did not know that any of "our soldiers," as she called us, were anywhere in the neighborhood. It was not necessary to use any precaution as to her, and she was permitted to pass on, feeling much happier for the encounter . . .

Colonel [Hilary Pollard] Jones, who had been entrusted with the command of all the artillery, had been quietly getting it into position out of sight, so as to be pushed by hand rapidly to the front when the time arrived to open on the enemy. When the men had become sufficiently refreshed, Hays' brigade, which was selected to make the assault, was moved to the front near to the edge of the woods next the enemy's position, with directions to General Hays to keep his men under cover until the artillery opened, and then to advance to the assault across the field and up the hill to the enemy's works, as soon as he should discover that the force occupying them was demoralized by the artillery fire . . .

About an hour before sunset, everything being ready, Jones caused his pieces to be run by hand to the front, and opened almost simultaneously with the whole twenty pieces upon the enemy, who thus received the first indication of our presence in that quarter. Of course he was taken by surprise and thrown into confusion. Our fire continued for about three-fourths of an hour very rapidly, being replied to, after the first consternation was over, by the enemy's guns, but in a very wild manner. Hays then advanced to the assault as directed, crossing the field in his front, ascending the hill—the slope of which was covered with abattis made by cutting the brush wood growing on it, and carrying the main work on the crest in handsome style, capturing some prisoners and six pieces of artillery, including those in the small redoubt, two of which were immediately turned on a body of the enemy's infantry seen approaching from the main fort to the assistance of these outer works.

The greater portion of the force occupying the captured works was enabled to make its escape towards the town, as it proved that this main work was open in the rear with wings thrown back from the two flanks of the bastion front presented to us. As soon as I saw Hays' men entering the works, I ordered Smith's brigade forward to their support, and directed Colonel Jones, whose guns had ceased firing when Hays advanced, to move the pieces on the left to the captured hill . . . I was of opinion that he would attempt an evacuation during the night, and I sent a courier to General Ewell with information of what I had accomplished, stating my opinion of the probability of the attempt to escape, but also informing him that I would renew the attack at light if the enemy was not gone . . .

As soon as it was light enough to see it was discovered that the enemy had evacuated his works and the town of Winchester during the night, taking the Martinsburg road, and some artillery was heard on the road which proved to be Johnson's guns near Stephenson's depot firing on the retiring enemy, whose retreat had been cut off by his division.

The brigades with me, including the detached regiments of Hoke's, were immediately ordered forward to the Martinsburg road for the purpose of taking up the pursuit. Gordon had advanced at light, as ordered, and finding the main fort unoccupied had pulled down the large garrison flag still left floating over that work. The 13th Virginia Regiment under Colonel [James B.] Terrill was immediately detailed by me as a guard for a large number of loaded wagons found standing outside of the town, and a considerable amount of stores left in the town by the enemy, and the rest of my command, as soon as Avery came up with Hoke's brigade, advanced in pursuit along the Martinsburg road, Gordon's brigade having preceded the others. On getting near Stephenson's depot, five or six miles from Winchester, I found that General Johnson's division had captured the greater part of Milroy's force, Milroy himself having made his escape with a small fraction of his command, principally mounted on the mules and horses taken from the wagons and artillery that had been left behind, and I therefore desisted from further pursuit.

An enemy flying for safety cannot be overtaken by a force on foot moving with arms in their hands, and as we had but a very small battalion of cavalry (that belonging to [James R.] Herbert's command, which did capture some prisoners), nothing was accomplished by the attempts made at further pursuit of Milroy, and he succeeded in getting in safety to Harper's Ferry . . . The enemy had abandoned the whole of his artillery, wagon trains, camp equipage, baggage, and stores, and twenty-five pieces of artillery with all their equipments complete, including those captured by Hays' brigade at the storming of the outer work, a very large number of horses and mules, and a quantity of ammunition, though in a damaged state, which fell into our hands . . . I sent off to Richmond, under guard, by the way of Staunton, 108 commissioned officers and 3,250 enlisted men as prisoners, much the larger portion of which had been captured by Johnson's division. Besides these there were left in Winchester several hundred sick and wounded prisoners.

My loss in the operations around Winchester was slight, consisting of 30 killed and 144 wounded, total 174, all but one killed and six wounded being from Hays' and Gordon's brigades.

Thomas Benton Reed [9th Louisiana], *A Private in Gray* (Camden, AR, 1905)

Saturday, June 13th—We moved before daylight, crossed the South and North Shenandoah Rivers and on to Winchester, seventeen miles. By noon we were thrown in line of battle . . . Late that night we were released and went away back in an old field and were permitted to lie down . . . We lay around until 10 or 11 o'clock, when we were ordered to fall in . . . Then the artillery formed in front of us, right on the crest of the hill. They placed thirty-two pieces, and when everything was in readiness we heard the report of a pistol, and those cannon were turned loose, and such a deafening noise! It seemed like the hill trembled under those cannon. The cannonading continued for about thirty minutes, then we were ordered to fall in, and "Forward march" was the next command. On we went, but when we got to the bottom of the hill our line was all broken, so we had to halt and form again. Then we moved, until we had gone half way, I suppose, when I heard Gen. Harry T. Hays give the command:

"Hoist those colors in the Ninth!"

I looked and saw a man raising our flag. A shell had burst near and a piece of it had struck our flag-bearer, James Stewart, on the head and killed him instantly. On we went and when we were within about one hundred yards of the enemy's breastworks we came to a kind of stockade. This was made of trees fallen or dragged, with the tops of them outward, forming the breastworks, and the small ends of the limbs were cut sharp. Now, we had to pass through this mass of stuff before getting to the rifle pits, but this did not stop us. The Major of the 7th Louisiana regiment was the first man to mount the works, and I was just behind him. He shouted out:

"Come on, boys!"

I shouted to him, "I am here," and mounted the breastworks. The Yankees did not know that we were on them until they saw us standing over them. Then you ought to have seen those fellows run, and as they ran down the hill we poured it into them, but they soon scampered away and we were in possession of the breastworks.

When things got kinder quiet the Colonel of the 9th regiment came up and fell on the breastworks almost tired to death, for he weighed 330 pounds, and had walked in this engagement. His name was William Peck.

Said he, and you could have heard him get his breath ever so far: "Bully! bully! by God! Bully!! for the old Ninth, by God!"

So we laughed at the Colonel's expense.

The Federals had a very strong fort, some six or eight hundred yards from the works we had taken, but another part of our army had come up on the other side and we had them penned in. We captured the whole thing about six thousand prisoners, with all of their stores, artillery, guns and ammunition, and we only lost one man of our company.

John Brown Gordon, *Reminiscences of the Civil War* (New York, 1903)

I was never in a battle without realizing that every moment might be my last; but I never had a presentiment of certain death at a given time or in a particular battle. There did come to me, on one occasion, a feeling that was akin to a presentiment. It was, however, the result of no supposed perception of certain coming fate, but an unbidden, unwelcome calculation of chances—suggested by the peculiar circumstances in which I found myself at the time. It was at Winchester, in the Valley of Virginia. My command was lying almost in the shadow of a frowning fortress in front, in which General Milroy, of the Union army, was strongly intrenched with forces which we had been fighting during the afternoon. In the dim twilight, with the glimmer of his bayonets and brass howitzers still discernible, I received an order to storm the fortress at daylight the next morning. To say that I was astounded at the order would feebly express the sensation which its reading produced; for on either side of the fort was an open country, miles in width, through which Confederate troops could easily pass around and to the rear of the fort, cutting off General Milroy from the base of his supplies, and thus forcing him to retire and meet us in the open field. There was nothing for me to do, however, but to obey the order. As in the night I planned the assault and thought of the dreadful slaughter that awaited my men, there came to me, as I have stated, a calculation as to chances, which resulted in the conclusion that I had not one chance in a thousand to live through it. The weary hours of the night had nearly passed, and by the dim light of my bivouac fire I wrote, with pencil, what I supposed was my last letter to Mrs. Gordon, who, as usual, was near me. I summoned my quartermaster, whose duties did not call him into the fight, and gave him the letter, with directions to deliver it to Mrs. Gordon after I was dead. Mounting my horse, my men now ready, I spoke to them briefly and encouraged them to go with me into the fort. Before the dawn we were moving, and soon ascending the long slope. At every moment I expected the storm of shell and ball that would end many a life, my own among them; but on we swept, and into the fort, to find not a soldier there! It had been evacuated during the night.

Louis Leon, *Diary of a Tar Heel Confederate Soldier* (Charlotte, NC, 1913)

June 17

We crossed the Potomac River to-day at 1 P.M., and camped in Williamsport, Maryland, on the banks of the Potomac. Two miles to-day. The river is knee-deep.

June 18

The people are mixed in their sympathies, some Confederates and some Yankees.

June 19

Left at 8 A.M., and seven miles took us to Hagerstown, Md. Here the men greeted us very shabby, but the ladies quite the reverse. This town has 5,000 inhabitants, and is a very pretty town. We camped on the Antietam.

June 20 and 21

Raining hard.

June 22

Left this morning at 8 o'clock, got to Middleburg, Pa., at 11, passed through it, and got to Green Castle at half past one. Eleven miles to-day. The people seemed downhearted, and showed their hatred to us by their glum looks and silence, and I am willing to swear that no prayers will be offered in this town for us poor, ragged rebels.

Henry B. McClellan, *The Life and Campaigns of Major-General J.E.B. Stuart: Commander of the Cavalry of the Army of Northern Virginia* (Boston, 1885)

The night of the 23^d^ of June was most inclement. A pitiless rain poured without cessation from the clouds, and the land was drenched. Although the shelter of the old house at the Cross Roads was available, at bedtime Stuart ordered his blanket and oil-cloths to be spread under a tree in the rear of the house, and directed me to sleep on the front porch, where I could readily light my candle and read any despatches which might come during the night . . . It was late in the night when a courier arrived from army headquarters, bearing a despatch marked "confidential." Under ordinary circumstances I would not have ventured to break the seal; but the rain poured down so steadily that I was unwilling to disturb the general unnecessarily, and yet it might be important that he should immediately be acquainted with the contents of the despatch. With some hesitation I opened and read it. It was a lengthy communication from General Lee, containing the directions upon which Stuart was to act. I at once carried it to the general and read it to him as he lay under the dripping tree. With a mild reproof for having opened such a document, the order was committed to my charge for the night, and Stuart was soon asleep. It is much to be regretted that a copy of this letter cannot now be produced. A diligent search has failed to find it, and as General Stuart did not forward a copy of it with his report, I presume it was destroyed during our subsequent march. But I have many times had occasion to recall its contents, and I find that my recollection of it is confirmed by several passages in General Stuart's report.

The letter discussed at considerable length the plan of passing around the enemy's rear. It informed General Stuart that General Early would move upon York, Pa., and that he was desired to place his cavalry as speedily as possible with that, the advance division of Lee's right wing. The letter suggested that, as the roads leading northward from Shepherdstown and Williamsport were already encumbered by the infantry, the artillery, and the transportation of the army, the delay which would necessarily occur in passing by these would, perhaps, be greater than would ensue if General Stuart passed around the enemy's rear. The letter further informed him that, if he chose the latter route, General Early would receive instructions to look out for him and endeavor to communicate with him; and York, Pa., was designated as the point in the vicinity of which he was to expect to hear from Early, and as the possible (if not the probable) point of concentration of the army. The whole tenor of the letter gave evidence that the commanding general approved the proposed movement, and thought that it might be productive of the best results, while the responsibility of the decision was placed upon General Stuart himself . . .

Having received his orders on the night of the 23^d^ of June, General Stuart prepared on the 24th to execute them. The three brigades of [Wade] Hampton, Fitz[hugh] Lee, and W.H.F. Lee, the latter under the command of Colonel [John Randolph] Chambliss, were ordered to rendezvous that night at Salem, and Robertson's and Jones' brigades, under command of Brigadier-General B[everly] H. Robertson, "were left in observation of the enemy on the usual front, with full instructions as to following up the enemy in case of withdrawal, and joining our main army." . . .

The three brigades selected to accompany Stuart rendezvoused at Salem during the earlier part of the night of the 24th, and at one o'clock on the same night marched out for Haymarket, passing through Glasscock's Gap early in the morning. As Stuart approached Haymarket it was discovered that Hancock's corps, marching northward, occupied the road upon which he expected to move. A brisk artillery fire was opened upon the marching column, and was continued until the enemy moved a force of infantry against the guns. Not wishing to disclose his force, Stuart withdrew from Hancock's vicinity after capturing some prisoners and satisfying himself concerning the movement of that corps. This information was at once started to General Lee by a courier bearing a despatch written by General Stuart himself. It is plain from General Lee's report that this messenger did not reach him; and unfortunately the despatch was not duplicated. Had it reached General Lee the movement of Hancock's corps would, of itself, have gone far to disclose to him the intentions of the enemy as to the place where a passage of the Potomac was about to be effected.

It was now clearly impossible for Stuart to follow the route originally intended; and he was called upon to decide whether he should retrace his steps and cross the Potomac at Shepherdstown, or by making a wider détour continue his march to the rear of the Federal army . . . Upon reaching Dranesville Hampton's brigade was sent to Rowser's Ford, and made the passage early in the night; but the Potomac was so wide, the water so deep, and the current so strong, that the ford was reported impracticable for the artillery and ambulances. Another ford in the vicinity was examined, under circumstances of great danger, by Captain R.B. Kennon of Stuart's staff, but it was found to offer no better prospect of success, and Stuart determined to cross at Rowser's, if it were within the limits of possibility . . . It was past noon when Stuart entered Rockville. While halting for the purpose of destroying the telegraph line, and to procure supplies, information was brought of the approach from Washington of a large train of wagons on the way to Meade's army. Lieutenant Thomas Lee, 2nd South Carolina Cavalry, with four men from his regiment, dashed along the train and routed its small guard. Although some of the wagons in the rear had turned about and were moving rapidly toward Washington, Lee reached the one foremost in the retreat, and halted and turned it about within sight of the defences of the city . . .

Had General Lee gained the battle of Gettysburg . . . the persistency with which Stuart held on to these wagons, and the difficulties he surmounted in transporting them safely through an enemy's country during the next three days and nights of incessant marching and fighting, would have been the cause of congratulation. But Gettysburg was lost to the Confederate arms, and not through Stuart's fault; and every circumstance which might have contributed to a different result will be judged in the light of the final catastrophe. Considered from this point of view, it must be acknowledged that the capture of this train of wagons was a misfortune . . .

The best information which Stuart could obtain seemed to indicate that the Confederate army was concentrating in the vicinity of Shippensburg. After a short rest at Dover, on the morning of the 1st of July, Stuart pressed on toward Carlisle, hoping there to obtain provisions for his troops, and definite information concerning the army. From Dover he sent Major A[ndrew] R[eid] Venable, of his staff, on the trail of Early's troops, and at a later hour of the day Captain Henry Lee, of Fitz Lee's staff, was sent toward Gettysburg on a similar errand. Stuart had reached Carlisle before either of these officers could return with a report . . .

Stuart himself, with Fitz Lee's and Chambliss' commands, reached Gettysburg on the afternoon of the 2d, and took position on the Confederate left. For eight days and nights the troops had been marching incessantly. On the ninth night they rested within the shelter of the army, and with a grateful sense of relief which words cannot express.

John W. Phillips, *History of the Eighteenth Regiment of Cavalry, Pennsylvania Volunteers* (New York, 1909)

The 30th day of June, 1863, brought the first real engagement in which the 18th Pennsylvania Cavalry took part as a regiment. It was known that the dashing Confederate cavalry leader, General J.E.B. Stuart, with his command, had been, in the contests of the previous days, cut off and separated from the main army of General Lee, and was moving in the vicinity of where we then were; but his precise whereabouts were unknown. The mission of [Judson] Kilpatrick's cavalry was in part to intercept him and prevent his return to join Lee, but it was not thought we were in such close proximity to him as we in fact were on this 30th of June. We left Littlestown early in the morning and moved in the direction of Hanover. The 18th Pennsylvania Cavalry had the rear of the line, and Lieutenant H[enry] C[lay] Potter, with about forty men from L and M companies, had the extreme rear of the regiment with orders to keep a sharp lookout for the enemy. Just after the main body of the brigade had passed through Hanover, and the 18th had entered the town, this rear guard was suddenly attacked by the enemy, who appeared on a nearly parallel road, and Potter was driven upon the main part of the regiment, which had reached Hanover, as stated, and had halted in the main street of the town, accepting the hospitalities of the good people of the place. For a moment all was confusion. The impetuous charge of the enemy brought some of their troops in the midst of our men, and hand-to-hand contests were had with the sabre. In a few moments the 18th rallied, and with the 5th New York Cavalry drove the charging party back on their reserves. They, in turn, charged us and drove us back, when a second time they were driven back. The enemy then changed their position to the right and one of the Michigan regiments was pushed forward to meet them there. The 18th Pennsylvania and the 5th New York were dismounted and pushed forward as skirmishers, and the enemy were driven out of the town.

The losses to the 18th in this battle were three killed, twenty-four wounded, and fifty-seven missing. The command left Hanover about 2 P.M. and moved rapidly in the direction of Harrisburg. We passed through Abbottstown and reached Berlin, fifteen miles from Harrisburg, bivouacing there on the night of July 1st. All that day as we marched, the distant boom of the cannon could be heard in the direction of Gettysburg, for there was then going on the terrible contest of the first day. On the 2d of July, we turned back and moved rapidly toward Gettysburg. The sound of the conflict was sufficient guide. The peaceful and fertile fields of Pennsylvania never looked prettier than they did that day, as they waved with their weight of golden grain, all unconscious of the carnage that was reddening the fields of the beautiful valley of Gettysburg. We all felt that the contest was on which would decide the Nation's fate. On we rode, no man left his place, no man faltered, as with set lips and mayhap blanched faces, we moved on to Gettysburg. Passing through Abbotstown and New Oxford, we came to Hunterstown late in the evening, and here for the first time saw the smoke of the battle and met the enemy. They charged our column, but were repulsed after a short engagement. At dark we fed our horses and lay down on the grass to rest, expecting to bivouac for the night, but soon "boots and saddles" sounded, and we moved silently around the left of the enemy's line, and early on the morning of July the 3d, we joined the main army on the heights of Gettysburg. Halting only for a short rest at the junction of Rock Creek and Baltimore Pike, our ([Elon] Farnsworth's) brigade moved rapidly to the left of the Union line, passing Little Round Top and Big Round Top . . . This position, with but slight changes, was maintained until the battle ended with the Waterloo of the Rebellion.

THE MARCH UP

The first elements of Lee's army to cross the Potomac northward were the cavalrymen of Albert Jenkins's brigade, who forded the river on June 15th, at Williamsport. They moved quickly up through Hagerstown, Maryland, and reached Chambersburg, Pennsylvania, by the 16th. Lee's infantry and artillery were not far behind. Edward Johnson's division (from Richard Ewell's corps) reached the Potomac on June 18th and crossed at Boteler's Ford, followed the next day by Robert Rodes's division; A.P. Hill's corps and Longstreet's corps followed by June 26th. With Ewell in the lead, the Army of Northern Virginia swept northeastward, up the Cumberland Valley. With Jenkins's cavalry in the lead, Rodes's division reached Carlisle by June 28th and sent the Pennsylvania state capital at Harrisburg into an uproar. Ewell's remaining division, under Jubal Early, struck directly eastward from Chambersburg, routing a scratched-together force of Pennsylvania militia as Early made his way into the crossroads town of Gettysburg, and then pushing on to York and Wrightsville on the Susquehanna River. Lee himself was at Hagerstown by June 26th and, along with Longstreet's corps, was outside Chambersburg by June 28th.

The Union army, by contrast, was left to play catch-up. Joseph Hooker did not get the Army of the Potomac into pursuit until June 12th, and its seven infantry corps only began crossing the Potomac on June 25th in a drizzling rain. Hooker chose this moment to quarrel with General-in-Chief Henry Wager Halleck over who had jurisdiction over other Union forces in the region. When Halleck refused to give Hooker control of the Union garrison at Harpers Ferry, Hooker fired off a resignation letter on June 27th, which both Halleck and Lincoln coldly accepted. Hooker's replacement in command, George Meade, was notified of his new (and not particularly welcome) appointment the next day.

Still, no one had crossed the state line into Pennsylvania until June 30th, when the army mustered for pay. A brigade of nine-months Vermont volunteers was pulled out of its comfortable billet in the defenses of Washington and hurried up to join the Army of the Potomac, but their commanding officer lamented that "just before we arrived at Emmettsburg [Maryland] the men fell out badly in consequence of exhaustion."

Lee issued strictly worded orders on June 21st, forbidding free foraging by Confederates on the Pennsylvania countryside. These orders were later held up as evidence of a kind of Confederate noblesse oblige, which would be contrasted smartly with the behavior of Union armies in the South. In practice, Lee's orders were ignored at almost every level, and Confederate commanders turned a blind eye to widespread confiscation of property and supplies across the path of the rebel forces. The most egregious example was the rounding up of the free black population of south-central Pennsylvania towns—Chambersburg, Mercersburg, Greencastle, Waynesboro—to be herded southward for sale as slaves on the Richmond slave markets. As many as five hundred black Pennsylvanians disappeared into slavery, while hundreds more took to the roads eastward to stay ahead of the invaders. "I can see them yet," wrote one Pennsylvanian, "men and women with bundles as large as old-fashioned feather ticks [mattresses] slung across their backs, almost bearing them to the ground. Children also, carrying their bundles, and striving in vain to keep up with their seniors."

One of the most detailed observers of Confederate behavior was the Swiss-born Philip Schaff, one of the most celebrated church historians of his time, and in 1863 the Professor of Church History and Biblical Literature in the German Reformed Church's theological seminary in Mercersburg. Nothing impressed Schaff more than the glee with which the rebels chased down any "contrabands"—the term coined in 1861 to justify Federal emancipation of slaves as "contraband of war"—they might find. That sight alone, wrote Schaff, was "sufficient to settle the slavery question for every humane mind."

The dismay of Schaff and other Pennsylvanians at the Confederate sweep through their towns was more than matched by the fright that seized the state on the eastern side of the Susquehanna River. Governor

Andrew Gregg Curtin issued a proclamation on June 12th, followed by a second one on June 26th, calling for the recruitment of sixty thousand temporary "emergency militia," but the response was scanty. Louis Moreau Gottschalk, the New Orleans–born composer and piano virtuoso, was then on tour in Pennsylvania and saw the roads leading east from Harrisburg choked with fleeing civilians. Similar scenes of confusion were repeated at Gettysburg and York when Jubal Early's division showed up there. When Early moved (on June 28th) to seize the mile-and-a-quarter-long railroad bridge over the Susquehanna at Wrightsville, there was even a possibility that the Confederates would make a lodgment on the east side of the river. Only a shrewd delaying action by Pennsylvania militia under Colonel Jacob Gellert Frick allowed the bridge to be burned before Early could capture it.

By that moment, however, Robert E. Lee already had other plans. Henry T. Harrison, a spy for Lieutenant General Longstreet, reported to Longstreet and Lee on the night of June 28th that the Army of the Potomac was in Maryland and that George Meade was now in command. "Harrison gave us the first complete account of the operations of the enemy since Hooker left our front," wrote Moxley Sorrel, Longstreet's chief of staff. "He brought his report down to a day or two, and described how they were even then marching in great numbers in the direction of Gettysburg, with intention apparently of concentrating there" and "also informed us of the removal of Hooker and the appointment of George Meade to command of the Army of the Potomac."

Satisfied that the Federals were sufficiently disorganized by their pursuit that they could be turned-upon and defeated piecemeal, Lee ordered a concentration of Longstreet's, Hill's, and Ewell's corps at Gettysburg. "That afternoon General Lee was walking with some of us in the road in front of his head-quarters," remembered Longstreet, "and said, 'To-morrow, gentlemen, we will not move to Harrisburg as we expected, but will go over to Gettysburg and see what General Meade is after.'" George Meade, on the other hand, was thrust into command of an army whose exact whereabouts, piece by piece, were at first unknown to him. Determined to play his new game cautiously, Meade began planning a defensive line behind Pipe Creek, just below the Pennsylvania-Maryland state line, which would cover any approaches by Lee toward Washington or Baltimore.

"General Orders, No. 72" (June 21, 1863), *The War of the Rebellion: A Compilation of the Official Records of the Union and Confederate Armies* (Washington, DC, 1881-1901), Series 1, Vol. 27 (pt 3)

While in the enemy's country, the following regulations for procuring supplies will be strictly observed, and any violation of them promptly and rigorously punished.

I. No private property shall be injured or destroyed by any person belonging to or connected with the army, or taken, excepting by the officers hereinafter designated.

II. The chiefs of the commissary, quartermaster's, ordnance, and medical departments of the army will make requisitions upon the local authorities or inhabitants for the necessary supplies for their respective departments, designating the places and times of delivery. All persons complying with such requisitions shall be paid the market price for the articles furnished, if they so desire, and the officer making such payment shall take duplicate receipts for the same, specifying the name of the person paid, and the quantity, kind, and price of the property, one of which receipts shall be at once forwarded to the chief of the department to which such officer is attached.

III. Should the authorities or inhabitants neglect or refuse to comply with such requisitions, the supplies required will be taken from the nearest inhabitants so refusing, by the order and under the directions of the respective chiefs of the departments named.

IV. When any command is detached from the main body, the chiefs of the several departments of such command will procure supplies for the same, and such other stores as they may be ordered to provide, in the manner and subject to the provisions herein prescribed, reporting their action to the heads of their respective departments, to whom they will forward duplicates of all vouchers given or received.

V. All persons who shall decline to receive payment for property furnished on requisitions, and all from whom it shall be necessary to take stores or supplies, shall be furnished by the officer receiving or taking the same with a receipt specifying the kind and quantity of the property received or taken, as the case may be, the name of the person from whom it was received or taken, the command for the use of which it is intended, and the market price. A duplicate of said receipt shall be at once forwarded to the chief of the department to which the officer by whom it was executed is attached.

VI. If any person shall remove or conceal property necessary for the use of the army, or attempt to do so, the officers hereinbefore mentioned will cause such property, and all other property belonging to such person that may be required by the army, to be seized, and the officer seizing the same will forthwith report to the chief of his department the kind, quantity, and market price of the property so seized, and the name of the owner.

By command of General R.E. Lee:

R[obert] H. CHILTON, Assistant Adjutant-General

"Jenkins's Raid into Pennsylvania," *The Rebellion Record: A Diary of American Events, with Documents*, ed. Frank Moore (New York, 1864), Vol. 7

On Sunday evening, June fourteenth, the dark clouds of contrabands commenced rushing upon us, bringing the tidings that General Milroy's forces at Martinsburgh had been attacked and scattered, and that the rebels, under General Rhodes, were advancing upon Pennsylvania. With due allowance for the excessive alarm of the slaves, it was manifest that the rebels were about to clear out the Shenandoah valley, and, that once done, the Cumberland, with all its teeming wealth, would be at rebel mercy. On Sunday night our people were much excited, and the question of protection became one of paramount interest. To inquiries, the authorities at Washington answered that the aspect of the war just at present rendered it unwise to divide or weaken the army of the Potomac, and that Pennsylvania must furnish her own men for her defence. A call from the President was issued to that effect, which is noticed elsewhere.

On Monday morning [June 15th] the flood of rumors from the Potomac fully confirmed the advance of the rebels, and the citizens of Chambersburgh and vicinity, feeling unable to resist the rebel columns, commenced to make prompt preparation for the movement of stealable property. Nearly every horse, good, bad, and indifferent, was started for the mountains as early on Monday as possible, and the negroes darkened the different roads northward for hours, loaded with household effects, sable babies, etc., and horses and wagons and cattle crowded every avenue to places of safety. About nine o'clock in the morning the advance of Milroy's retreating wagon-train dashed into town, attended by a few cavalry, and several affrighted wagon-masters, all of whom declared that the rebels were in hot pursuit; that a large portion of the train was captured, and that the enemy was about to enter Chambersburgh. This startling information, coming from men in uniform, who had fought valiantly until the enemy had got nearly within sight of them, naturally gave a fresh impetus to the citizens, and the skedaddle commenced in magnificent earnestness and exquisite confusion. Men, women, and children, who seemed to think the rebels so many cannibals, rushed out the turnpike, and generally kept on the leading thoroughfares as if they were determined to be captured, if the rebels were anywhere within range and wanted them. We watched the motley cavalcade rush along for a few hours, when it seems to have occurred to someone to inquire whether the rebels were not some distance in the rear; and a few moments of reflection and dispassionate inquiry satisfied the people that the enemy could not be upon us for several hours at least. The railroad men were prompt and systematic in their efforts to prepare for another fire, and by noon all the portable, property of the company was safely under control, to be hauled and moved at pleasure. The more thoughtful portion of our people, who felt it a duty to keep out of rebel hands, remained until the cutting of telegraph communication south, and the reports of reliable scouts rendered it advisable to give way to the guerrilla army of plunderers.

Greencastle being but five miles north of the Maryland line, and in the direct route of the rebels, was naturally enough in the highest state of excitement on Sunday night and Monday morning. Exaggerated rumors had of course flooded them, and every half-hour a stampede was made before the imagined rebel columns. Hon. John Rowe at last determined to reconnoitre, and he mounted a horse and started out toward Hagerstown. A little distance beyond he was captured by a squad of rebels, and held until General Jenkins came up. Jenkins asked Rowe his name, and was answered correctly.

He subsequently asked Mr. ——— who was with Rowe, what Rowe's name was, and upon being told that the name had been given to him correctly, he insisted that the Major had been an officer in the United States service. Mr. ——— assured Jenkins that the Major had never been in the service, and he was satisfied. (Jenkins had evidently confounded Major Rowe with his son, the gallant Lieutenant-Colonel [D. Watson] Rowe, of the One Hundred and Twenty-sixth.) Jenkins then asked Mr. ——— whom he had voted for at the last Presidential election. He answered that he had voted for Lincoln. To which Jenkins gave the following chaste and classic reply: "Get off that horse, you ——— abolitionist." The horse was surrendered, and the same question was propounded to Major Rowe, who answered that he had voted for [Stephen A.] Douglas, and had scratched every [John C.] Breckinridge man off his ticket. Jenkins answered: "You can ride your horse as long as you like—I voted for Douglas myself." He then demanded to know what forces were in Greencastle, and what fortifications. Major Rowe told him that the town was defenceless; but Jenkins seemed to be cautious lest he might be caught in a trap. He advanced cautiously, reconnoitred all suspicious buildings, and finally being fully satisfied that there was not a gun in position, and not a man under arms, he resolved upon capturing the town by a brilliant charge of cavalry. He accordingly divided his forces into two columns, charged upon the vacated streets, and reached the centre of the town without the loss of a man! This brilliant achievement, so soon after entering Pennsylvania, seemed to encourage the gallant guerrilla chief to still more daring deeds, and he immediately commenced to empty stables and capture every article within his reach that seemed to suit the fancy of his men. He announced in terms unfit for ears polite that he had come to burn and destroy, and that he would begin at Greencastle. Major Rowe informed him that he could burn Greencastle, but that he would end his depredations and his mundane career at about that point. Jenkins pondered as he blustered, and Jenkins didn't burn and destroy. He probably forgot to apply the torch. Generous teaching of memory!

The rebels were evidently under the impression that forces would be thrown in their way at an early hour, and they pushed forward for Chambersburgh. About eleven o'clock on Monday night they arrived at the southern end of the town, and the same intensely strategic movements exhibited at Greencastle were displayed here. Several were thrown forward cautiously to reconnoitre, and a few of our brave boys captured them and took their horses. This taste of war whetted the appetite of Jenkins, and he resolved to capture the town by a brilliant dash, without so much as a demand for surrender. He divided his forces into several columns—about two hundred in advance as a forlorn hope, to whom was assigned the desperate task of charging upon the empty undefended streets, store-boxes, mortar-beds [a wooden box for mixing mortar or plaster], etc., of the ancient village of Chambersburgh. Every precaution that strategy could invent was taken to prevent failure. Men were detailed to ride along the columns before the charge was made, bawling out as loudly as possible to plant artillery at different points, although the redoubtable Jenkins had not so much as a swivel in his army. The women and children having been sufficiently frightened by the threatened booming of artillery, and all things being in readiness, the forlorn hope advanced, and the most desperate charge ever known in the history of war—in Chambersburgh at least—was made. Down the street came the iron clatter of hoofs, like the tempest with a thousand thunderbolts; but the great plan had failed in one particular, and the column recoiled before it reached the Diamond. A mortar-bed on the street . . . had not been observed in the reconnoitring of the town, nor had willing copperheads advised him of it. His force was hurled against it; down went some men and bang went a gun. To strike a mortar-bed and have a gun fired at the same time was more than the strategy of Jenkins had bargained for; and the charge was broken and fell back. A few moments of fearful suspense, and the mortar-bed was carefully reconnoitred, and the musket report was found to be an accidental discharge of a gun in the hand of one of his own men, who had fallen. With a boldness and dash worthy of Jenkins, it was resolved to renew the attack without even the formality of a council of war. Again the steeds of war thundered down the street, and, there being nothing in the way, overcame all opposition, and the borough of Chambersburgh was under the rule of Jenkins. Having won it by the most determined and brilliant prowess, Jenkins resolved that he would be magnanimous, and would allow nothing to be taken from our people—excepting such articles as he and his men wanted.

Jenkins had doubtless read the papers in his day, and knew that there were green fields in the "Green Spot;" and what is rather remarkable, at midnight he could start for a forty-acre clover-patch belonging to [Alexander K. McClure] the editor of the *Repository*, without so much as stopping to ask where the gate might be found. Not even a halt was called to find it; but the march was continued until the gate was reached, when the order "File right!" was given, and Jenkins was in clover. Happy fellow thus to find luxuriant and extensive clover as if by instinct. By way of giving the devil his due, it must be said that, although there were over sixty acres of wheat, and eighty acres of corn and oats in the same field, he protected it most carefully, and picketed his horses so that it could not be injured. An equal care was taken of all other property about the place, excepting half a dozen of our fattest Cottswell [Cotswald] sheep, which were necessary, it seems, to furnish chops, etc., for his men. No fences were wantonly destroyed, poultry was not disturbed, nor did he compliment our blooded cattle so much as to test the quality of their steak and roasts. Some of his men cast a wistful eye upon the glistening trout in the spring; but they were protected by voluntary order, and save a few quarts of delicious strawberries, gathered with every care, after first asking permission, nothing in the gardens or about the grounds was taken. Having had a taste of rebel love for horses last October, when General Stuart's officers first stole our horses, and then supped and smoked socially with us, we had started to the mountains slightly in advance of Jenkins's occupation of the town, and, being unable to find them, we are happy to say that General Jenkins didn't steal our new assortment.

However earnest an enemy Jenkins may be, he don't seem to keep spite, but is capable of being very jolly and sociable when he is treated hospitably. For prudential reasons the editor was not at home to do the honors at his own table; but Jenkins was not particular, nor was his appetite impaired thereby. He called upon the ladies of the house, shared their hospitality, behaved in all respects like a gentleman, and expressed very earnest regrets that he had not been able to make the personal acquaintance of the editor. We beg to say that we reciprocate the wish of the General, and shall be glad to make his acquaintance personally—"when this cruel war is over." . . .

Horses seemed to be considered contraband of war, and were taken without the pretence of compensation; but other articles were deemed legitimate subjects of commerce even between enemies, and they were generally paid for after a fashion. True, the system of Jenkins would be considered a little informal in business circles; but it's his way, and our people agreed to it perhaps, to some extent, because of the novelty, but mainly because of the necessity of the thing. But Jenkins was liberal—eminently liberal. He didn't stop to higgle about a few odd pennies in making a bargain . . . Doubtless our merchants and druggists would have preferred greenbacks to confederate scrip that is never payable, and is worth just its weight in old paper; but Jenkins hadn't greenbacks, and he had confederate scrip, and such as he had he gave unto them. Thus he dealt largely in our place. To avoid the jealousies growing out of rivalry in business, he patronized all the merchants, and bought pretty much everything he could conveniently use and carry. Some people, with the antiquated ideas of business, might call it stealing to take goods and pay for them in bogus money; but Jenkins calls it business, and for the time being what Jenkins calls business, was business. In this way he robbed all the stores, drug-stores, etc., more or less, and supplied himself with many articles of great value to him.

Jenkins, like most doctors, don't seem to have relished his own prescriptions. Several horses had been captured by some of our boys, and notice was given by the General Commanding that they must be surrendered or the town would be destroyed. The city fathers, commonly known as the town council, were appealed to in order to avert the impending fate threatened us. One of the horses, we believe, and some of the equipments were found and returned, but there was still a balance in favor of Jenkins. We do not know who audited the account, but it was finally adjusted by the council appropriating the sum of nine hundred dollars to pay the claim. Doubtless Jenkins hoped for nine hundred dollars in "greenbacks," but he had flooded the town with confederate scrip, pronouncing it better than United States currency, and the council evidently believed him; and, desiring to be accommodating with a conqueror, decided to favor him by the payment of his bill in confederate scrip. It was so done, and Jenkins got just nine hundred dollars' worth of nothing for his trouble. He took it, however, without a murmur, and doubtless considered it a clever joke.

Sore was the disappointment of Jenkins at the general exodus of horses from this place. It limited his booty immensely. Fully five hundred had been taken from Chambersburgh and vicinity to the mountains, and Jenkins's plunder was thus made just so much less. But he determined to make up for it by stealing all the arms in the town. He therefore issued an order requiring the citizens to bring him all the arms they had, public or private, within two hours; and search and terrible vengeance were threatened in case of disobedience. Many of our citizens complied with the order, and a committee of our people was appointed to take a list of the persons presenting arms. Of course very many did not comply, but enough did so to avoid a general search and probable sacking of the town. The arms were assorted—the indifferent destroyed, and the good taken along.

On Tuesday a few of Milroy's cavalry, escaping from Martinsburgh, were seen by the redoubtable Jenkins hovering in his front. Although but thirteen in number, and without the least appetite for a battle with his two thousand men, he took on a fright of huge proportions, and prepared to sell his command as dearly as possible. Like a prudent general, however, he provided fully for his retreat. The shrill blast of the bugle brought his men to arms with the utmost possible alacrity; his pickets were called in to swell the ranks; the horses and baggage, consisting principally of stolen goods, were sent to the rear, south of the town; the surgeon took forcible possession of all our buildings, houses, barns, sheds, etc., to be used as hospitals, and especially requested that their wounded should be humanely treated in case of their sudden retreat without being able to take them along. The hero of two brilliant cavalry charges upon undefended towns was agitated beyond endurance at the prospect of a battle; and instead of charging upon a little squad of men, who were merely observing the course of his robberies, he stood trembling in battle array to receive the shock. No foe was nearer than the State capital, over fifty miles distant, and there the same scene was being presented. Jenkins in Chambersburgh, and the militia at Harrisburgh, were each momentarily expecting to be cut to pieces by the other. But these armies, alike terrible in their heroism, were spared the deadly clash of arms, inasmuch as even the most improved ordnance is not deemed fatal at a range of fifty miles. Both armies, as the usual reports go, having accomplished their purpose retired in good order.

As a rule, we believe that private houses were not sacked by Jenkins's forces; but there were some exceptions. The residences of Messrs. [Franz] Dengler and [Joseph] Gipe, near Chambersburgh, were both entered (the families being absent) and plundered of clothing, kettles, and other articles. Bureaus and cupboards were all emptied of their contents, and such articles as they wanted were taken. We have not learned of any instances of the kind in town.

A very few of our citizens exhibited the craven spirit of the genuine copperhead, but Jenkins and his men, in no instance, treated them with even courtesy. That they made use of some such creatures to obtain information, cannot be doubted; but they spurned all attempts to claim their respect because of professed sympathy with their cause. To one who desired to make fair weather with Jenkins, by ardent professions of sympathy with the South, he answered: "Well, if you believe we are right, take your gun and join our ranks." It is needless to say that the cowardly traitor did not obey. To another he said: "If we had such men as you in the South we would hang them." They say, on all occasions, that there are but two modes of peace—disunion or subjugation, and they stoutly deny that the latter is possible . . .

Quite a number of negroes, free and slave—men, women, and children—were captured by Jenkins and started South to be sold into bondage. Many escaped in various ways, and the people of Greencastle captured the guard of one negro train and discharged the negroes; but, perhaps, full fifty were got off to slavery. One negro effected his escape by shooting and seriously wounding his rebel guard. He forced the gun from the rebel and fired, wounding him in the head, and then skedaddled. Some of the men were bound with ropes, and the children were mounted in front or behind the rebels on their horses. By great exertions of several citizens some of the negroes were discharged.

The southern border of this county has been literally plundered of everything in the stock line, excepting such as could be secreted.

Philip Schaff, "The Gettysburg Week," *Scribner's Magazine* (July 1894)

This is the third time within less than a year that the horrible civil war, now raging through this great and beautiful country, has been brought to our very doors and firesides. First, during the Rebel invasion of Maryland, in September, 1862, when forty thousand Rebel troops occupied Hagerstown, and sent their pickets to within five miles of this place, and kept us in hourly fear of their advance into Pennsylvania, until they were defeated at Antietam. In October followed the bold and sudden Rebel raid of Stuart's cavalry to Mercersburg and Chambersburg, in the rear of our immense army then lying along the upper Potomac. At that time they took about eight prominent citizens of this place prisoners to Richmond (released since, except Mr. P[erry] A. Rice, editor of the *Mercersburg Journal*, who died in Richmond [in February, 1863]), and deprived the country of hundreds of horses. Now we have the most serious danger, an actual invasion of this whole southern region of Pennsylvania by a large portion of the Rebel army of Lee, formerly under command of the formidable Stonewall Jackson, now under that of General Ewell. The darkest hour of the American Republic and of the cause of the Union seems to be approaching. As the military authorities of the State and the United States have concluded to fortify Harrisburg and Pittsburg, and to leave Southern Pennsylvania to the tender mercies of the advancing enemy, we are now fairly, though reluctantly, in the Southern Confederacy, cut off from all newspapers and letters and other reliable information, and so isolated that there is no way of safe escape, even if horses and carriages could be had for the purpose. I will endeavor on this gloomy and rainy day to fix upon paper the principal events and impressions of the last few days.

Sunday, June 14th

Rumors reached us of the advance of the Rebels upon our force at Winchester, Va., and of the probable defeat of General Milroy.

Monday, the 15th

On my way to my morning lecture to complete the chapter on the conversion of the Germanic races to Christianity, I heard that the advance of the Rebels had reached Hagerstown and taken possession of that town. Rumors accumulated during the day, and fugitive soldiers from Milroy's command at Winchester and at Martinsburg, most of them drunk, made it certain that our force in the valley of Virginia was sadly defeated, and that the Rebels were approaching the Potomac in strong force. On the same evening, their cavalry reached Greencastle and Chambersburg, endeavoring to capture Milroy's large baggage-train, which fled before them in the greatest confusion, but reached Harrisburg in safety.

Tuesday, the 16th

We felt it necessary to suspend the exercises of the Seminary, partly because it was impossible to study under the growing excitement of a community stricken with the panic of invasion, partly because we have no right to retain the students when their State calls them to its defence. We invited them all to enlist at the next recruiting station for what are seminaries, colleges, and churches if we have no country and home? We closed solemnly at noon with singing and the use of the Litany.

Tuesday, Wednesday, and Thursday, June 16th-18th

Passed under continued and growing excitement of conflicting rumors. Removal of goods by the merchants, of the horses by the farmers; hiding and burying of valuables, packing of books; flight of the poor contraband negroes to the mountains from fear of being captured by the Rebels and dragged to the South. Arrests of suspicious persons by some individual unknown to us, yet claiming authority as a sort of marshal. One of these persons, from Loudon County, Va., was shut up for a while in the smoke-house of the Seminary, under my protest. I concluded to stay with my family at the post of danger, trusting in God till these calamities be passed. There is now no way of escape, and no horses and carriages are within reach. All communication cut off. These rumors of war are worse than war itself. I now understand better than ever before the difference of these two words as made by the Lord, Matt. xxiv.6. ["And ye shall hear of wars and rumours of wars"] The sight of the Rebels was an actual relief from painful anxiety.

Friday, the 19th

Actual arrival of the Rebel cavalry, a part of General Jenkins's guerilla force, which occupied Chambersburg as the advance of the Rebel army. They were under command of Colonel [Milton] Ferguson, about two hundred strong. They had passed through town the night previous on their way to McConnelsburg, and returned to-day after dinner with a drove of about two hundred head of cattle captured at McConnelsburg, and valued at $11,000, and about one hundred and twenty stolen horses of the best kind, and two or three negro boys. They rode into town with pointed pistols and drawn sabres . . . Long conversation with Col Ferguson. He said in substance: I care nothing about the right of secession, but I believe in the right of revolution. You invaded our rights, and we would not be worthy the name of men if we had not the courage to defend them. A cowardly race is only fit for contempt. You call us Rebels; why do you not treat us as such? Because you dare not and cannot. You live under a despotism; in the South the Habeas Corpus is as sacredly guarded as ever. You had the army, the navy, superiority of numbers, means, and a government in full operation; we had to create all that with great difficulty; yet you have not been able to subdue us, and can never do it. You will have to continue the war until you either must acknowledge our Confederacy, or until nobody is left to fight. For we will never yield. Good-by, I hope when we meet again we will meet in peace. The colonel spoke with great decision, yet courteously. The Rebels remained on their horses, and then rode on with their booty towards Hagerstown. The whole town turned out on the street to see them. I felt deeply humbled and ashamed in the name of the government. The Rebels were very poorly and miscellaneously dressed, and equipped with pistols, rifles, and sabres, hard-looking and full of fight, some noble, but also some stupid and semi-savage faces. Some fell asleep on their horses. The officers are quite intelligent and courteous, but full of hatred for the Yankees.

Saturday, the 20th

Appearance of about eighty of Milroy's cavalry [Co. C, 1st New York Cavalry], who had made their escape from Winchester in charge of the baggage-train, and returned from Harrisburg under Captain [William Henry] Boyd, of Philadelphia. They were received with great rejoicing by the community, took breakfast, fed their horses, and then divided into two parties in pursuit of some Rebels, but all in vain. They then went to Shippensburg, I believe, and left us without protection.

Sunday, the 21st

Received mail for the first time during a week, in consequence of the temporary withdrawal of the Rebel advance from Chambersburg. But on Monday all changed again for the worse.

Monday and Tuesday, 22d, 23rd

Squads of Rebel cavalry stealing horses and cattle from the defenceless community. No star of hope from our army or the State government. Harrisburg in confusion. The authorities concluded to fortify Harrisburg and Pittsburg, and to leave all Southern Pennsylvania exposed to plunder and devastation, instead of defending the line and disputing every inch of ground. No forces of any account this side of Harrisburg, and the Rebels pouring into the State with infantry and artillery. The government seems paralyzed for the moment. We fairly, though reluctantly, belong to the Southern Confederacy, and are completely isolated. The majority of the students have gradually disappeared, mostly on foot . . .

Wednesday, the 24th

An eventful day, never to be forgotten. As we sat down to dinner the children ran in with the report, The Rebels are coming, the Rebels are coming! The advance pickets had already occupied the lane and dismounted before the gate of the Seminary. In a few minutes the drum and fife announced the arrival of a whole brigade of seven regiments of infantry, most of them incomplete, one only two hundred strong, with a large force of cavalry and six pieces of artillery, nearly all with the mark U.S., and wagons captured from Milroy and in other engagements. Their muskets, too, were in part captured from us at the surrender of Harpers Ferry in October last . . . The brigade was commanded by Gen. Stewart [George Hume Steuart], of Baltimore, a graduate of West Point (not to be confounded with the famous cavalry Stuart, who made the raid to Mercersburg and Chambersburg last Oct.). The major of the brigade, Mr. [William W.] Goldsborough, from Baltimore, acts as marshal and rode up to the Seminary. He is distantly related to my wife. I had some conversation with him, as with many other officers and privates. This brigade belongs to the late Stonewall Jackson's, now to Ewell's, command, and has been in fifteen battles, as they say. They are evidently among the best troops of the South, and flushed with victory. They made a most motley appearance, roughly dressed, yet better than during their Maryland campaign last fall; all provided with shoes, and to a great extent with fresh and splendid horses, and with U.S. equipments. Uncle Sam has to supply both armies. They seem to be accustomed to every hardship and in excellent fighting condition. The whole force was estimated at from three thousand to five thousand men. General Stewart and staff called a few of the remaining leading citizens together and had a proclamation of Lee read, dated June 21st, to the effect that the advancing army should take supplies and pay in Confederate money, or give a receipt, but not violate private property. They demanded that all the stores be opened. Some of them were almost stripped of the remaining goods, for which payment was made in Confederate money . . . Towards evening they proceeded towards McConnelsburg . . . They hurt no person, and upon the whole we had to feel thankful that they behaved no worse.

Thursday, the 25th

The town was occupied by an independent guerilla band of cavalry, who steal horses, cattle, sheep, store-goods, negroes, and whatever else they can make use of, without ceremony, and in evident violation of Lee's proclamation read yesterday. They are about fifty or eighty in number, and are encamped on a farm about a mile from town. They are mostly Marylanders and Virginians, and look brave, defiant, and bold. On Thursday evening their captain, with a red and bloated face, threatened at the Mansion House to lay the town in ashes as soon as the first gun should be fired on one of his men. He had heard that there were firearms in town, and that resistance was threatened. He gave us fair warning that the least attempt to disturb them would be our ruin. We assured him that we knew nothing of such intention, that it was unjust to hold a peaceful community responsible for the unguarded remarks of a few individuals, that we were non-combatants and left the fighting to our army and the militia, which was called out, and would in due time meet them in open combat. They burned the barn of a farmer in the country who was reported to have fired a gun, and robbed his house of all valuables. On Friday this guerilla band came to town on a regular slave-hunt, which presented the worst spectacle I ever saw in this war. They proclaimed, first, that they would burn down every house which harbored a fugitive slave, and did not deliver him up within twenty minutes. And then commenced the search upon all the houses on which suspicion rested. It was a rainy afternoon. They succeeded in capturing several contrabands, among them a woman with two little children. A most pitiful sight, sufficient to settle the slavery question for every humane mind.

Saturday, the 27th

Early in the morning the guerilla band returned from their camping-ground, and drove their booty, horses, cattle, about five hundred sheep, and two wagons full of store goods, with twenty-one negroes, through town and towards Greencastle or Hagerstown. It was a sight as sad and mournful as the slave-hunt of yesterday. They claimed all these negroes as Virginia slaves, but I was positively assured that two or three were born and raised in this neighborhood. One, Sam Brooks, split many a cord of wood for me. There were among them women and young children, sitting with sad countenances on the stolen store-boxes. I asked one of the riders guarding the wagons: Do you not feel bad and mean in such an occupation? He boldly replied that he felt very comfortable. They were only reclaiming their property which we had stolen and harbored. Mrs. [Ellen Robinson] McFarland, a Presbyterian woman, who had about three hundred sheep taken by the guerillas, said boldly to one: So the Southern chivalry have come down to sheep-stealing. I want you to know that we regard sheep thieves the meanest of fellows. I am too proud to ask any of them back, but if I were a man I would shoot you with a pistol. The Rebel offered her his pistol, upon which she asked him to give it to her boy, standing close by her. Among the goods stolen was the hardware of Mr. [John] Shirts, which they found concealed in a barn about a mile from town. They allowed him to take his papers out of one box, and offered to return the goods for $1,200 good federal money, remarking that they were worth to them $5,000, as hardware was very scarce in Virginia. He let them have all, and took his loss very philosophically. Mr. [William D.] McKinstry estimates his loss in silks and shawls and other dry goods, which the guerillas discovered in a hiding-place in the country, at $3,000. The worst feature is that there are men in this community who will betray their own neighbors! In the Gap they took from Mrs. [Mary] Unger a large number of whiskey-barrels, and impressed teams to haul them off. They say they will bring $40 per gallon in the South. I pity Mrs. Unger, but am glad the whiskey is gone; would be glad if someone had taken an axe and knocked the barrels to pieces . . . I expect these guerillas will not rest until they have stripped the country and taken all the contraband negroes who are still in the neighborhood, fleeing about like deer. My family is kept in constant danger, on account of poor old Eliza, our servant, and her little boy, who hide in the grain-fields during the day, and return under cover of the night to get something to eat. Her daughter Jane, with her two children, were captured and taken back to Virginia . . .

These guerillas are far worse than the regular army, who behaved in an orderly and decent way, considering their mission. One of the guerillas said to me, We are independent, and come and go where and when we please. It is to the credit of our government that it does not tolerate such outlaws. Already the scarcity of food is beginning to be felt. No fresh meat to be had; scarcely any flour or groceries; no wood. The harvest is ripe for cutting, but no one to cut it. And who is to eat it? The loss to the farmers in hay and grain which will rot on the fields is incalculable . . . I hear from a drover that the Rebel army has been passing all day from Hagerstown to Chambersburg in great force. Perhaps their advance-guard is in Harrisburg by this time . . . Hooker is said to be behind them in Frederick, Md.

SUNDAY, THE 28TH

Thanks be to God we had a comparatively quiet Sunday. Dr. [Thomas] Creigh preached in our church. Small congregation, few country people, all on foot. In the evening . . . we see camp-fires in the Gap.

MONDAY, THE 29TH

[Brigadier-General John Daniel] Imboden's brigade encamped between here and the Gap. Infantry, artillery, and cavalry. They came from Western Virginia, Cumberland, and Hancock. They clean out all the surrounding farm-houses. They have discovered most of the hiding-places of the horses in the mountains, and secured to-day at least three hundred horses.

TUESDAY, THE 30TH

This morning Gen. Imboden, with staff, rode to town and made a requisition upon this small place of five thousand pounds of bacon, thirty barrels of flour, shoes, hats, etc., to be furnished by eleven o'clock; if not complied with, his soldiers will be quartered upon the citizens. If they go on this way for a week or two we will have nothing to eat ourselves. They say as long as Yankees have something, they will have something. Gen. Imboden, who is a large, commanding, and handsome officer, said within my hearing, You have only a little taste of what you have done to our people in the South. Your army destroyed all the fences, burnt towns, turned poor women out of house and home, broke pianos, furniture, old family pictures, and committed every act of vandalism. I thank God that the hour has come when this war will be fought out on

Pennsylvania soil. This is the general story. Everyone has his tale of outrage committed by our soldiers upon their homes and friends in Virginia and elsewhere. Some of our soldiers admit it, and our own newspaper reports unfortunately confirm it. If this charge is true, I must confess we deserve punishment in the North. The raid of [Col. James] Montgomery in South Carolina, the destruction of Jacksonville in Florida, of Jackson in Miss., and the devastation of all Eastern Va., by our troops are sad facts. A large part of the provision demanded was given. Imboden made no payment, but gave a sort of receipt which nobody will respect. In the afternoon Imboden's brigade broke up their camp a little beyond the toll-gate, and marched through town on the way to Greencastle. They numbered in all only about eleven hundred men, including three hundred cavalry, six pieces of cannon, fifty wagons, mostly marked U. S., and a large number of stolen horses from the neighborhood . . . Imboden remarked to a citizen in town, that if he had the power he would burn every town and lay waste every farm in Pa.!

Wednesday, July 1st

We hoped to be delivered from the Rebels for awhile, but after dinner a lawless band of guerillas rode to town stealing negroes and . . . taking what they wanted and wantonly destroying a good deal. This was the boldest and most impudent highway robbery I ever saw. Such acts I should have thought impossible in America after our boast of superior civilization and Christianity in this nineteenth century. Judge [James Oliver] Carson asked one of these guerillas whether they took free negroes, to which the ruffian replied: Yes, and we will take you, too, if you do not shut up! How long shall this lawless tyranny last? But God rules, and rules justly. To-day I saw three Richmond papers, the last of June 24th, half sheets, shabby and mean, full of information from Northern papers of the Rebel invasion of Maryland and Pa., and full of hatred and bitterness for the North, urging their Southern army on to unmitigated plunder and merciless retaliation. Dr. [Samuel] Seibert walked from Chambersburg. So did Mr. [Isaac J.] Stine. They say that terrible outrages are committed by the soldiers on private citizens. One was shot to get his money, another was stripped naked and then allowed to run. Hats are stolen off the head in the street and replaced by Rebel hats.

Dr. [Benjamin] Schneck, walking to his lots, just out of Chambersburg, was asked for the time by a soldier. He pulled out his old gold watch, inherited from father and grandfather. The Rebel instantly pointed his bayonet at the Dr.'s breast and said, Your watch is mine. Another soldier, apparently coming to his relief, touched his pocket, pointing his bayonet from behind, and forced him to give up his pocket-book with $57, all he had. This comes from Dr. S. himself, through Dr. Seibert . . . In the evening and during the night this party drove all the remaining cows away from the neighborhood towards the Potomac. This reminds one of the worst times of the Dark Ages (the *Faustrecht*), where might was right, and right had no might . . .

Louis Moreau Gottschalk, *Notes of a Pianist* (Philadelphia, 1881)

June 15, 1863

The town is all in commotion. A despatch has been received announcing the invasion of the State by three columns of Rebels, marching on the capital. The despatch is placarded on all the street corners . . . 5 p.m. Another despatch from the Governor of Pennsylvania calling all able-bodied citizens to arms. The Confederates, says the despatch, have seized Martinsburg, and are making forced marches on Hagerstown . . . I go out into the streets. The crowds multiply and increase every moment . . . A volunteer military band (the only one in Williamsport) draws up in battle array on the principal square; is it necessary for me to say that it is composed of Germans (all the musicians in the United States are Germans)? There are five of them: A cornet á piston with a broken-down constitution (I speak of the instrument), a cavernous trombone, an ophicleide [a keyed brass instrument] too low, a clarionet too high, a sour-looking fifer—all of an independent and irascible temper, but united for the moment through their hatred of time and their desire vigorously to cast off its yoke. I must confess that they succeeded to that extent that I am doubtful whether they played in a major or minor key.

Fresh despatches received excite the greatest consternation. The Confederates are marching on Harrisburg. The crowd is stirred up;

patriotic meetings are organized. An old gentleman in black clothes, with a large officer's scarf [sash] around his waist, harangues from the porch of the hotel many of his friends. The band strikes up, and marches through the streets, which fills the people with military ardour, thanks to the strains, more noisy than harmonious, of this performing cohort. With all this, the chances for the concert this evening are rather dubious. The receipts, which promised famously this morning, are suddenly paralyzed.

11 P.M.

I played this evening, after all, before a very respectable audience, which listened with marked interest and a more sustained attention than I always meet with in the audiences of small towns. My little piece entitled the 'Union' [*The Union: Paraphrase de Concert on the National Airs Star Spangled Banner, Yankee Doodle & Hail Columbia*, 1862] was much applauded; it suited the moment.

WILLIAMSPORT, JUNE 16, 4 O'CLOCK IN THE MORNING

A fresh telegram from the Governor orders all the National Guards to hurry to the defence of the State capital . . .

Decidedly, Hagerstown is in possession of the Confederates. The Governor enjoins the people to place before their doors all the empty barrels which they may have to dispose of; they will use them on the fortifications which are to be thrown up at Harrisburg. All along the road we see the agriculturists in arms, in battle array and performing military evolutions. They all seem disposed to obey the command of the Governor, who orders all able-bodied men to the field to meet the enemy, and to take the Susquehanna as the line for battle. A traveller whom we took up at the last station assures us that the Confederate Army is not more than thirty miles from Harrisburg. Everybody is frightened . . .

1 P.M.

A mile this side of Harrisburg the road is completely obstructed by freight trains, wagons of all sorts, and in fine by all the immense mass of merchandise, etc., which for the last twelve hours has been concentrated near the town to avoid capture or burning by the rebels. The train stops at the middle of the bridge over the Susquehanna—why? . . .

The city expects to be attacked every moment. Three thousand persons are at work throwing up entrenchments. The clergy (many hundred persons), in a meeting which took place on this subject, have placed themselves at the disposition of the Governor, to be employed for the defence of the city. Priests, pastors, rectors, ministers of all denominations, are at this moment engaged in wheeling barrows full of earth and in digging pits for the sharpshooters . . .

2 P.M.

A battery of artillery passes at full gallop. We are crushed in the midst of the crowd . . . Numerous groups stand before the telegraph office. The rebels, the despatches announce, are eighteen miles off. All the shops are closed, and most of the houses from the garret to the cellar . . .

A long convoy comes in with ten locomotives in front. It brings cannons, caissons, and many steam-engines in course of construction, which have been sent to Harrisburg to prevent their falling into the hands of the enemy. The confusion is at its height. Cattle bellowing, frightened mules, prancing horses, the noisy crowd, the whistling locomotives . . . The station is full of locomotives. I have counted thirty at a time. They look frightened like those around them. Puffing, out of breath, rushing forward, striking and bellowing at each other—I seemed to see a horrible troop of ante-diluvian animals flying before a geological flood. The train leaves in a few moments; it consists of eight or nine cars, in which are piled at least two thousand persons. We are like herrings in a barrel. The women are sitting on each other, the men all standing, and the children are everywhere: not one inch of room which is not occupied. We are dying from thirst; the heat is intolerable . . .

The panic increases. It is no longer a flight, it is a flood—a general *sauve qui peut* [stampede]. It would seem, seeing the precipitation with which the inhabitants abandon their city, that the rebels were already in sight. Trunks, boxes, bundles of clothes, furniture, mattresses, kitchen utensils, and even pianos, are piled pell-mell on the road. Carriages, carts, chariots, indeed all the vehicles in the city have been put in requisition. The poor are moving in wheelbarrows. A trader has attached to his omnibus, already full, a long file of spring carts, trucks, buggies, whose owners had probably no horses, and drags them along to the great displeasure of his team, which sweat, froth, and fall, under the increased weight of the load.

"The Union Cavalry Service" (July 15, 1863), *The Rebellion Record: A Diary of American Events, with Documents*, ed. Frank Moore (New York, 1864), Vol. 7

Stuart and Early, the marauding chiefs of the rebel army . . . had demanded tribute in almost every town visited by them, and threatened to destroy the towns unless their demands were promptly met. In some towns the citizens nobly refused to comply, but prepared rather to sacrifice their property than to yield to the invader. In many places, I regret to say, the reverse of all this was acted upon. At York, a town of twelve thousand inhabitants, the chief burgomaster, a man named [David] Small, rode seven miles to surrender the town, and before any demand had been made for its surrender. General Early condescended to say, that if in the course of his peregrinations York was visited, he would consider the surrender as an ameliorating circumstance. Visiting the place, he demanded a ransom of one hundred thousand dollars and a supply of provisions and clothing for his whole command. A committee of citizens was actually formed, and forty-five thousand dollars in greenbacks and the required provisions were turned over to the Early aforesaid, who magnanimously offered to spare the town then, provided the balance of the money demanded was paid upon his return, which he said would be within a few days. Fortunately, General [Judson] Kilpatrick's troops frightened this pink of generals away, and the citizens of York and vicinity were saved the opportunity of further humiliating themselves . . .

On the Saturday previous to arriving in Hanover, one hundred and fifty of Stuart's cavalry entered that place, and did pretty much as they pleased, not one of the three thousand inhabitants daring to remonstrate or raise a finger in self-defence. In fact, it appears they met more friends than enemies—for they found those who gave them information as to the movements of our troops, and were thereby enabled to make the sudden attack they did upon the rear of General [Elon J.] Farnsworth's brigade the following Tuesday. Indeed, I have had in my possession a letter written by Fitz-Hugh Lee, and addressed to General Stuart on the very morning of the attack, giving a correct account of General Kilpatrick's movements, "obtained," he says, "from a citizen, and is reliable." There was no "reliable citizen" in all Pennsylvania to inform General Kilpatrick of the approach of General Stuart upon the rear of General Farnsworth's brigade; and our commanders throughout the campaign in that State, labored under almost as many disadvantages as if campaigning in an enemy's country. Indeed, not until we arrived near Gettysburgh, could any valuable information as to the enemy's movements be obtained. In conversation with the editor of a paper in Hanover, whom I accidentally met, after showing him the letter of Fitz-Hugh Lee, I made the remark that the rebels appeared to have a great many sympathizers in that vicinity. He replied: "I don't know as to that, but you see this is a very strong Democratic county, and the Democrats were opposed to the removal of McClellan!" Leading and active Union men were pointed out by the traitors, who seek to mask their treason under the garb of Democracy in this town, that they might be plundered by the marauders. One man, a jeweller, was thus pointed out, and his stock in trade, though concealed, was unearthed, and divided among the rebel soldiers, in Hanover, and at other points, particularly in York County, the enemy found warm friends ready to welcome them, and actually received some recruits for their army. Women at the Washington Hotel in York degraded themselves by waving their handkerchiefs in token of welcome to the rebel troops, and there were a number of citizens who spread tables for the officers, and invited them to their houses. At Mechanicsville, one "Democrat" was so buoyant, that he mounted a sword, and guided the rebel column to the railroad junction, where they destroyed a large amount of property. There seemed to be a perfect understanding between the enemy and men whose loyalty had been questioned before. One of this class recovered nine horses from Stuart . . . The keeper of a hotel in Abbotstown, who, I regret to say, was once a leading "Wide Awake" [a youth movement for Lincoln's election in 1860], also manifested his pleasure at receiving a visit from the rebels. Fortunately, even the Democrats of York County have seen all they wish of rebels—a column of whom can be smelled as far as a slave-ship. A majority of the women in Hanover and elsewhere are truly loyal. They cared for the wounded—even taking them from the streets while bullets were flying around promiscuously. They furnished provisions to the soldiers, and in most instances, positively refusing to receive any pay. In one instance, a citizen voluntarily exchanged horses with a scout to enable the latter to escape.

"The Fight at Wrightsville," *Philadelphia Inquirer* (June 30, 1863)

Columbia, Pa., June 29, 5 a.m.

The conflict near Wrightsville, Pa., commenced about half-past six o'clock on Sunday evening last. Colonel Frick, with a regiment composed of men from the interior counties of Pennsylvania [27th Pennsylvania Emergency Militia] . . . aided by about two companies of volunteer negroes, held the enemy, supposed to consist of eight thousand men, at bay for at least forty-five minutes, retreating in good order and burning the bridge over the Susquehanna to prevent the crossing of the rebel cavalry . . .

The intrenchments of Colonel Frick were thrown up across the centre of the valley leading from Wrightsville, opposite Columbia, to York. They were simply trenches constructed by negroes, and commanded the turnpike approach to the Susquehanna. Had they been supported on each adjacent hill by other works, the position would have been tenable, but Colonel Frick had not a sufficient number of men to protect himself from a flank movement. The rebels came not only in his front, but sent flanking parties along roads leading to the river, which skirted his position on either side . . . It soon became apparent that a retreat was necessary.

The rebel batteries throwing shell into the intrenchments were stationed at various points. That the range of their guns was great, was evident from the fact that some of the shell passed over our troops, and either fell into the river beyond Wrightsville or into the town itself, doing an execution among the peaceable inhabitants, the extent of which is as yet unknown. As we stated yesterday, nearly all of the women and children had remained at Wrightsville.

In order to insure the safety of the command, should a retreat become necessary, a train of coal-cars was drawn across the entrance to the bridge, on the Wrightsville side of the River, leaving between them only an opening sufficient for the passage of our men. These cars protected the retreat during the time that a party of workmen, with torpedoes and axes, were preparing the structure for demolishment. After our men had all retired, closely followed by the rebel cavalry, the torch was applied to the fourth span, and before the flames could be checked by the enemy they had enveloped the entire span and were making rapid headway toward the two ends, which they reached. The remains of the bridge, on Monday morning, consisted only of the piers, which stretched themselves across the river—more than a mile wide—like giant's stepping-stones.

It was almost eight o'clock in the evening of Sunday when the fire first gained headway, and the scene was magnificent. Some of the arches remained stationary even when the timbers were all in flames, seeming like a fiery skeleton bridge whose reflection was pictured in the water beneath. The moon was bright, and the blue clouds afforded the best contrast possible to the red glare of the conflagration. The light in the heavens must have been seen for many miles. Some of the timbers as they fell into the stream seemed to form themselves into rafts, which floated down like infernal ferry-boats of the region pictured by DANTE.

The heavy fog this (Monday) morning, at the hour this is written, prevents any object over the river from being distinctly seen. The flames do not appear, however, to have extended to any dwelling in Wrightsville, although two or three board-yards above the town were destroyed. Another yard below the town still contains sufficient lumber for the enemy to construct as many rafts as may seem desirable, but it is impossible to see whether the rebel guns are planted in its vicinity, or on the hills which come out naked and abrupt, with fields upon their tops, to the very edge of the river. One fact is certain, and the truth may as well be told, Columbia is completely at the mercy of the enemy, who, from the opposite hills just mentioned, can shell every building in the town . . .

"The Latest News!" *Lancaster Examiner* (July 1, 1863)

The Rebels retreated from York about 2 o'clock on yesterday (Tuesday) morning towards Gettysburg, followed during the morning by those from Wrightsville. They also made a hasty exit from in front of Harrisburg toward Carlisle and Chambersburg . . . These movements of the Rebel army indicate that Gen. Lee is massing his troops for the purpose of engaging the army of the Potomac, and that a decisive battle between these two armies may be expected daily. The battle ground will probably be in the Gettysburg valley. The Confederate government have doubtless risked every thing upon the result of this battle, which, from present indications, promises to be one of the most bloody of the war.

Charles Augustus Stevens, *Berdan's United States Sharpshooters in the Army of the Potomac, 1861–1865* (St. Paul, 1892)

The two regiments were now assigned to [Brigadier-General John Henry Hobart] Ward's 2^{d} brigade of [Major-General David Bell] Birney's 1st division of the 3^{d} corps; the 3^{d} division having been consolidated with the 1st and 2^{d}. Moving northward, for miles could their lines be traced by the clouds of dust that enveloped them, many to meet a soldier's death—face to the front. On the 12th, after marching 25 miles, they bivouacked for a day, Company A being detailed for outpost duty, watching the enemy who appeared in force on the left bank of the Rappahannock. Thence pressing hurriedly on *via* Catlett's Station, they reached the dry and parched plains of Manassas on or about the 15th, suffering greatly from the effects of the sun's heat, causing at times sunstroke and debilitation. It was reported that more than 200 members of the 3[d] corps were sunstruck. Water being scarce, also added to their troubles; for while on a hot march it could be drank too freely to their injury, yet was it a great and necessary relief, when used in moderation. By the time they halted near Fairfax and Centreville, the troops were in need of rest after their hurried and exhaustive march. About this time, June 17th, Pleasanton's cavalry had another brush with the enemy, at Aldie . . . The appointment of Gen. Meade was a surprise both to himself and to the army. For the soldiers at that time would hardly have chosen him in preference to Slocum, Hancock, Sickles or Reynolds.

"Pipe Creek Circular" (July 1, 1863), *The War of the Rebellion: A Compilation of the Official Records of the Union and Confederate Armies* (Washington, DC, 1881-1901), Series 1, Vol. 27 (pt 1)

HEADQUARTERS ARMY OF THE POTOMAC, TANEYTOWN, JULY 1, 1863

From information received, the commanding general is satisfied that the object of the movement of the army in this direction has been accomplished, *viz.* the relief of Harrisburg, and the prevention of the enemy's intended invasion of Philadelphia, &c, beyond the Susquehanna. It is no longer his intention to assume the offensive until the enemy's movements or position should render such an operation certain of success.

If the enemy assume the offensive, and attack, it is his intention, after holding them in check sufficiently long, to withdraw the trains and other impedimenta; to withdraw the army from its present position, and form line of battle with the left resting in the neighborhood of Middleburg, and the right at Manchester, the general direction being that of Pipe Creek. For this purpose, General Reynolds, in command of the left, will withdraw the force at present at Gettysburg, two corps by the road to Taneytown and Westminster, and, after crossing Pipe Creek, deploy toward Middleburg. The corps at Emmitsburg will be withdrawn, via Mechanicsville, to Middleburg, or, if a more direct route can be found leaving Taneytown to their left, to withdraw direct to Middleburg.

General Slocum will assume command of the two corps at Hanover and Two Taverns, and withdraw them, *via* Union Mills, deploying one to the right and one to the left, after crossing Pipe Creek, connecting on the left with General Reynolds, and communicating his right to General Sedgwick at Manchester, who will connect with him and form the right.

The time for falling back can only be developed by circumstances. Whenever such circumstances arise as would seem to indicate the necessity for falling back and assuming this general line indicated, notice of such movement will be at once communicated to these headquarters and to all adjoining corps commanders.

The Second Corps now at Taneytown will be held in reserve in the vicinity of Uniontown and Frizellburg, to be thrown to the point of strongest attack, should the enemy make it. In the event of these movements being necessary, the trains and impedimenta will all be sent to the rear of Westminster. Corps commanders, with their officers commanding artillery and the divisions, should make themselves thoroughly familiar with the country indicated, all the roads and positions, so that no possible confusion can ensue, and that the movement, if made, be done with good order, precision, and care, without loss or any detriment to the morale of the troops.

The commanders of corps are requested to communicate at once the nature of their present positions, and their ability to hold them in case of any sudden attack at any point by the enemy.

This order is communicated, that a general plan, perfectly understood by all, may be had for receiving attack, if made in strong force, upon any portion of our present position.

Developments may cause the commanding general to assume the offensive from his present positions.

The Artillery Reserve will, in the event of the general movement indicated, move to the rear of Frizellburg, and be placed in position, or sent to corps, as circumstances may require, under the general supervision of the chief of artillery.

The chief quartermaster will, in case of the general movement indicated, give directions for the orderly and proper position of the trains in rear of Westminster.

All the trains will keep well to the right of the road in moving, and, in case of any accident requiring a halt, the team must be hauled out of the line, and not delay the movements.

The trains ordered to Union Bridge in these events will be sent to Westminster.

General headquarters will be, in case of this movement, at Frizellburg; General Slocum as near Union Mills as the line will render best for him; General Reynolds at or near the road from Taneytown to Frizellburg.

The chief of artillery will examine the line, and select positions for artillery.

The cavalry will be held on the right and left flanks after the movement is completed. Previous to its completion, it will, as now directed, cover the front and exterior lines, well out.

The commands must be prepared for a movement, and, in the event of the enemy attacking us on the ground indicated herein, to follow up any repulse.

The chief signal officer will examine the line thoroughly, and at once, upon the commencement of this movement, extend telegraphic communication from each of the following points to general headquarters near Frizellburg, *viz.* Manchester, Union Mills, Middleburg, and the Taneytown road.

All true Union people should be advised to harass and annoy the enemy in every way, to send in information, and taught how to do it; giving regiments by number of colors, number of guns, generals' names, &c. All their supplies brought to us will be paid for, and not fall into the enemy's hands.

Roads and ways to move to the right or left of the general line should be studied and thoroughly understood. All movements of troops should be concealed, and our dispositions kept from the enemy. Their knowledge of these dispositions would be fatal to our success, and the greatest care must be taken to prevent such an occurrence.

By command of Major-General Meade:

S[eth] WILLIAMS, Assistant Adjutant-General

George G. Meade to Henry Wager Halleck (July 1, 1863, noon), *The War of the Rebellion: A Compilation of the Official Records of the Union and Confederate Armies* (Washington, DC, 1881-1901), Series 1, Vol. 27 (pt 1)

Ewell is massing at Heidlersburg. A.P. Hill is massed behind the mountains at Cashtown. Longstreet somewhere between Chambersburg and the mountains.

The news proves my advance has answered its purpose. I shall not advance any, but prepare to receive an attack in case Lee makes one. A battle-field is being selected to the rear, on which the army can be rapidly concentrated, on Pipe Creek, between Middleburg and Manchester, covering my depot at Westminster.

If I am not attacked, and I can from reliable intelligence have reason to believe I can attack with reasonable degree of success, I will do so; but at present, having relieved the pressure on the Susquehanna, I am now looking to the protection of Washington, and fighting my army to the best advantage.

1 P.M.

The enemy are advancing in force on Gettysburg, and I expect the battle will begin today.

GEO. G. MEADE

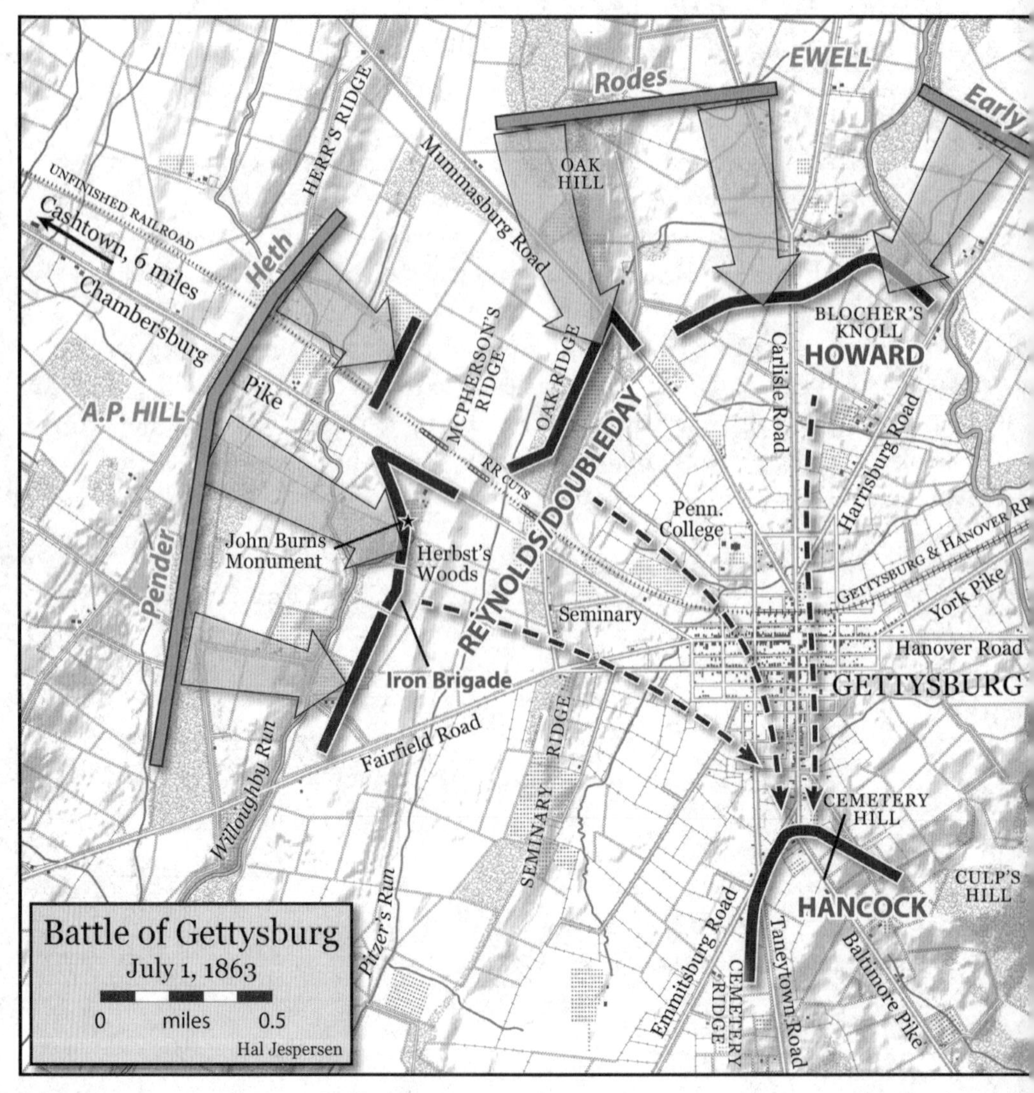

Battle of Gettysburg
July 1, 1863
0 miles 0.5
Hal Jespersen
EWELL
Rodes
Early
OAK HILL
HERR'S RIDGE
Mummasburg Road
UNFINISHED RAILROAD
Cashtown, 6 miles
Heth
Chambersburg
Pike
A.P. HILL
MCPHERSON'S RIDGE
OAK RIDGE
RR CUTS
REYNOLDS/DOUBLEDAY
BLOCHER'S KNOLL
HOWARD
Carlisle Road
Harrisburg Road
Penn. College
GETTYSBURG & HANOVER RR
York Pike
Hanover Road
GETTYSBURG
John Burns Monument
Herbst's Woods
Pender
Seminary
Iron Brigade
Fairfield Road
Willoughby Run
SEMINARY RIDGE
Pitzer's Run
CEMETERY HILL
HANCOCK
CULP'S HILL
Emmitsburg Road
CEMETERY RIDGE
Taneytown Road
Baltimore Pike

THE FIRST DAY

On June 29th, Robert E. Lee ordered a concentration of the Army of Northern Virginia around Gettysburg for July 1st. This would involve recalling Jubal Early's division of Ewell's Corps from the Susquehanna River, Ewell's other two divisions from Carlisle, moving A.P. Hill's and Longstreet's two corps eastward from Chambersburg, all with a view to having Hill arrive first and "proceed through Gettysburg towards York," followed by Longstreet arriving on the west side of the town, and Ewell coming down from the north. There, they would be in easy supporting distance of each other, "moving toward one common centre ... like a huge machine." They would then be ready to pounce together on the first elements of the Army of the Potomac to arrive in the Gettysburg vicinity or stand together to repel a Union attack.

What Lee had not fully anticipated was the speed with which the Army of the Potomac was moving under its new commander, George Meade. Lee believed that "the enemy are still at Middleburg [Maryland], and have not yet struck their tents."

But three of the Army of the Potomac's seven infantry corps—the 1st, 3rd, and 11th—were already in motion toward the Pennsylvania state line under the temporary oversight of John Reynolds, along with a division of cavalry under Major-General John Buford. And while Meade was focused on establishing a defensive shield at Pipe Creek, Reynolds favored "striking" the Confederates "as soon as possible" lest they "strip the State of everything." By June 30th, Reynolds was already at Moritz Tavern, only seven miles south of Gettysburg, and Buford cantered into Gettysburg with his troopers the same day and began establishing picket lines (or videttes) west and north of the town.

The lead division of Hill's Corps, under Major-General Harry Heth, was also on the road toward Gettysburg that day, and his first brigade (under James Johnston Pettigrew) blundered into Buford's pickets west of the town that afternoon on the Chambersburg-Cashtown pike. In the absence of J.E.B. Stuart's three brigades to brush them away, Heth was unsure of what might lie behind the Yankee cavalry and pulled back. But when he appealed to Hill that evening, Hill authorized him to press ahead, since the general understanding on the Confederate side was that this was nothing more than a screen, and any infantry he might encounter were probably only militia, like the ones Early had encountered five days previously. "The only force at Gettysburg is cavalry," Hill assured Heth, "probably a detachment of observation."

Early the next morning, through ground haze and drizzle, Heth renewed his push eastward along the pike, and collided with one of Buford's outposts on Knoxlyn Ridge, about three miles from the center of Gettysburg, where the first shots of the battle were exchanged with troopers of the 8th Illinois cavalry. Still lacking certainty about his opposition, Heth deployed his infantry for a fight, only to have the Union cavalrymen mount up and fall back to the next ridgeline. Buford's horsemen kept this up for almost three hours, at each point forcing Heth to waste valuable time in deployment lest there really be something more substantial behind them.

As it turned out, there was. By the time Heth's infantry had pushed to within sight of Gettysburg's Lutheran Theological Seminary, John Reynolds had arrived from Moritz Tavern, followed closely by his 1st Corps, and its three infantry divisions under Abner Doubleday, James Samuel Wadsworth (a onetime Republican candidate for governor of New York), and John Cleveland Robinson. As Heth's lead Confederate brigades (under John J. Archer and Joseph Davis) moved to attack the last ridgeline before the Seminary, Doubleday's infantry division struck them head-on. One Yankee brigade—the Iron Brigade, composed of five Western regiments—threw Archer's rebels backward, capturing Archer himself. Wadsworth's Federals trapped one of Joseph R. Davis's Mississippi regiments in an unfinished railroad cutting and compelled most of the Mississippians to surrender. The battle of Gettysburg was in full cry.

In the years after the battle, Harry Heth would have to bear the burden of explaining how he had managed to bring on the fight so clumsily. Heth struggled to shift as much of the blame as he could onto the shoulders of the absent J.E.B. Stuart, and in truth this really was the moment when the screening services provided by Civil War cavalry could have yielded the Confederacy their best reward. But Heth also found another defense: need. His men were in want of shoes, and since Gettysburg was said to have ample supplies of them, his determination to enter the town was perfectly understandable. Heth made a faint allusion to shoes in his after-action report, but with the passage of time, Heth increasingly made the pursuit of shoes a full justification for his determination to advance on Gettysburg. There really was no unusual supply of shoes in Gettysburg, nor do the quartermaster returns for his units reveal any extraordinary want of shoes among his men. But Heth felt the blame for Gettysburg more than he liked to admit, and Stuart and shoes were his indulgence tickets.

Heth's advance was not the only pressure on the Federals, either. John Reynolds was fatally shot in the opening moments of the encounter, and by noon, Confederate infantry from Ewell's corps were moving down from the north onto the 1st Corps' flank. They could have made matters very bleak indeed for the Federals, except for another series of botched rebel assaults along Oak Ridge, northwest of town, and for the arrival of two fresh Union divisions from Oliver Otis Howard's 11th Corps, who extended the Federal defense of the town in an arc from west of Gettysburg to its north. The balance, however, swung back to the Confederates by two o'clock, with the arrival of Jubal Early's rebels alongside the rest of Ewell's corps north of the town, and then the personal appearance of Robert E. Lee, riding in from Cashtown.

Lee had not expected, or wished, to fight "a general engagement" on

July 1st, much less do it in the piecemeal fashion managed by Hill and Ewell. But with Early's approach from the north, and more of Hill's corps from the west, Lee judged that a coordinated attack could succeed in smashing the Yankee defenses north and west of Gettysburg. At approximately three o'clock, Ewell's and Hill's massed troops struck the 1st and 11th Corps, breaking up the 11th Corps north of the town and sending it fleeing through Gettysburg's streets to Cemetery Hill, where the town graveyard perched on the south fringe of the town. The Federals defending the Lutheran Seminary were also pushed backward into the town, and as the dusk came on, it appeared that Lee had won a decisive, even if unplanned, victory.

Except that he hadn't, at least not yet. Otis Howard rallied the defeated men of the 1st and 11th Corps on Cemetery Hill; Henry Warner Slocum's 12th Corps arrived as the light faded and was dispatched to hold the neighboring knoll known as Culp's Hill; and Winfield Scott Hancock arrived as a personal observer for George Meade to determine whether the rest of the Army of the Potomac should be committed to the fight. Hancock sent back a positive report, and by midnight Meade had joined Howard on Cemetery Hill. The 3rd and 2nd Corps would arrive at Gettysburg before morning, and the 5th and 6th Corps would soon join them.

Almost as a compensation for having misjudged the closeness of the Army of the Potomac to Gettysburg that morning, Lee suggested Ewell move more aggressively in clearing the Federals off Cemetery Hill and Culp's Hill. But even here, Lee was misreading the closeness and speed of Union forces, since his directions to Ewell lacked the kind of urgency that would have moved Ewell at any cost. Lee assumed that the rest of Meade's troops were still sufficiently far away that the next morning would allow the Confederates to drive away what remained of the 1st and 11th Corps of the Army of the Potomac. They could then create a defensive position of their own around Cemetery Hill, on which the rest of the bloodied Union army could batter itself to death over the next two or three days, much as they had done at Fredericksburg the previous December.

Most of the people in the town of Gettysburg either fled the town or (rather than risk abandoning their homes to looting) cowered in their basements. A few, however, managed to find roles to play in the battle. Michael Jacobs, the mathematics professor at Gettysburg's Pennsylvania College, took detailed meteorological readings of each day's fighting, continuing a practice Jacobs had begun in 1840 and which made him one of the pioneer meteorologists of the country. At least four Gettysburg civilians tried to join the fight, one attaching himself to the 56th Pennsylvania and another to the 16th Maine. (They were not entirely welcomed, since the regiments' officers feared they were more likely to shoot their own men by accident than any Confederates.)

The most famous of these civilians was John Burns, who wandered over to the 150th Pennsylvania armed with an old flintlock musket. The officers of the 150th politely suggested he join the nearby 7th Wisconsin. There, Burns blazed away until he was wounded and left on the field. Captured by the Confederates, he could easily have been shot as an armed guerilla. But Burns talked his way out of his dilemma by passing himself off as a farmer who had been trying to herd his cattle out of harm's way. After the battle, Burns would become one of the minor heroes of Gettysburg, the subject of paintings (by Xanthus Russell Smith), poems (by Bret Harte), and numerous newspaper stories.

"Letter from Major-General Henry Heth, of A.P. Hill's Corps, A.N.V.," *Southern Historical Society Papers* 4 (September 1877)

The failure to crush the Federal army in Pennsylvania in 1863, in the opinion of almost all the officers of the Army of Northern Virginia, can be expressed in five words—the absence of our cavalry.

Train a giant for an encounter and he can be whipped by a pigmy—if you put out his eyes. The eyes of an army are its cavalry. Before Ewell crossed the Potomac General Lee wrote to General Stuart, commanding the cavalry, in substance, as follows: "Ewell will cross the Potomac on a certain day, at a certain point. Hill will follow Ewell, crossing on a given day at a given point; Longstreet will hold the gaps in the mountains and protect the crossing of these two corps; after Hill has crossed Longstreet will vacate the gaps, and follow Hill; on Longstreet vacating the gaps in the mountains, you will seize them and protect Longstreet's crossing; then follow Longstreet, throw yourself on the right flank of the army, watch the enemy, give me all the information you can gather of his movements, and collect supplies."

General Stuart, probably thinking he could carry out General Lee's orders, and at the same time make a brilliant dash toward and threatening Washington, worked by his right flank, separating himself from Longstreet, crossing the Potomac between the enemy and Washington city—making a swoop toward Washington, then turning west to join the Army of Northern Virginia, when he found the enemy had crossed the Potomac and were between him and that army. This necessitated his riding entirely around the Federal army, and brought him, whether from necessity or not, I cannot say, to Carlisle, Pa. From this point he struck south and joined the Army of Northern Virginia, *being late in the evening of July second*. It is thus evident that so far as deriving any assistance from his cavalry from the [25th] of June to the evening of July 2, it might as well have had no existence. Every officer who conversed with General Lee for several days previous to the battle of Gettysburg, well remembers having heard such expressions as these: "Can you tell me where General Stuart is?" "Where on earth is my cavalry?" "Have you any news of the enemy's movements?" "What is the enemy going to do?" "If the enemy does not find us, we must try and find him, in the absence of our cavalry, as best we can!" The eyes of the giant were out; he knew not where to strike; a movement in any direction might prove a disastrous blunder.

I have stated above that General Lee's purpose in invading Pennsylvania was to break up the enemy's combinations, to draw him from our own territory, and to subsist his army on that of the enemy's. While this is true, his intention was to strike his enemy the very first available opportunity that offered—believing he could, when such an opportunity offered, crush him . . . This determination to strike his enemy was not, from the position he found himself, consequent upon invasion, but from a leading characteristic of the man. General Lee, not excepting Jackson, was the most aggressive man in his army. This cannot and will not be contradicted, I am satisfied. General Lee, had he seen fit, could have assumed a defensive position, and popular opinion in the Northern States would have forced the commander of the Federal army to attack.

And further, to corroborate the fact that General Lee was not compelled to attack Meade "where Meade chose to wait for him," I will show, I am confident, that the "Battle of Gettysburg" was the result purely of *an accident*, for which I am probably, more than anyone else, accountable. Napoleon is said to have remarked that "a dog fight might determine the result of a great battle." Almost as trivial a circumstance determined the battle of Gettysburg being fought at Gettysburg. It is well known that General Meade had chosen another point as his battlefield. On the 29th of June, 1863, General Lee's army was disposed as follows: Longstreet's corps, at or near Chambersburg; Ewell's corps, which had been pushed east as far as York, had received orders to countermarch and concentrate on Hill's corps, which lay on and at the base of South Mountain; the leading division (Heth's) occupying Cashtown, at the base of the mountain; the cavalry not heard from, probably at or near Carlisle. Hearing that a supply of shoes was to be obtained in Gettysburg, eight miles distant from Cashtown, and greatly needing shoes for my men, I directed General Pettigrew to go to Gettysburg and get these supplies.

On the 30th of June General Pettigrew, with his brigade, went near Gettysburg, but did not enter the town, returning the same evening to Cashtown, reporting that he had not carried out my orders, as Gettysburg was occupied by the enemy's cavalry, and that some of his officers reported hearing drums beating on the farther side of the town; that under these circumstances he did not deem it advisable to enter Gettysburg. About this time General Hill rode up, and this information was given him. He remarked, "the only force at Gettysburg is cavalry, probably a detachment of observation. I am just from General Lee, and the information he has from his scouts corroborates that I have received from mine, that is, the enemy are still at Middleburg, and have not yet struck their tents." I then said, if there is no objection, I will take my division to-morrow and go to Gettysburg and get those shoes! Hill replied, "None in the world."

On July 1st I moved my division from Cashtown in the direction of Gettysburg, reaching the heights, a mile (more or less) from the town, about 9 o'clock a.m. No opposition had been made and no enemy discovered. While the division was coming up I placed several batteries in position and shelled the woods to the right and left of the town. No reply was made. Two brigades were then deployed to the right and left of the railroad leading into Gettysburg, and, with the railroad as a point of direction, were ordered to advance and occupy Gettysburg. These brigades, on moving forward, soon struck the enemy, which proved to be Reynolds' corps of the Federal army, and were driven back with some loss. This was the first intimation that General Lee had that the enemy had moved from the point he supposed him to occupy, possibly thirty miles distant.

My division was then formed in a wooded ravine to the right of the railroad, the ground rising in front and in rear. The enemy was evidently in force in my front. General [Robert] Rodes, commanding a division of Ewell's corps, . . . was following a road running north of Gettysburg. Rodes hearing the firing at Gettysburg, faced by the left flank and approached the town. He soon became heavily engaged, and seeing this, I sought for and found General Lee. Saying to the General: "Rodes is very heavily engaged, had I not better attack?" General Lee replied: "No; I am not prepared to bring on a general engagement to-day—Longstreet is not up." Returning to my division, I soon discovered that the enemy were moving troops from my front and pushing them against Rodes. I reported this fact to General Lee and again requested to be permitted to attack. Permission was given. My division numbered some seven thousand muskets. I found in my front a heavy skirmish line and two lines of battle. My division swept over these without halting. My loss was severe. In twenty-five minutes I lost twenty-seven hundred men, killed and wounded. The last I saw or remember of this day's fight was seeing the enemy in my front completely and utterly routed, and my division in hot pursuit. I was then shot and rendered insensible for some hours . . .

The fight at Gettysburg on July 1 was without order or system, the several divisions attacking the enemy in their front as they arrived on the field—nor do I see how there could have been a systematic plan of battle formed, as I have, I think, clearly shown that we accidentally stumbled into this fight.

Captain Amasa Dana [8th Illinois Cavalry] in Theodore W. Bean, "Who Fired the Opening Shots!" *Philadelphia Weekly Times* (February 2, 1878)

On the 30th of June, 1863, the Eighth Illinois Cavalry with the First Cavalry Division, encamped a short distance in front of the town of Gettysburg; a portion of the regiment being detailed for picket duty, I, with Company E, encamped about a mile west from the town on the Cashtown road, holding the larger portion of the company in reserve and placing videttes from three to four miles still further out and across the pike and railroad. About daylight on the 1st of July the report came in from Lieutenant Jones, in charge of the pickets, that the enemy were within sight; and a short time afterward, perhaps fifteen minutes, while on my way out with the reserve, the report met me that the enemy were moving toward us. When I reached the outposts, about sunrise, I could see the enemy's skirmish line advancing slowly, and reaching from right to left across the Cashtown road, as we thought, for a distance of a mile and a half, concealed at intervals by timber, but evidently a continuous line formed for advancing. A short distance in the rear of this skirmish line, in the open road, in our front, were columns of infantry deploying into the woods, evidently forming their line of battle. I immediately forwarded a report of my observations to headquarters, then dismounting my entire company and sending the horses to the rear, called in the pickets and formed the first line with twenty men including myself. This line was formed a few hundred yards in the rear of the picket line held during the night, the position being more favorable for observation—it ran across the pike and railroad bed—Lieutenant Marcellus E. Jones, Eighth Illinois Cavalry, *firing the first shot* a little after sunrise, before leaving the outpost. The enemy advanced steadily, though slow and cautiously. Our first position proved to be well-taken—in our front there was a large open field. Scattering my men to the right and left at intervals of thirty feet, and behind post-and-rail fences, I directed them to throw up their carbine sights for eight hundred yards, then taking rest on the top rail we gave the enemy the benefit of long range practice, from a long, but much attenuated line. The firing was rapid from our carbines, and at the distance induced the belief of four times the number of men actually present, as . . . the line in our front halted, artillery was brought up, and the woods to our rear was shelled vigorously, no one being within range of their shells save the orderlies carrying our reports to and from the front . . . We retired, and continued to take new positions, and usually held out as long as we could without imminent risk of capture . . . We had been driven from three positions successively in less than one hour before support reached us . . . This condition of things continued for an hour or perhaps an hour and a half; the enemy feeling his way with the greatest caution until toward 7:30 to 8 o'clock a.m., when the fury of the attack upon our single line of battle was almost more than we could bear. All the troops of the First Brigade were now on the single line of battle—to our right the Second Brigade could be seen for a distance of two miles severely engaged, with two squadrons of the Seventeenth Pennsylvania Cavalry . . . From 8 to 10 o'clock the unequal conflict was maintained, yielding ground to the enemy step by step, suffering severe loss in officers and men, with many of our led horses . . . Our ammunition was now almost exhausted, and it was becoming painfully evident that the Seminary Ridge, on which this fierce struggle was raging, would have to be abandoned unless additional support speedily reached us. It was at this hour that the advanced infantry [Abner Doubleday's division of the Army of the Potomac's 1st Corps] was seen going into position. Then we felt assured and our carbines were willing to fire their last bullet, as many of them did before leaving the line to their equally courageous comrades, fresh and eager for the fray.

Charles Henry Veil to David McConaughy (April 7, 1864), MS-022: The Papers of David McConaughy, 1823-1902, Gettysburg College Special Collections

General Reynolds encamped near a tavern between Emmitsburg [Maryland] & Gettysburg, the night previous to the battle. Early on the morning of July 1st he . . . put the troops in motion, and being in command of the Left Wing at the time, Consisting of the 1st, 3rd & 11th Corps, he moved on ahead of the troops, probably several miles. When within about 3 miles of town, he recd a note from General Buford, Commanding Cavalry at Gettysburg, that the enemy was advancing on the Cashtown road, but did not state what the force was supposed to be. The Genl sent an aid to Genl Wadsworth Commanding 1st Divn of the 1st Corps, to close up his divn and come on, while the Genl rode to the front. When we got within about ½ mile of town we met a citizen on horseback who appeared to be much frightened. The Genl stopped and enquired what the trouble was. The man stated that our Cavalry was fighting . . . When we got into town we saw that there was considerable excitement so the Genl rode to the front at once—Found Genl Buford engaged on [a] ridge in front of [the] Seminary—(McPhersons farm I think). Just as we arrived there the enemy opened a Battery from a position in the Road in front of a house (have heard since that it was at the old toll Gate). The General ordered Genl Buford to hold the enemy in check as long as possible, to Keep them from Getting into town, and at the same time sent orders to Genl Sickles Comdg 3rd Corps & Genl Howard 11th to come on as fast as possible. The Genl then rode back, to town, went up a back street (By [John] Burns house) to the Emmitsburg road & out about ½ mile, when he ordered his escort to tear down all the fences, and make way for the troops to get across the fields to the Seminary. About this time the head of Column of 1st Corps Came in and filed across the fields at a point a little to the left of the Seminary. When we arrived at the Seminary Genl Bufords Cavalry on [the] right of [the] Cashtown Road was being driven back in disorder. The Genl at once ordered 1 Brigade of 1st Div^{n} to Cross the road, and take position . . . also ordered a Brigade of 1st Div^{n} to take position on [the] left of [the] Cashtown Road . . . These troops had to form under a heavy artillery fire, and had no sooner got into line than the enemy advanced his infantry . . . and both lines met near the top of the ridge. The action had now commenced in real earnest. The Genl rode along in rear of our line towards the woods on our left (Called I believe McPhersons, though I heard while in Gettysburg that they belonged to Mr. Herbst) . . . The Enemy then pushed on, and was now not much more than 60 paces from where the Genl was. Minnie Balls were flying thick. The Genl turned to look towards the Seminary. (I suppose to see if the other troops were coming on, & as he did so, a Minnie Ball struck him in the back of the neck, and he fell from his horse, dead. He never spoke a word, or moved a muscle after he was struck. I have seen many men killed in action, but never saw a ball do its work so *instantly* as did the ball which struck General Reynolds, a man who Knew not what fear or danger was, in a word, was one of our very best Generals . . . The last words the lamented General spoke were—*"Forward men forward for Gods sake and drive those fellows out of those woods*," meaning the enemy.)

When the General fell the only persons who were with him was Capts [Robert M.] Mitchell & [Edward C.] Baird, and myself. When he fell we Sprang from our horses. The Genl fell on his left side. I turned him on his back, glanced over him but could see no wound except a bruise above his left eye. We were under the impression that he was only stunned. This was all done in a glance. I caught the Genl under the Arms while each of the Capts. took hold of his legs, and we commenced to carry him out of the woods towards the Seminary. When we got outside of the woods, the Capts. left me to Carry the word to the next officers in Command of his death. I in the Meantime got some help from some of the orderlies who came up about this time, & we carried the body towards the Seminary, really not knowing where to take it to, as the enemy appeared to be coming in on our right and left. When we arrived at the Seminary I concluded to Carry the body to the

Emmitsburg Road & done so, Carrying it to Mr. George's house, (a small stone house) as we were laying him down, I first found the wound in the back of the neck. I then saw that the Genl was dead—I almost forgot to tell you that in Crossing the fields between the woods where he was Killed & the Semy, he gasped a little and I thought he was coming to his senses. We stopped a moment & I gave him a drop of water from a canteen but he would not drink. It was his last struggle . . .

Alanson Henery Nelson [57th Pennsylvania], *The Battles of Chancellorsville and Gettysburg* (Minneapolis, 1899)

The fall of Gen. Reynolds . . . was a great loss to the army, the country and its cause. He was a West Point graduate, had seen service in the Mexican war and on the frontier and War of Rebellion from the first, a Pennsylvanian, a gallant officer, none more patriotic. He said to Gen. Doubleday: "We must fight the enemy as soon as we can find them, or they will ruin the state of Pennsylvania." He had no idea of fighting and falling back. If he had lived he would have made haste to order up Sickles' third corps and requested Gen. Slocum of the twelfth corps to come to his support, who was not more than five miles from Gettysburg . . . When Gen. Hooker placed Gen. Reynolds in command of the left wing of the army, Reynolds turned over the command of the corps to Doubleday, and on the morning of July 1st, Gen. Reynolds was encamped with the first corps at Marsh creek, and when Gen. Buford's cavalry command fired the three successive cannon shots, the signal that had been agreed upon as a notice that the enemy had attacked the cavalry, and that Gen. Reynolds was to move the infantry forward to their support . . .

Reverend Michael Colver, "Reminiscences of the Battle of Gettysburg," 1902 *Spectrum*, Gettysburg College Special Collections

I entered the Sophomore class in 1860 and was a senior when the famous and decisive battle of the rebellion was fought. As it may well be supposed Gettysburg was in a state of agitation during almost the whole of my college and seminary life—the prescribed theological course being then but two years . . . We all had a knowledge of a few troops in and around the town, brought there, perhaps, because of the rebel invasion of the week previous, but we were entirely ignorant of the near approach of the main body of either army. A company of students—about sixty in number—had enlisted in the three months service, and the few of us who remained went to prayers and recitations as usual on the morning of July 1, 1863. Preparing for the second recitation—11 o'clock—I walked from my room on the second to the first floor—book in hand—and passing out of the building toward Linnaean Hall I was called to by a student (Watkins) from his room on the third floor and asked whether I heard "shooting." I replied "no"—but instantly heard the ominous sounds. I proposed to him that we go to the cupola of the Seminary as a point of observation. He suggested we get permission from the faculty. My crude reply was "let the faculty go to grass and you come on." Whither the faculty went I did not learn, but he came down and we went to the place named . . .

We saw, not far distant from us, pickets of both armies exchanging bullets—saw the first batteries planted on our side—saw the first charge made on our dismounted cavalry and heard a shell from the first rebel battery pass in close proximity to our ears. This was all we desired just then to see and hear. The half dozen of us in the cupola left our lofty perch rather unceremoniously, passed rapidly out of the building and down the walk at the head of the 1st army corps which had arrived and was in line ready to march to the scene of action. My former companion and I became separated but Miller of Harper's Ferry and myself went to "Cemetery Ridge" to get a position for observance at longer range. On arriving there we were at once accosted by a chaplain who said, "if you young men will remain with me you may be the means of saving some valuable lives." Only a few more words were exchanged when some uniformed men, mounted on horseback, approached us. I inquired of the chaplain what that meant. He said it was his "brother's staff coming to prepare to plant a battery here." These words were scarcely more than spoken when a shell from the rebel ranks scattered chaplain, Miller and myself. After this I wandered alone, being driven from place to place by the sound of cannon balls which did not pass comfortably high enough in air.

William H. Harries, "The Iron Brigade in the First Day's Battle at Gettysburg" (October 8, 1895), *Glimpses of the Nation's Struggle: Papers Read Before the Minnesota Commandery of the Military Order of the Loyal Legion of the United States, 1892–1897*, ed. Edward D. Neill (St. Paul, 1898)

General [John J.] Archer, whose brigade was in our front, evidently refused to be borne to the rear with his troops and was taken prisoner together with about two hundred and fifty of his men. I can recall now, something of General Archer's personal appearance as he appeared to me that day. He wore a splendid gray uniform and while I was looking him over, the lieutenant of my company stepped up to him and said, "I'll relieve you of that sword"; it was a beautiful steel-scabbard sword that he handed over to Lieutenant D[ennis] B. Daily. General Archer was sent to the rear with his men and as he was being taken back, General Doubleday rode up and said: "Good-morning, Archer, how are you? I am glad to see you." General Archer replied, "Well, I am not glad to see you by a ——— sight." General Doubleday shrugged his shoulders, straightened up in his saddle and said: "Take him to the rear; take him to the rear." They had been classmates at West Point and the meeting was far less pleasant to Archer than to Doubleday [Archer actually graduated from Princeton, Class of 1835]. When General Archer's Brigade broke to the rear, some of his men would occasionally dodge behind trees and fire and while this was going on General Reynolds rode up to the edge of the grove with his aides, [Major William] Riddle and [Captain Craig W.] Wadsworth, and was killed by one of these retreating Confederates.

Lieutenant-Colonel Rufus Dawes, *Service with the Sixth Wisconsin Volunteers* (Marietta, OH, 1890)

Excepting the Sixth Wisconsin, the whole of Wadsworth's division was hotly engaged in battle with the enemy. Lieutenant Meredith Jones came with orders from General Doubleday. He said, "General Doubleday directs that you move your regiment at once to the right." I immediately gave the order to move in that direction at a double quick. Captain J.D. Wood came and rode beside me, repeating the order from General [Solomon]

Meredith and saying the rebels were "driving [Colonel Lysander] Cutler's men." The guns of [Captain James A.] Hall's battery could be seen driving to the rear, and Cutler's men were manifestly in full retreat . . .

The regiment halted at the fence along the Cashtown Turnpike, and I gave the order to fire. In the field, beyond the turnpike, a long line of yelling Confederates could be seen running forward and firing, and our troops of Cutler's brigade were running back in disorder. The fire of our carefully aimed muskets, resting on the fence rails, striking their flank, soon checked the rebels in their headlong pursuit. The rebel line swayed and bent, and suddenly stopped firing and the men ran into the railroad cut, parallel to the Cashtown Turnpike. I ordered my men to climb over the turnpike fences and advance. I was not aware of the existence of the railroad cut, and at first mistook the manuever of the enemy for retreat, but was undeceived by the heavy fire which they began at once to pour upon us from their cover in the cut. Captain John Ticknor, always a dashing leader, fell dead while climbing the second fence, and many were struck on the fences, but the line pushed on. When over the fences and in the field, and subjected to an infernal fire, I first saw the Ninety-Fifth New York regiment coming gallantly into line upon our left. I did not then know or care where they came from, but was rejoiced to see them. Farther to the left was the fourteenth Brooklyn regiment, but I was then ignorant of the fact. Major Edward Pye appeared to be in command of the

Ninety-Fifth New York. Running to the major, I said, "We must charge." The gallant major replied, "Charge it is." "Forward, charge!" was the order I gave, and Major Pye gave the same command. We were receiving a fearfully destructive fire from the hidden enemy. Men who had been shot were leaving the ranks in crowds. With the colors at the advance point, the regiment firmly and hurriedly moved forward, while the whole field behind streamed with men who had been shot, and who were struggling to the rear or sinking in death upon the ground. The only commands I gave, as we advanced, were, "Align on the colors! Close up on the colors! Close up on the colors!" The regiment was being so broken up that this order alone could hold the body together. Meanwhile the colors fell upon the ground several times but were raised again by the heroes of the color guard. Four hundred and twenty men started in the regiment from the turnpike fence, of whom about two hundred and forty reached the railroad cut. Years afterward I found the distance passed over to be one hundred and seventy-five paces. Every officer proved brave, true, and heroic in encouraging the men to breast the deadly storm, but the real impetus was the eager and determined valor of our men who carried muskets in the ranks. I noticed the motions of our "Tall Sycamore," Captain J[oseph] H. Marston, who commanded company E. His long arms were stretched out as if to gather his men together and push them forward. At a crisis he rose to his full height, and he was the tallest man in the regiment, excepting Levi Steadman of company I, who was killed on this charge. How the rebels happened to miss Captain Marston I cannot comprehend. Second Lieutenant O[rrin] B. Chapman, commanding company C, fell dead while on the charge. The commission of Lieutenant Thomas Kerr as captain of Company D, bears the proud date of July first, 1863—in recognition of his conduct. The rebel color was seen waving defiantly above, the edge of the railroad cut. A heroic ambition to capture it took possession of several of our men. Corporal [George Dulton] Eggleston, of company H, sprang forward to seize it, and was shot and mortally wounded. Private [Harry] Anderson, of his company, furious at the killing of his brave young comrade, recked [reckoned] little for the rebel color, but he swung aloft his musket and with a terrific blow split the skull of the rebel who had shot young Eggleston. This soldier was well known in the regiment as "Rocky Mountain Anderson." Lieutenant William N. Remington was shot and severely wounded in the shoulder, while rushing for the color.

Into this deadly melee came Corporal Francis A. Waller, who seized and held the rebel battle flag. His name will forever remain upon the historic record, as he received from Congress a medal for this deed.

My notice that we were upon the enemy, was a general cry from our men of: "Throw down your muskets! Down with your muskets!" Running forward through our line of men, I found myself face to face with hundreds of rebels, whom I looked down upon in the railroad cut, which was, where I stood, four feet deep. Adjutant [Edward P.] Brooks, equal to the emergency, quickly placed about twenty men across the cut in position to fire through it. I have always congratulated myself upon getting the first word. I shouted: "Where is the colonel of this regiment?" An officer in gray, with stars on his collar, who stood among the men in the cut, said: "Who are you?" I said: "I command this regiment. Surrender, or I will fire." The officer replied not a word, but promptly handed me his sword, and his men, who still held them, threw down their muskets. The coolness, self-possession, and discipline which held back our men from pouring in a general volley saved a hundred lives of the enemy, and as my mind goes back to the fearful excitement of the moment, I marvel at it. The fighting around the rebel colors had not ceased when this surrender took place. I took the sword. It would have been the handsome thing to say, "Keep your sword, sir," but I was new to such occasions, and when six other officers came up and handed me their swords, I took them also. I held this awkward bundle in my arms until relieved by Adjutant Brooks. I directed the officer in command, Major John A. Blair, of the Second Mississippi regiment, to have his men fall in without arms. He gave the command, and his men (seven officers and two hundred and twenty-five enlisted men) obeyed.

Orson Blair Curtis, *History of the Twenty-Fourth Michigan of the Iron Brigade* (Detroit, 1891)

Leaving Emmitsburg behind on Tuesday, June 30, the Iron Brigade, with the Sixth Wisconsin in advance, crossed the Pennsylvania line, being in the van of the Potomac Army. It moved on five miles, nearly to Greenmount, Adams County, Pennsylvania, 160 miles from the starting point on the Rappahannock, and bivouacked about noon near Marsh Creek, where the men were mustered for pay . . . At an early hour on

Wednesday morning, July 1, the men partook of their frugal meal of hardtack, pork and coffee, as usual. The Pennsylvania line had been reached and the forces of the enemy must be met very soon, though none suspected that the foe was within a few hours' march. Before resuming the daily journey it was deemed proper to assemble the regiment for prayer. During Chaplain [William] Way's invocation, cartridges and hardtack were distributed among the men. Time was precious and not to be lost . . .

Hastening across the fields the Iron Brigade's right wing halted on the crest of a ridge looking down into a wooded ravine, from which blazed a shower of bullets from Archer's Tennessee Brigade. Its left wing, consisting of the Twenty-fourth Michigan, swung clear around into the forest in the rear of this Tennessee Brigade . . . The Twenty-fourth Michigan was on the extreme left of the Iron Brigade during the charge, and swept over the hill, down across Willoughby Run, swinging clear around the ravine in which was Archer's forces, most of whom were thus captured with General Archer himself. It was a victory indeed, but at the cost of precious lives, including its valiant color-bearer, Sergeant Abel G. Peck. The regiment then about-faced and drove the uncaptured foe over the crest and a hundred yards beyond, but soon after withdrew to the eastern side of the stream and hastily formed, during which Lieutenant-Colonel Mark Flanigan lost a leg . . .

General Meredith of the Iron Brigade was soon wounded and left the field. Some historians have assigned Colonel Morrow to the command of the Iron Brigade for the rest of the fight, but in a private letter from Colonel Henry A. Morrow to the author, in 1890, he disclaimed any command on that day of the Iron Brigade, saying that Colonel [William W.] Robinson of the Seventh Wisconsin took Meredith's place after the latter was wounded . . . Soon after, [John Mercer] Brockenbrough and Pettigrew's brigades attacked the Twenty-fourth Michigan and Nineteenth Indiana, in front and left flank, as if to crush them. Other troops came down upon the Seventh and Second Wisconsin as if to drive them in . . . The Nineteenth Indiana fought valiantly, but overpowered by flanking numbers, with a disadvantage of position, they were forced back after severe loss and formed on a new line. This exposed the Twenty-fourth Michigan to a terrible cross fire, the men falling like grass before the scythe . . . The enemy had now approached a little within the first line of battle of the Twenty-fourth Michigan, where they were held for some time, the work of death going on

without ceasing. They were the Twenty-sixth North Carolina . . . their old antagonists who now were heard by our own wounded to exclaim: "Here are those black-hat fellows again! This is no militia."

The Second Line of Battle of the Twenty-fourth Michigan was speedily formed. Meanwhile, a desperate resistance was made against [Brigadier-General Alfred Moore] Scales' Confederate Brigade on our right, which the rest of the Iron Brigade, chiefly the Seventh and Second Wisconsin, aided by Battery B, Fourth U. S. Artillery from another section of the field, almost annihilated . . . Overwhelmed again, it was forced to take another new position beyond a small ravine. On this Third Line of Battle its third color-bearer was killed, and Major Edwin B. Wight (acting as Lieutenant-Colonel) lost an eye . . . Scarcely a fourth of the regiment taken into action could now be rallied . . . The Twenty-fourth regiment had now retired from the woods into the open field towards the Seminary. A Fourth Line of Battle was next attempted. The last of the color-guard planted the flag around which to rally the men . . .

Colonel Morrow took the flag to rally the remnant of his devoted band of Wayne County boys and men, when a private took the colors from his hands and was instantly killed by the Colonel's side . . . A Fifth Line of Battle was attempted where he planted the colors. On this new line, while waiving his sword over his head to rally the men, Captain [Malachi J.] O'Donnell was instantly killed, and Lieutenant [Newell] Grace received two wounds, both of which were mortal. Gradually contesting every foot of ground, step by step, frequently almost surrounded, through and out of the woods and over the open field, what was now left of the Twenty-fourth had been forced back to the friendly rail fence barricade just west of the Seminary. Its Sixth Line of Battle was attempted to be formed at this place. It fought for a time, during which Colonel Morrow, holding aloft the bullet-riddled flag, received a wound in his head and was forced to leave the field, first turning the command of the regiment over to Captain A[lbert] M. Edwards . . . This was the last stand made by the Union troops on that part of the field . . . Captain Edwards, still carrying the flag, led the way through the town to the Cemetery, followed by only twenty-six of the Twenty-fourth Michigan, in comparative good order . . . Of the Twenty-fourth Michigan only ninety-nine men and three officers could be rallied to the flag, out of 496 who followed it into action that morning . . .

The noble and stalwart Color-Sergeant, Abel G. Peck, in whose keeping the colors were placed . . . yielded up his life in their defense, early in the morning fight, being the first man of the regiment killed in this battle. Before they touched the ground, as Peck fell, Color-Corporal Charles Bellore of E sprang forward and seizing the colors, bore them aloft as the troops advanced to the capture of Archer's Brigade. Bellore, too, was killed in McPherson's woods near the second line of battle. Private August Earnest of K now took the colors . . . When Earnest dropped dead, the flag fell with him at the feet of First Sergeant Everard B. Welton of H, who reached forward and picked it up, holding it till Colonel Morrow ran to him and took the thrice prostrated flag from his hands. He gave it to Color-Corporal Andrew Wagner of F, who boldly waved it in the face of the advancing foe . . . Wagner in turn, the last of the Color Guard, was shot and fell with the colors. Colonel Morrow took them from under Wagner, and, assuring him that his wound was not mortal, himself bore them until Private William Kelly of E came up and took them, saying: "The Colonel of the Twenty-fourth Michigan shall not carry the colors while I am alive." In an instant after his lifeless body lay at the feet of the Colonel! After the death of the brave Kelly, the flag was carried for a time by Private Lilburn A. Spaulding of K, when Colonel Morrow again took it . . . What became of the colors or who took them after Colonel Morrow was wounded, will ever remain a mystery known only to the God of heaven and the brave spirit of him in whose possession they were found. Soon after assuming command, Captain A.M. Edwards saw the flag lying on the ground in the hand of a dead or dying soldier boy, who was reclining on his right side, his gun being near him. Captain Edwards took the flag from the young soldier's hands . . . and . . . bore it through the town to the Cemetery, where he planted it near a battery, and sat down on a grave stone . . . Seven of the Companies had not a single officer left, and the other three companies but one officer each. B had but ten men left, C had but three, D had eleven, I had only eight, and so on.

Charles Carleton Coffin, "Memories of Gettysburg," *Stories of Our Soldiers: War Reminiscences by "Carleton," and by Soldiers of New England* (Boston, 1893)

On the 30th we were at Marsh Run, two miles north of Emmittsburg and within five miles of Gettysburg: It was here that Charles F. Weakley, a brave boy living with his father in the mountains in the vicinity (his mother being dead), joined us . . . He came to Sergeant Anson B. Barton of Company A, Twelfth Massachusetts, while the Sergeant was filling his canteen from a stream. He was brimful of patriotism and wanted to join us and "fight the rebels." . . . Barton brought the little fellow into camp, where Capt. [Erastus L.] Clark . . . was convinced that he meant business, and took him to Col. [James L.] Bates . . . So he was taken into the company and supplied with such odds and ends in the way of equipments as we could collect. He went into battle with us next day, behaved like a veteran, and was wounded in two places . . .

Weakley was treated in Mulberry Street Hospital, Harrisburg, Pa., from July 24 to Oct. 8,1863, when . . . he was discharged from the hospital and sent home, never having been enlisted or mustered into the service. I ascertained also that young Weakley enlisted after his Gettysburg exploit . . . Charles F. Weakley enlisted Dec. 18, 1863, in Company G, Thirteenth Pennsylvania Cavalry, and served until Nov. 23, 1864, when he was found drowned near camp, his drowning being due to epileptic seizure. Evidence submitted to the Pension Office shows that he was born in Carroll county, Md., Sept. 2,1841.

Abner Ralph Small, *The Sixteenth Maine Regiment in the War of the Rebellion, 1861-1865* (Portland, ME, 1886)

Lieutenant [Isaac H.] Thompson, of Company G, noticed a stranger to the regiment, standing about fifteen paces in rear of line, loading and firing independently. Thinking the man might do mischief to his comrades, Thompson went to him, said something in his low, peculiar tone, and, receiving a reply, immediately knocked him down, and then raising him from the ground by the collar, kicked him rapidly to the rear, much to the merriment and satisfaction of the men, who didn't care to be shot in the back. Lieutenant G[eorge] A. Deering, of Company G, sheathed his sword, and seizing a musket from a fallen man, went into the ranks. He was evidently excited, and every once in a while would forget to return his rammer after loading, hence would send it over to the enemy. The peculiar swishing noise made by the rammer, as it hurried through the wood, was laughable to the boys, and must have been a holy terror to the rebels.

Isaac R. Trimble, "The Battle and Campaign of Gettysburg," *Southern Historical Society Papers* 26 (January-December 1898)

The battle was over and we had won it handsomely. General Ewell moved about uneasily, a good deal excited, and seemed to me to be undecided what to do next. I approached him and said: "Well, General, we have had a grand success; are you not going to follow it up and push our advantage?"

He replied that "General Lee had instructed him not to bring on a general engagement without orders, and that he would wait for them."

I said, that hardly applies to the present state of things, as we have fought a hard battle already, and should secure the advantage gained. He made no rejoinder, but was far from composure. I was deeply impressed with the conviction that it was a critical moment for us and made a remark to that effect.

As no movement seemed immediate, I rode off to our left, north of the town, to reconnoitre, and noticed conspicuously the wooded hill northeast of Gettysburg (Culp's), and a half mile distant, and of an elevation to command the country for miles each way, and overlooking Cemetery Hill above the town. Returning to see General Ewell, who was still under much embarrassment, I said: "General, there," pointing to Culp's Hill, "is an eminence of commanding position, and not now occupied, as it ought to be by us or the enemy soon. I advise you to send a brigade and hold it if we are to remain here." He said: "Are you sure it commands the town?" "Certainly it does, as you can see, and it ought to be held by us at once." General Ewell made some impatient reply, and the conversation dropped.

By night (it was then about 3:30), that hill—Culp's—the key of the position around Gettysburg was occupied by part of the 12th Corps, Slocum's, and reinforced the next day.

On the 2nd and 3rd determined efforts were made by us to gain this hill, but without success, and fearful loss.

On our extreme right, west of Round-top Hill, General Longstreet had reached a point three or four miles from Gettysburg, with but slight opposition.

That night from daylight to late at night, General Lee was anxiously reconnoitering the ground and frequently expressed a wish to attack the enemy that night or early in the morning. Why his wish was not carried out I don't feel at liberty to explain. Nothing however was done, nor a gun fired, until next day late in the afternoon.

Henry Eyster Jacobs, "Meteorology of the Battle: Notes by Rev. Dr. Jacobs," *Gettysburg Star and Sentinel* (August 11, 1885)

The entire period of the invasion is remarkable for being one of clouds, and, for that season of the year, of low temperature. From June 15th until July 22nd, 1863, there was not an entirely clear day. On the evening before the entrance into our town of Gen. Gordon's division, viz: June 25th, at 8 p.m., a rain began, which some may remember in connection with the arrival of the advance guard of the 25th [26th] Pa. [Emergency] militia, under Lieut. [William F.] Hinkle, of the college company. This rain continued at intervals until Saturday, June 27th, at 7 a.m. . . . At all the observations made on Saturday and Sunday, and until the nine o'clock observation of Monday night, the entire sky was covered with clouds. On the day before the battle, both at 7 a.m., and 2 p.m., the obscuration was again complete, with cumulo-stratus clouds moving from S.S.E. At 9 p.m., only four-tenths of the heavens were covered. During these days of sombre suspense, the records of the wind are those of almost an entire calm. The thermometer registers as follows during this period:

	7 a.m.	2 p.m.	9 p.m.
June 25th,	59	51	63
" 26th,	60	63	62
" 27th,	61	63	67
" 28th,	63	67	68
" 29th,	66	72	69
" 30th,	68	79	71

First Day. All through the first day, the entire sky was covered with clouds, viz: cumulo-stratus at 7 a.m. and 2 p.m.; and cirro-stratus at 9 p.m. A very gentle southern breeze, (2 miles per hour).

Thermometer:

7 a.m.	2 p.m.	9 p.m.
72	76	74

Second Day. At 8 a.m., sky still covered, (cumulo-stratus). At 2 p.m., three-tenths are clear. At 9 p.m., there are cirrus clouds; wind as on preceding day.

Thermometer:

7 a.m.	2 p.m.	9 p.m.
74	81	76

Third Day. At 8 a.m., sky again completely covered with cumulo-stratus clouds; at 2 p.m., only four-tenths of the heavens are covered, but with cumulus or the massive thunder-cloud of summer; at 9 p.m., seven-tenths cumulus. Wind S. S.W., very gentle. Thunder storm in neighborhood at 6 p.m. The thunder seemed tame, after the artillery firing of the afternoon.

Thermometer:

7 a.m.	2 p.m.	9 p.m.
73	87	76

SATURDAY, THE FOURTH.-Rain in showers at 6 a.m.

Thermometer:

7 a.m.	2 p.m.	9 p.m.
69	72	70

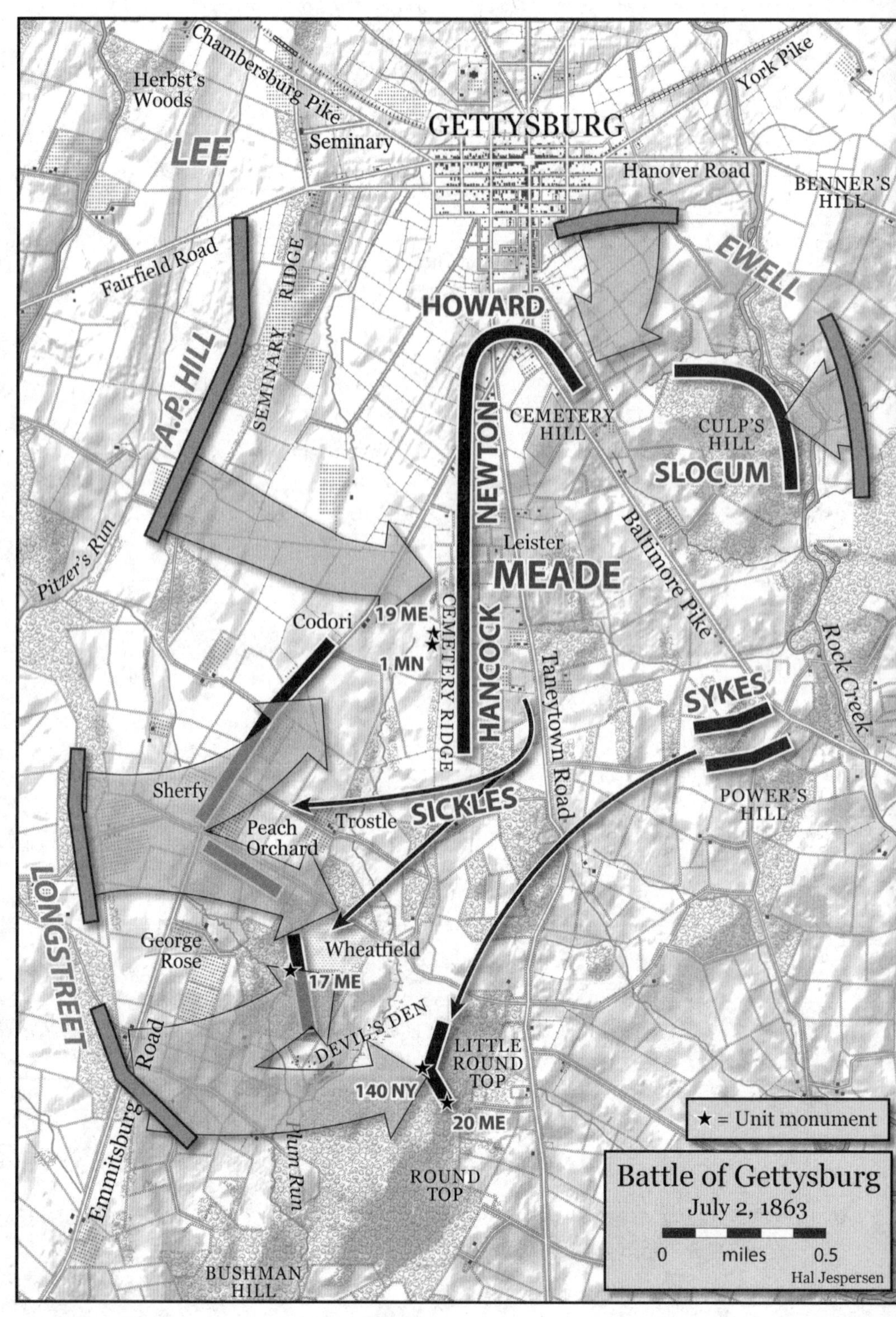
Chambersburg Pike
Herbst's Woods
GETTYSBURG
York Pike
Seminary
LEE
Hanover Road
BENNER'S HILL
Fairfield Road
SEMINARY RIDGE
EWELL
HOWARD
A.P. HILL
NEWTON
CEMETERY HILL
CULP'S HILL
SLOCUM
Pitzer's Run
Leister
MEADE
Baltimore Pike
Codori
19 ME
1 MN
CEMETERY RIDGE
HANCOCK
Taneytown Road
Rock Creek
SYKES
Sherfy
SICKLES
POWER'S HILL
Peach Orchard
Trostle
LONGSTREET
George Rose
Wheatfield
17 ME
DEVIL'S DEN
Road
LITTLE ROUND TOP
140 NY
20 ME
★ = Unit monument
Emmitsburg
Plum Run
ROUND TOP
Battle of Gettysburg
July 2, 1863
0 miles 0.5
Hal Jespersen
BUSHMAN HILL

THE SECOND DAY

George Meade arrived at Gettysburg during the night of July 1st and set about arranging his forces around the defensive position established by Oliver Otis Howard and Winfield Scott Hancock on Cemetery Hill and Culp's Hill. Dan Sickles and the 3rd Corps, and Hancock's own 2nd Corps, arrived by dawn and were positioned along a low ridge that ran south like a tail from Cemetery Hill, to be known as Cemetery Ridge; the 5th Corps under George Sykes and the 6th Corps under John Sedgwick were expected sometime that morning. For the moment, the five infantry corps Meade had in hand would form a long arc, beginning on the right at Culp's Hill (held by Henry Slocum's 12th Corps and the battered remnants of the 1st Corps), crossing Baltimore Pike to Cemetery Hill and Howard's

11th Corps, and then bending southward along Cemetery Ridge to the 2nd and 3rd Corps. Just out of reach beyond the left flank of the 3rd Corps were two hills that would later become known simply as Little and Big Round Top. Big Round Top was too thickly wooded to be of much use to Meade, but Little Round Top's west-facing side had been cleared by logging, and Meade posted a Signal Corps detachment there to communicate by coded flag wigwags with other detachments posted on prominent heights for miles around.

Meade expected that the Army of Northern Virginia would renew its attack on the morning of July 2nd by striking Cemetery Hill. Actually, Lee was already planning something different. At first light, he dispatched one of his staff engineers, Captain Samuel R. Johnston, southward to be sure no new Federal troops had arrived in the night. Johnston was to "reconnoiter along the enemy's left and report as soon as possible." Johnston afterward claimed that he worked southward as far as "the round top across the Emmitsburg road and got up on the slope of round top, where I had a commanding view," and found no new Union reinforcements.

This hardly seems credible, since John Buford's cavalry had been posted along that line, and Little Round Top had been occupied by the Union signalers. Both the 2nd Corps and the 3rd Corps of the Army of the Potomac had arrived on that ground by the early morning of July 2nd, and were taking up their positions along Cemetery Ridge. Nevertheless, once Johnston's reconnaissance confirmed that there were no new additions to the Federal defenders from the day before, Lee put Longstreet's Corps into motion, heading southward (and parallel to Cemetery Ridge) with a view toward curling eastward, then northward, and striking Cemetery Hill from behind, just as he had done two months before at Chancellorsville.

This did not go smoothly: It took some time to bring all of Longstreet's Corps up to the starting point near Lee's headquarters on the Cashtown-Chambersburg Pike, and the entire movement did not jump off until well into the afternoon. But the real flaw in the plan was Johnston's initial reconnaissance. The engineer had somehow missed the arrival of two entire corps of the Army of the Potomac, and it could be said pretty fairly that it was *that* moment, and not in some misjudgment by Stuart, Heth, or Longstreet, that the Confederates lost the battle.

Meade's expectation that the Confederate attack would fall on

Cemetery Hill bothered Daniel Sickles. As it was, Sickles and Meade mistrusted each other politically and personally, and Sickles suspected that his 3rd Corps had been posted to the far left of the Army of the Potomac's position to keep it from sharing in any laurels the Yankees might win. Sickles eventually became so agitated that he began to imagine a major Confederate concentration facing his own position, and after fruitlessly badgering Meade for permission to move, took it on himself to order his entire corps to advance several hundred yards beyond Cemetery Ridge, to the Emmitsburg Road. When Meade finally learned of Sickles's movement, he rode down to deliver a countermand to Sickles personally—only to be surprised at that moment when Confederate artillery and infantry indeed emerged from the woods opposite Sickles's position. It was Longstreet's flank attack, at last ready to strike. Meade had no choice but to tell Sickles to hold his place, while Meade looked to bring up reinforcements from his just-arrived 5th Corps.

In the months after the battle, Meade and Sickles would descend into a furious controversy. Meade and his admirers dismissed Sickles as a reckless incompetent whose change of position had endangered the entire Army of the Potomac. Sickles (or possibly one of his staffers, writing in the New York newspapers under the pseudonym "Historicus") argued that his change of position had saved an unimaginative Meade and the Union army from destruction.

The attack Lee had planned for July 2nd involved two divisions of Longstreet's Corps (under John Bell Hood and Lafayette McLaws) and a division borrowed from Powell Hill, under Richard Heron Anderson. However, the wheels began to go off the plan almost at once. Longstreet's long swing downward toward the Round Tops was delayed when it was forced to reroute the attack to avoid detection by the signal detachment on Little Round Top, and again when they prepared to make their turn toward Cemetery Hill, only to discover the 3rd Corps barring their way. After consultation with Lee, Longstreet concluded to drive ahead anyway, Hood's and McLaws's divisions overrunning the Yankee defenders at the Emmitsburg Road.

Unhappily, John Bell Hood was knocked out of the action almost at the start by a Federal shell splinter, and without his direction, his division pushed straight eastward over a granite outcropping known as Devil's Den and then onto Little Round Top, rather than turning to the left to attack Cemetery Hill. This triggered a sharp fight for control of Little Round Top, in which a Federal brigade from the newly arrived 5th Corps, under Colonel Strong Vincent, held off one attack, and quick Federal reinforcements, led by Colonel Patrick O'Rorke, fended off another.

The rest of Longstreet's attacks steamrollered Sickles's outnumbered corps. Joseph Kershaw's South Carolina brigade overran Federal defenders along a stony ridge behind the George Rose farm and pushed them into a wheat field behind the ridge. William Barksdale's Mississippi brigade smashed through Federal defenses around Joseph Sherfy's peach orchard and forced the 9th Massachusetts Light Artillery to make a desperate last stand at the Abraham Trostle barn. Cadmus Wilcox's Alabama brigade was only kept from rolling over the wrecked remainder of the 3rd Corps by a near-suicidal charge by the 1st Minnesota. Dan Sickles himself went down with a leg-shattering wound at the Trostle barn, struggling all the while to keep up his usual bravado while he was carried off.

Even with its temporary derailment by the 3rd Corps, Lee's plan came perilously close to working, and may have succeeded had it not been for the initiative shown by numerous Union line officers in making key decisions. On Little Round Top, it was Lieutenant-Colonel Joshua Lawrence Chamberlain ordering a bayonet attack that took the Confederates by surprise. In the Rose wheat field, it was Lieutenant-Colonel Charles Merrill (whose brother was fighting for the Confederacy) and the 17th Maine holding off an overwhelming assault by one of Hood's Georgia brigades as Merrill told his men that "they would stay there and hold the ground with the bayonet until the last man had fallen." It was also Lieutenant-Colonel Francis Heath, of the 19th Maine, countermanding orders from a temporarily deranged Federal division commander from the 3rd Corps for the 19th to turn their weapons on their own fellow Yankees. It was even Chaplain William Corby, giving absolution to the 2nd Corps' Irish Brigade before it went into action in the Rose wheat field.

Sickles's wound would require the amputation of a leg; that amputation and the death of John Reynolds the day before are the highest-ranking casualties of the battle. Overall, the Confederates in Hood's, McLaws's, and Anderson's divisions lost around six thousand in killed, wounded, and missing; the Union defenders may have lost even more. The wonder is that there were not more casualties, especially among the civilians trembling in their cellars in the town. Only one civilian—Mary Virginia "Jennie" Wade—was killed by gunfire, early on the morning of July 3rd. Other Gettysburg residents, like fifteen-year-old Albertus McCreary, ventured around Gettysburg, almost oblivious of the danger. The soldiers knew better, especially on the night of July 2nd, as their sergeants called roll, and the steady tick of the names of the missing gave them their first indication of the dreadful toll Gettysburg was demanding.

Isaac Rusling Pennypacker, *General Meade* (New York, 1901)

Meade's preparations for an attack from his right [Culp's Hill and Cemetery Hill] in the early morning . . . had naturally demanded from him a large share of personal attention. Upon the arrival of the Sixth Corps in the middle of the afternoon he moved the Fifth Corps, in reserve on the right, to a position in reserve on the left, one of those numerous movements from wing to wing of his army made by the army commander during the battle, to which the final victory was largely due. In the morning he had sent instructions to Sickles that the Third Corps was to hold the line from Hancock's left to Little Round Top, relieving [Brigadier-General John White] Geary, who had orders from Meade to rejoin his corps upon being relieved by Sickles, and Geary had sent to Sickles a staff officer with instructions to explain the position and its importance, and to ask, if troops could not be sent to hold it, that Sickles would send an officer to see the ground and post the Third Corps troops when they did come. Twice during the early morning, Meade had dispatched a staff officer to Sickles urging him to get into position, and, in reply to the second message, received at seven o'clock, Sickles had said that he was then moving into position. Again, at eleven o'clock, Meade told Sickles that his right was to be Hancock's left and his left on Round Top, which General Meade pointed out to him.

While the Fifth Corps was moving to the left, a little before four o'clock in the afternoon, Meade rode to that part of the line for the purpose of inspecting the location of his own troops, and as far as possible that of the enemy, and of ordering an attack from there with the troops now assembling in that part of the field. On arriving at the left, Meade saw, to his amazement, that Sickles had thrown forward his line so that his right flank, instead of connecting with the left of Hancock, was from a half to three quarters of a mile in front of Hancock, leaving a large gap between the right of the Third Corps and the left of the Second, and that the left flank of the Third Corps, instead of resting on Little Round Top, was in advance of it, and that the Third Corps line, instead of being a prolongation of that held by Hancock, formed an angle, one side of which ran along the Emmitsburg road as far as the Peach Orchard, from which apex the other side was thrown back to the Devil's Den, the two lines delighting a foe by the opportunity which they offered for destruction from a raking artillery fire.

Riding rapidly to the front, Meade told Sickles that he had advanced his line beyond the support of the army; that he was in danger of being attacked and of losing his artillery, to support which would involve the abandonment of all the rest of the line adopted for the army. The staff and other officers in the vicinity listened to the conversation with the keenest interest. In his reply Sickles was perfectly deferential and polite. He expressed regret that he had occupied a position which did not meet with General Meade's approval, offered to withdraw his troops to that ridge which the army commander had intended they should hold, and, in explanation of his forward movement, which had excited the amazement of those who witnessed it, said that the ground to which he had advanced was higher than that which he left. To his offer to withdraw, Meade said: "I wish to God you could, but the enemy will not permit it." To Sickles's claim that his change of position was justified by the greater elevation of the advanced position, Meade replied: "General Sickles, this is in some respects higher ground than that to the rear; but there is still higher ground in front of you, and if you keep on advancing you will find constantly higher ground all the way to the mountains." . . .

Seeing at a glance the impossibility of withdrawing Sickles's corps, Meade had hurried away the members of his staff after artillery and infantry to support the corps and to prevent, if possible, a rout which might imperil the safety of the whole army. Thus suddenly made aware that his plan for occupying Little Round Top with Sickles's troops had miscarried, Meade directed [Brigadier-General Gouverneur Kemble] Warren, his chief of engineers, to see that that important position was made secure, and he also sent Colonel [Addison Gordon] Mason, of his staff, away upon the same errand.

"The Battle of Gettysburg. Important Communication from an Eye Witness," *New York Herald* (March 12, 1864)

General Sickles saw at once how necessary it was to occupy the elevated ground in his front towards the Emmettsburg road, and to extend his lines to the commanding eminence, known as the Roundtop, or Sugarloaf Hill. Unless this were done the left and rear of our army would be in the greatest danger. Sickles concluded that no time was to be lost, as he observed the enemy massing large bodies of troops on their right (our left). Receiving no orders, and filled with anxiety, he reported in person to General Meade and urged the advance he deemed so essential. "Oh," said Meade, "generals are apt to look for the attack to be made where they are." Whether this was a jest or a sneer Sickles did not stop to consider, but begged Meade to go over the ground with him instantly, but the commander-in-chief declined this on account of other duties. Yielding, however, to the prolonged solicitations of Sickles, General Meade desired [Brigadier-] General [Henry Jackson] Hunt, chief of artillery, to accompany Sickles and report the result of their reconnoissance. Hunt concurred with Sickles as to the line to be occupied—the advance line from the left of the Second corps to Roundtop Hill—but he declined to give any orders until he had reported to General Meade, remarking, however, that he (General Sickles) would doubtless receive orders immediately . . .

General Meade at length arrived on the field. The following colloquy ensued, which I gathered from several officers present:

"Are you not too much extended, General," said Meade. "Can you hold this front?"

"Yes," replied Sickles, "until more troops are brought up, the enemy are attacking in force, and I shall need support."

General Meade then let drop some remark, showing that his mind was still wavering as to the extent of the ground covered by the Third corps.

Sickles replied, "General, I have received no orders. I have made these dispositions to the best of my judgment. Of course I shall be happy to modify them according to your views." "No," said Meade, "I will send you the Fifth corps, and you may send for support from the Second corps."

"I shall need more artillery," added Sickles.

"Send for all you want," replied Meade, "to the artillery reserve. I will direct General Hunt to send you all you ask for."

The conference was then abruptly terminated by a heavy shower of shells. Sickles received no further orders that day. There is no doubt I may venture to add, that Sickles' line was too much extended for the number of troops under his command, but his great aim was to prevent the enemy getting down his flank to the Roundtop alluded to . . .
Historicus

John Coxe, "At Gettysburg," *Confederate Veteran* 21 (September 1913), 433-434

I was a private in Company B, 2[d] South Carolina Volunteers, Kershaw's Brigade, McLaws's Division, Longstreet's Corps. On the 29th of June, 1863, we marched from Chambersburg and bivouacked at a little town called Longwood, near the Caledonia Iron Works and also near the foot of South Mountain, on the west side. The iron works had been burned by the Confederates a few days before. On the night of the 30th there was a heavy rain, and we passed the forenoon of the 1st of July in cooking, eating, and drying our wet blankets. The little town was built on both sides of the pike and was very long, therefore we changed its name and called it "Longstreet."

So far we had heard of no enemy, but knew that Ewell was ahead of us somewhere. About 2 p.m. the sun came out vigorously, and almost immediately the order to swing knapsacks and "fall in" was given with sharp emphasis, and in less than twenty minutes the command was marching rapidly north along the pike . . . The slope up the mountain was gradual, but not very steep at any point. Near the summit . . . all of a sudden the distant sound of cannon coming through the gap from the east side of the mountain struck our ears and threw us into extreme alertness . . . At a clearing just east of the top we saw clouds of smoke hanging like a pall over the valley beyond; but by this time, which was after sunset, the firing had ceased and we heard no more noise of battle . . .

I was up at dawn the next morning and walked a little forward on the pike . . . I saw straight ahead a large building on a low hill partly surrounded by trees. I didn't know it then, but that was the famous seminary where Lee stood and watched most of the fighting at Gettysburg. I was on the edge of the McPherson wood. The town was on the left, obscured by hills and woods . . . Soon after sunrise we were called into ranks and marched slowly forward on the pike. Still no noise. Just before reaching the seminary we passed a brigade cooking breakfast on the left of the pike, and some of the men told us that they were in the fight on the day before. Coming to the foot of the seminary hill . . . we halted and lay around for at least two hours, during which Gen. A.P. Hill and staff rode over from the west . . . and then slowly on up through the woods toward the seminary . . .

Shortly after General Hill passed, a Confederate field gun was fired from the wooded hill to the right of the seminary. We hear the shell explode in the distance and adjusted our ears for the next shot. But it didn't come, and we never knew why that single shot broke the quietness all around us.

At last we were brought to attention and marched in column through open woods . . . Proceeding about half a mile, another halt was called and we lay around another hour. Meanwhile we heard desultory picket firing in the distance on our left. With several others I walked to the left about one hundred yards to an opening in the woods. We looked across a field and road and saw the famous peach orchard beyond. To the right of the orchard and farther away we saw two cone-shaped hills partly covered with scrubby timber. These were the now celebrated Round Tops, the smaller of the two being on the left. The field to the right of the peach orchard extended as far as we could see from that point. The light skirmishing was going on in the peach orchard which was so densely green that we couldn't see the men of either party. We were sharply called back to the ranks and cautioned not to expose ourselves to the view of the enemy.

Soon after this, hearing a noise in the rear, we looked and saw General Hood at the head of his splendid division riding forward parallel to us about fifty yards to the left. This explained our last halt . . . It seemed to take an age for Hood's men and train of artillery to pass us; and when finally it did get by, our division followed, [Brigadier-General Paul Jones] Semmes's brigade leading. But it didn't take us long to reach the open near the Emmitsburg Pike and in plain view of both Round Tops and the peach orchard. I looked and saw a Yankee flag waving signals from the apex of little Round Top. Indeed we were so much exposed to view that the enemy had no trouble counting the exact numbers under Hood . . . However, we were placed behind a stone fence along the west side of the pike and ordered to lie down . . . By this time the sun was observed to be getting down toward the top of South Mountain to the west and in our rear. Then suddenly we heard Hood's cannon . . . open on the right and the furious reply of the Federal guns. Then pretty soon a few sharp bugle notes were heard and then boom! boom! boom! blazed away [Henry Coalter] Cabell's guns at the Federal batteries near the peach orchard . . . A little to the right I saw General Longstreet and staff dismounted behind the stone fence watching the effects of our shots through their field glasses. I don't know how long this awful cannonade lasted (probably twenty minutes), but as it began to slacken we were ordered to scale the stone fence behind which we were standing. This was quickly done and then we were on the Emmitsburg Pike . . .

Our line, formed in perfect order of battle, faced a little to the left so as to sweep the Federal batteries near the peach orchard. Just before the order, "Forward, march" was given I saw General Kershaw and staff immediately in our rear dismounted. About halfway from our start at the pike to the Federal batteries was a little down grade to a small depression. We went along in perfect order, the 15th South Carolina being on the right. As yet we could see no Federal infantry, because it was covered by the woods in the rear of the batteries; but we saw plainly that their artillerists were loading their guns to meet our assault . . . Just as our left struck the depression in the ground every Federal cannon let fly at us with grape. O the awful deathly surging sounds of those little black balls as they flew by us, through us, between our legs, and over us! Many, of course, were struck down, including Captain [Robert C.] Pulliam, who was instantly killed. Then the order was given to double-quick, and we were mad and fully determined to take and silence those batteries at once . . .

We were now so close to the Federal gunners that they seemed bewildered and were apparently trying to get their guns to the rear . . .

However, it wasn't long till the Federal infantry in great force advanced to the rim of the bluff and began to pour lead down upon us; but they soon found out that bullets could go uphill with death in their songs as well as downhill . . . We fought in that position for nearly half an hour, when to our surprise the thunder and roar of the Federal cannon and musketry in our front suddenly stopped, and the next moment we heard a tremendous Rebel cheer, followed by an awful crash of small arms, coming through the woods on our left front and from the direction of the peach orchard. Then one of our officers shouted and said: "That's help for us! Spring up the bluff, boys!" And we did so . . .

Emerging from the woods on the other side, we drove the enemy across a wheat field and on to the western slopes of Little Round Top, up which they scampered in great disorder . . . At that time, and while putting on a [percussion] cap for another shot, a bullet from little Round Top tore open my right coat sleeve from wrist to elbow, but I wasn't hurt much. At the farther edge of the wheat field we were met by shots from Federal cannon on the apex of little Round Top, but all went high over us. Of course every one of us expected to go right on and capture that famous hill, which at that time seemed easy to do . . .

The wheat field and woods were blue with dead and wounded Federals . . . I felt sorry for the wounded enemy, but we could do little to help them. Just before dark I passed a Federal officer sitting on the ground with his back resting against a large oak tree. He called me to him, and when I went he politely asked me to give him some water. There was precious little in my canteen, but I let him empty it. His left leg was crushed just above the ankle, the foot lying on the ground sidewise. He asked me to straighten it up in a natural position and prop it with rocks, and as I did so I asked him if the movement hurt him. "There isn't much feeling in it now," replied he quietly. Then before leaving him I said: "Isn't this war awful?" "Yes, yes," said he, "and all of us should be in better business." He wore large red whiskers and was large and fine-looking. I shall never forget his profuse thanks for the little service I was able to render him.

"Seventeenth Maine Regiment," *Maine At Gettysburg: Report of Maine Commissioners*, ed. Charles Hamlin *et al* (Portland, ME, 1898)

Before daybreak of July 2d Colonel [Philippe Régis] de Trobriand received orders to come up to Gettysburg. The brigade marched rapidly, but cautiously, up the Emmitsburg road, arriving near Gettysburg late in the forenoon. The regiment was under command of Lieutenant-Colonel [Charles B.] Merrill, ably seconded by Major [George W.] West. As it passed northerly along the road beyond the Peach Orchard . . . the regiment filed off the road to the east and, passing through grass fields and across lots, halted near a growth, where the hungry boys made a hasty luncheon of hard tack and coffee. In the line, which Sickles was forming, de Trobriand first occupied the ridgy, wooded ground between the Peach Orchard and the Wheatfield. The Wheatfield was of triangular shape, about 400 yards each side; the highest portion was bounded by a cross road running along by the Peach Orchard and easterly across the north slope of Little Round Top. The Wheatfield sloped down southerly from this road, and along its westerly side by a wood, to quite low ground, making a corner near a branch of Plum Run, with a thick alder growth on the west; the third or southerly side was bounded by an open growth of sizable trees, a stone-wall intervening, and this wood separated the Wheatfield from Devil's Den . . .

The Seventeenth was at first placed south of the Peach Orchard, supporting the skirmish line of the 3d Mich. De Trobriand had two regiments at the front, to the left of the latter—the 5th Mich., whose skirmishers connected to the 3d [Michigan], near the [George] Rose barn, also the 110th Penn., a small regiment. The largest regiment in the brigade, the 40th N.Y., was in the wood, in reserve, behind these. The ball opened by a shot from a battery at the Peach Orchard, soon taken up by Smith's battery at Devil's Den, the latter drawing fire from the enemy's batteries near the Emmitsburg road farther south. [Brigadier-General] John [Henry Hobart] Ward's brigade extended from Devil's Den, through the wood, nearly to the Wheatfield . . . There was a gap between Ward and de Trobriand at the south corner of the Wheatfield. To occupy this gap the Seventeenth Maine was hastened upon the double-quick by the left, taking up its position at the stone-wall, the right of the regiment extending beyond the wall to the alders. Sometime after, the 40th N.Y. was also taken from de Trobriand and sent to Ward's left rear, in the Plum Run valley. Shortly after 4 p.m. the Seventeenth planted its colors at the stone-wall on the southern edge of the historic Wheatfield . . .

The Seventeenth . . . was swung back to a slight rail fence which, starting from the stone-wall at nearly a right angle, formed the boundary of the real wheat field. Thus two fronts were presented by the regiment, forming a salient angle at the stone-wall . . . The tables were turned. As the veterans of Georgia moved directly forward upon the 5th Mich. and 110th Penn., who received them face to face, this new line of the right wing of the Seventeenth took them in flank. They changed front to match the flank line of the Seventeenth and again advanced, and thus exposed their left to the reliable men of the 5th Mich. Meanwhile the enemy, that was not affected by this flanking fire, pressed forward, even up to the stone-wall, and a desperate struggle at close quarters ensued for this coveted position. At the salient angle was company B, with H, K and C at the right; at the left of B was G the color company, and on its left, along the stone-wall, were D, I, F, A and E. All received a raking fire, particularly G, B and H, but all remained steadfast, and routed the enemy, some of whom were taken prisoners, their color-bearer, who had advanced nearly to our line, narrowly escaping capture . . .

Longstreet now brought in [Brigadier-General Joseph Brevard] Kershaw's South Carolina brigade of [Major-General Lafayette] McLaws' division . . . to assault the Orchard from the south, as it advanced, and at the same time secure a foothold at the Wheatfield, thus taking de Trobriand in the right flank and rear . . . as they advanced, [Brigadier-General George "Tige"] Anderson's brigade also made another attack . . . Again the Seventeenth at the stone-wall held the enemy at bay; at its angle it repelled the attempts of Anderson after a long and persistent struggle; but Kershaw forced back the Fifth corps forces at the "loop" and struck the flank of de Trobriand's brigade in the woods. Pushing ahead for a junction with Anderson, a portion of the assailants made for the west corner of the Wheatfield through the thick alder growth, happily there, which both impeded their rush and broke the solidity of their ranks; they emerged through the alders within fifty paces of the flanking right wing of the Seventeenth, which awaited them at the rail fence. Here were a hundred muskets, in the hands of steady veterans, to receive them: "Aim low, boys!

make every shot tell!" With the most frantic efforts to re-form his lines for a charge, the enemy was unsuccessful; the men dropped as they emerged from the alders; in a few minutes they gave it up and retreated out of sight. The Seventeenth breathed easier . . .

But the attack of Kershaw, forcing [Brigadier-General James] Barnes away, in turn compelled the 5th Mich, and 110th Penn. to move rearward. Kershaw thus gained lodgment in the woods west of the Wheatfield, considerably in rear of the position of the Seventeenth. [Capt. George B.] Winslow's battery, posted at the north side of the field, withdrew from its position. The Seventeenth was thus left alone, far in advance of its brother regiments and well outflanked upon its right by Kershaw. It was ordered back across the field in line of battle to the cross road before spoken of. Another attack followed before a new general line could be arranged. The enemy seeing the retrograde movement across the Wheatfield, at once moved up to the abandoned stone-wall and over it, and also to the edge of the woods west of the Wheatfield. General [David Bell] Birney rode up, saw the desperate situation, and also saw the Seventeenth Maine near him, which had just squatted down in the cross road and had sent for ammunition . . . Birney called upon the Seventeenth for a charge. He placed himself at the head of the regiment, and with a cheer and a rush it moved down into the Wheatfield. The enemy disappeared over the stone-wall and into the woods.

It was past 6 o'clock. General Sickles had just been wounded. Birney was notified and took command of the corps. Leaving the Seventeenth, he went to another part of the field, but he was not unmindful of the situation he left; the gallant 5th Mich. was brought up and extended the line of the Seventeenth to the right; the two small brigades of Barnes, who had retired from the front woods, were now resting in the woods one hundred yards in rear of the Wheatfield, but not engaged; General Birney had sent to Hancock for Second corps troops. At last, at just about 6:40 o'clock, deliverance came. [Brigadier-General John Curtis] Caldwell's division of the Second corps readily assumed the battle on that portion of the line. Cross' brigade went in where Ward's right had rested; after this, [Colonel Patrick] Kelly's [Irish] brigade advanced, in line of battle, through and beyond the small remnant of the Seventeenth Maine and 5th Mich., into the edge of the wood, with a rush upon Kershaw's troops, with whom the Maine and Michigan veterans had been contending. The Seventeenth, thus relieved, collected and took along its wounded who were disabled on the field, and then, in good order, finally left the Wheatfield . . .

It may not be amiss to state briefly the events of that evening, on this part of the field, after the Seventeenth was relieved. [Colonel Edward] Cross' brigade advanced upon the enemy posted behind the west end of the Wheatfield stone-fence . . . A hot contest ensued for thirty or forty minutes, the enemy holding his ground, when the regulars of [Brigadier-General Romeyn Beck] Ayres' division, Fifth corps, came in up to the east side of the Wheatfield and relieved Cross' brigade. Kelly's brigade, with that of [Brigadier-General Samuel Kosciuszko] Zook upon its right, fought fiercely with Kershaw in the woods where we left him, finally driving the latter out. About this time [Colonel John R.] Brooke, with his brigade of Caldwell's division, charged across the Wheatfield, almost unresisted by the used-up and disconnected troops of Anderson, Kershaw and Semmes . . . This was about 7 p.m., when, [Brigadier-General William] Barksdale having pushed back our regiments and batteries just north of the Peach Orchard, Longstreet brought up [Brigadier-General William Tatum] Wofford's fresh brigade . . . There was nothing to resist him; [Colonel William S.] Tilton's brigade of Barnes' division had been resting in [Abraham] Trostle's grove, in an excellent position to defend from Wofford, but had retired. Kershaw joined to Wofford, and . . . easily whirled out the three brigades of the Second corps, [Colonel Jacob Bowman] Sweitzer's brigade of the Fifth corps which was then in the Wheatfield, also the Regulars of Ayres, causing heavy loss, and advanced the Confederate line to the Plum Run valley, west of Little Round Top . . .

"Absolution Under Fire. An Incident in the Irish Brigade at Gettysburg," *Souvenir of the Re-union of the Blue and the Gray: On the Battlefield of Gettysburg, July 1, 2, 3, and 4, 1888*, ed. John Tregaskis (New York, 1888)

The troops that arrived upon the field or changed their positions did so leisurely and unmolested. Sickles came up and went into position on our left, and Geary took his division over to Culp's hill. About 10 o'clock picket firing was heard out towards Little Round Top, continuing at intervals until long after noon, at times becoming quite sharp. But three o'clock came, and still no signs of the general engagement. The boys had partly recovered from their fatigue, and were actually beginning to enjoy life; some of them indulged in a quiet game of euchre, while others toasted their hard tack or fried a little bacon at the small fires in the rear of the lines. Shortly after three o'clock, a movement was apparent on our left. From where we (Caldwell's Division) lay, the whole country in our front, and far to our left, away to the peach orchard and to Little Round Top, was in full view. Our division stood in brigade columns, and when it became evident that something was going to take place, the boys dropped their cards regardless of what was trump—even the man who held both bowers and the ace—and all gathered on the most favorable position to witness the opening of the ball. Soon the long lines of the Third Corps are seen advancing, and how splendidly they march. It looks like a dress parade, a review . . . Some one calls out, "There!" and points to where a puff of smoke is seen arising against the dark green of the woods. Another and another cloud until the whole face of the forest is enveloped, and the dread sound of the artillery comes loud and quick; shells are seen bursting in all directions along the lines. The bright colors of the regiment are conspicuous marks.

On, on a little and the shells burst around them in great numbers. The musketry begins, the infantry became engaged, and the battle extends along the whole front of Sickles' Corps. Now the sounds come from Little Round Top, and the smoke rises among the trees, and all the high and wooded ground to the left of the peach orchard seems to be the scene of strife. An hour passes and our troops give way and are falling back; but slowly, very slowly, every inch of ground fought for. The Third Corps is not in the habit of giving it up, and they hold their own well; but the odds are against them and they are forced to retire.

Now help is called for, and [Major-General Winfield Scott] Hancock tells Caldwell to have his division ready. Fall in! and the men run to their places. "Take arms!", and the four brigades of Zook, Cross, [Colonel John Rutter] Brooke and Kelly are ready for the fray. There is yet a few minutes to spare before starting, and the time is occupied in one of the most impressive religious ceremonies I have ever witnessed. The Irish Brigade [63rd, 69th and 88th New York, 28th Massachusetts, 116th Pennsylvania], which had been commanded formerly by General Thomas Francis Meagher, and whose green flag has been unfurled in every battle in which the Army of the Potomac had been engaged . . . stood in columns

of regiments, closed in mass. As a large majority of its members were Catholics, the Chaplain of the brigade, Rev. William Corby, proposed to give a general absolution to all the men before going into the fight. While this is customary in the armies of the Catholic countries in Europe, it was, perhaps, the first time it was ever witnessed on this continent . . . Father Corby stood on a large rock in front of the brigade. Addressing the men, he explained what he was about to do, saying that each one could receive the benefit of the absolution by making a sincere act of contrition and firmly resolving to embrace the first opportunity of confessing their sins, urging them to do their duty well, and reminding them of the high and sacred nature of their trust as soldiers, and the noble object for which they fought, ending by saying that the Catholic Church refuses Christian burial to the soldier who turns his back upon the foe or deserts his flag. The brigade was standing at "Order Arms." As he closed his address every man fell on his knees, with head bowed down. Then stretching his right hand towards the brigade, Father Corby pronounced the words of the absolution :

> *"Dominus noster Jesus Christus vos absolvat et ego, auctoritate ipsius, vos absolvo ab omni vinculo excommunicationis et interdicti in quantum possum et vos indigetis, deinde ego vos absolvo a peccatis vestris, in nomini Patris, et Filii, et Spritus Sancti. Amen."*

Nearby stood Hancock, surrounded by a brilliant throng of officers, who had gathered to witness this very unusual occurrence, and while there was profound silence in the ranks of the Second Corps, yet over to the left . . . the roar of the battle rose and swelled and re-echoed through the woods, making music more sublime than ever sounded through cathedral aisle. The act seemed to be in harmony with all the surroundings. I do not think there was a man in the brigade who did not offer up a heartfelt prayer. For some it was their last; they knelt there in their grave-clothes . . .

Joshua L. Chamberlain, "Through Blood and Fire at Gettysburg," *Hearst's Magazine* 23 (June 1913)

Warren, chief engineer of our army, sent by Meade to see how things were going on the left, drawn to Little Round Top by its evident importance, found to his astonishment that it was unoccupied except by a little group of signal-men, earnestly observing the movements over in the region of the Emmitsburg Road beyond the Devil's Den . . .

As we neared the summit of the mountain, the shot so raked the crest that we had to keep our men below it to save their heads, although this did not wholly avert the visits of tree-tops and splinters of rock and iron, while the boulders and clefts and pitfalls in our path made it seem like the replica of the evil "den" across the sweetly named Plum Run.

Reaching the southern face of Little Round Top, I found [Colonel Strong] Vincent there, with intense poise and look. He said with a voice of awe, as if translating the tables of the eternal law, "I place you here! This is the left of the Union line. You understand. You are to hold this ground at all costs!" I did understand—full well; but had more to learn about costs.

The regiment coming up "right in front" was put in position by a quite uncommon order, "on the right by file into line;" both that we should thus be facing the enemy when we came to a front, and also be ready to commence firing as fast as each man arrived. This is a rather slow style of formation, but this time it was needful. Knowing that we had no supports on the left, I despatched a stalwart company [Company B] under the level-headed Captain [Walter Goodale] Morrill in that direction, with orders to move along up the valley to our front and left, between us and the eastern base of the Great Round Top, to keep within supporting distance of us, and to act as the exigencies of the battle should require . . .

I released the pioneers and provost guard altogether, and sent them to their companies. All but the drummer boys and hospital attendants went into the ranks. Even the cooks and servants not liable to such service, asked to go in. Others whom I knew to be sick or footsore, and had given a pass to "fall out" on the forced marches of the day and night before, came up, now that the battle was on, dragging themselves along on lame and bleeding feet . . .

Our line looked towards the Great Round Top, frowning above us not a gunshot away, and raising grave thoughts of what might happen if the enemy should gain foothold there, even if impracticable for artillery . . . The other regiments of the brigade were forming on our right; the Eighty-third Pennsylvania, the Forty-fourth New York, and the Sixteenth Michigan . . .

Ten minutes had not passed. Suddenly the thunder of artillery and crash of iron that had all the while been roaring over the Round Top crests stopped short . . .

In a minute more came the roll of musketry. It struck the exposed right center of our brigade. Promptly answered, repulsed, and renewed again and again, it soon reached us, still extending. Two brigades of Hood's Division had attacked—Texas and Alabama. The Fourth Alabama reached our right, the Forty-seventh Alabama joined and crowded in, but gradually, owing to their echelon advance. Soon seven companies of this regiment were in our front. We had all we could stand . . .

When Warren saw us started for Little Round Top, looking still intently down, he saw Hood's two brigades breaking past the Third Corps' left and sweeping straight for Little Round Top. Then he flew down to bring reinforcement for this vital place and moment. He came upon the One Hundred and Fortieth New York, of [Brigadier-General Stephen Hinsdale] Weed's Brigade of our Second Division, just going in to Sickles' relief, and dispatched it headlong for Round Top. Weed was to follow, and Ayres' whole division—but not yet. Warren also laid hold of [Lieutenant Charles Edward] Hazlett, with his battery, D of the Fifth Regulars, and sent him to scale those heights—if in the power of man so to master nature. Meantime the tremendous blow of the Fourth and Fifth Texas struck the right of our brigade, and our Sixteenth Michigan reeled and staggered back under the shock. Confusion followed. Vincent felt that all was lost unless the very gods should intervene. Sword aloft and face aflame, he rushed in among the broken companies in desperate effort to rally them, man by man. By sheer force of his superb personality he restored a portion of his line, and was urging up the rest. "Don't yield an inch now, men, or all is lost!" he cried, when an answering volley scorched the very faces of the men, and Vincent's soul went up in a chariot of fire. In that agonizing moment, came tearing up the One Hundred and Fortieth New York, gallant [Colonel Patrick Henry] O'Rorke at the head. Not waiting to load a musket or form a line, they sprang forward into that turmoil. Met by a withering volley that killed its fine young colonel and laid low many of his intrepid officers and a hundred of his men, this splendid regiment, as by a providence we may well call divine, saved us all in that moment of threatened doom . . .

In the very deepest of the struggle while our shattered line had pressed the enemy well below their first point of contact, and the struggle to regain it was fierce, I saw through a sudden rift in the thick smoke our colors standing alone. I first thought some optical illusion imposed upon me. But as forms emerged through the drifting smoke, the truth came to view. The cross-fire had cut keenly; the center had been almost shot away; only two of the color-guard had been left, and they fighting to fill the whole space; and in the center, wreathed in battle smoke, stood the Color-Sergeant, Andrew Tozier. His color-staff planted in the ground at his side, the upper part clasped in his elbow, so holding the flag upright, with musket and cartridges seized from the fallen comrade at his side he was defending his sacred trust in the manner of the songs of chivalry. It was a stirring picture—its import still more stirring. That color must be saved, and that center too. I sent first to the regiment on our right for a dozen men to help us here, but they could not spare a man. I then called my young brother, Tom [Thomas Davee Chamberlain], the adjutant, and sent him forward to close that gap somehow; if no men could be drawn from neighboring companies, to draw back the salient angle and contract our center. The fire down there at this moment was so hot I thought it impossible for him to get there alive; and I dispatched immediately after him Sergeant [Reuel] Thomas whom I had made a special orderly, with the same instructions. It needed them both; and both came back with personal proofs of the perilous undertaking. It was strange that the enemy did not seize that moment and point of weakness . . .

Now came a longer lull. But this meant, not rest, but thought and action. First, it was to gather our wounded, and bear them to the sheltered lawn for saving life, or peace in dying; the dead, too, that not even our feet should do them dishonor in the coming encounter. Then—such is heavenly human pity—the wounded of our Country's foes; brothers in blood for us now, so far from other caring; borne to like refuge and succor by the drummer-boys who had become angels of the field.

In this lull I took a turn over the dismal field to see what could be done for the living, in ranks or recumbent; and came upon a manly form and face I well remembered. He was a sergeant earlier in the field of Antietam and of Fredericksburg; and for refusing to perform some menial personal service for a bullying quartermaster in winter camp, was reduced to the ranks by a commander who had not carefully investigated the case. It was a degradation, and the injustice of it rankled in his high-born spirit. But his well-bred pride would not allow him to ask for justice as a favor. I had kept this in mind, for early action. Now he was lying there, stretched on an open front where a brave stand had been made, face to the sky, a great bullet-hole in the middle of his breast, from which he had loosened the clothing, to ease his breathing, and the rich blood was pouring in a stream. I bent down over him. His face lightened; his lips moved. But I spoke first, "My dear boy, it has gone hard with you. You shall be cared for!" He whispered, "Tell my mother I did not die a coward!" It was the prayer of home-bred manhood poured out with his life-blood. I knew and answered him, "You die a sergeant. I promote you for faithful service and noble courage on the field of Gettysburg!" This was all he wanted. No word more. I had him borne from the field, but his high spirit had passed to its place. It is needless to add that as soon as a piece of parchment could be found after that battle, a warrant was made out promoting George Washington Buck to sergeant in the terms told him; and this evidence placed the sad, proud mother's name on the rolls of the Country's benefactors . . .

The silence and the doubt of the momentary lull were quickly dispelled. The formidable Fifteenth Alabama, repulsed and as we hoped dispersed, now in solid and orderly array—still more than twice our numbers—came rolling through the fringe of chaparral on our left. No dash; no yells; no demonstrations for effect; but settled purpose and determination! We opened on them as best we could. The fire was returned, cutting us to the quick.

The Forty-Seventh Alabama had rallied on our right. We were enveloped in fire, and sure to be over-whelmed in fact when the great surge struck us. Whatever might be otherwhere, what was here before us was evident; these far-outnumbering, confident eyes, yet watching for a sign of weakness. Already I could see the bold flankers on their right darting out and creeping catlike under the smoke to gain our left, thrown back as it was. It was for us, then, once for all. Our thin line was broken, and the enemy were in rear of the whole Round Top defense—infantry, artillery, humanity itself—with the Round Top and the day theirs.

Now, too, our fire was slackening; our last rounds of shot had been fired; what I had sent for could not get to us. I saw the faces of my men one after another, when they had fired their last cartridge, turn anxiously towards mine for a moment; then square to the front again. To the front for them lay death; to the rear what they would die to save. My thought was running deep. I was combining the elements of a "forlorn hope," and had just communicated this to Captain [Ellis] Spear of the wheeling flank, on which the initiative was to fall. Just then—so will a little incident fleck a brooding cloud of doom with a tint of human tenderness—brave, warm-hearted Lieutenant [Holman] Melcher, of the Color Company, whose Captain and nearly half his men were down, came up and asked if he might take his company and go forward and pick up one or two of his men left wounded on the field, and bring them in before the enemy got too near. This would be a most hazardous move in itself, and in this desperate moment, we could not break our line. I admired him. With a glance, he understood, I answered, "Yes, sir, in a moment! I am about to order a charge!"

Not a moment was to be lost! Five minutes more of such a defensive, and the last roll-call would sound for us! Desperate as the chances were, there was nothing for it, but to take the offensive. I stepped to the colors. The men turned towards me. One word was enough—"*BAYONET*!" It caught like fire, and swept along the ranks. The men took it up with a shout . . . The frenzied bayonets pressing through every space forced a constant settling to the rear. Morrill with his detached company and the remnants of our valorous sharpshooters who had held the enemy so long in check on the slopes of the Great Round Top, now fell upon the flank of the retiring crowd, and it turned to full retreat—some up amidst the crags of Great Round Top, but most down the smooth vale towards their own main line on Plum Run. This tended to mass them before our center. Here their stand was more stubborn. At the first dash the commanding officer I happened to confront, coming on fiercely, sword in one hand and big navy revolver in the other, fires one barrel almost in my face; but seeing the quick saber-point at his throat, reverses arms, gives sword and pistol into my hands and yields himself prisoner.

"Nineteenth Maine Regiment," *Maine at Gettysburg: Report of Maine Commissioners*, ed. Charles Hamlin *et al* (Portland, ME, 1898)

About 6:30 p.m. the Second division line of the Third corps, along the Emmitsburg road, was attacked on that front. A part of [Brigadier-General Andrew Atkinson] Humphreys' men, who held that part of the line along the road, after the division began to change front to rear, made their line of retreat so as to bring some of the Excelsior brigade towards the advanced position of the Nineteenth. The Confederates, impelled by the ardor imparted by success and superior numbers, came pressing upon their flank and rear, threatening to make the retreat a disastrous rout. Fearing this, General Humphreys, commanding the Second division of the Third corps, after changing his front to the rear, rode back to the Nineteenth, which was lying down, and ordered it to arise and stop with the bayonet the soldiers of his command, who had by that time drifted back to within one hundred and fifty paces. Colonel [Francis] Heath refused to obey the order, fearing that his men, once caught in the disorder caused by broken troops, would be swept to the rear. Then General Humphreys rode down the line of the Nineteenth giving the order himself. Colonel Heath followed countermanding it, and was obeyed by his men. As Humphreys' men passed to the rear some of them shouted to the Nineteenth, "Hang on, boys! we will form in your rear." Some of them did try to do this, for they were brave men . . .

Captain George L. Whitmore, of Bowdoinham, who heard the conversation between General Humphreys and Colonel Heath, says (in 1889) that when General Humphreys had tried to order the Nineteenth up in vain, he turned to Colonel Heath and ordered him to the rear. To this Captain Whitmore says Colonel Heath returned the reply, "I was placed here by an officer of higher rank for a purpose, and I do not intend to go to the rear. Let your troops form in the rear and we will take care of the enemy in front." General Hancock was the officer who had stationed the

Nineteenth. The Excelsior brigade [70th, 71st, 72nd, 73rd and 74th New York] succeeded for a moment in establishing a line, but soon drifted away in the smoke and confusion . . .

The Confederate battle line was now right upon the four hundred men from Maine, who arose unwaveringly to receive it. As the gray line emerged from the smoke, about fifty yards in front a tall color-bearer was first seen, running at double-quick and tossing his colors several yards in front of their line. In quick response to the order, given by the Colonel, "Drop that color-bearer," a private of the Nineteenth drew up his musket and fired. The Confederate colors went down, and at this instant the Nineteenth poured in its first volley. This fire evidently stopped the Confederates, as they returned it at once. For a short time, no one can tell how long, the two lines exchanged volleys. During this fire Captain [Isaac Warren] Starbird of the left company reported that a Confederate regiment was deploying on his flank. The Colonel went to that part of the line at once, and found the enemy in double column in the act of deploying. They were not over twenty-five yards from the left of the Nineteenth. The Colonel at once threw back the left files of Captain Starbird's company so as to pour an enfilading fire upon the Confederate regiment, at the same time telling Captain Starbird to "give it to them." The left company mustered that day forty men, and its volley, poured in at short range upon a body of men in column, had a terrible effect. The Confederate regiment melted away in the smoke and was seen no more.

George Clark [11th Alabama], "Wilcox's Alabama Brigade at Gettysburg," *Confederate Veteran* 17 (1909), 229-230

About sunrise the next morning (July 2) the brigade [8th, 9th, 10th, 11th and 14th Alabama] formed line and moved to the left and east, and on reaching the proper point fronted and began to move forward in line to the position assigned us for the battle. The 11th Alabama occupied the left of the line, and after moving forward a short distance entered a valley and an open wheat field, and when about halfway across the field were fired into by a brigade of Federal sharpshooters in the woods on our right and rear, which produced some confusion and a retreat back to the fence, so as to escape the fire from the rear. But just at this time the 10th Alabama came up on our right and immediately opposite the

Federals in the woods, and after a brisk musketry drove the enemy back and uncovered the right flank of the 11th Alabama, thus enabling the brigade to move forward in line and take position, which was done at another fence across the field.

Here we remained almost the entire day and until 4 p.m. The sun was fiercely hot, and there was no shade or other protection for the men. Here they sweltered and sweated and swore until about four in the afternoon, when the engagement began on the right.

Our brigade commander [Brigadier-General Cadmus Marcellus Wilcox] during the morning took occasion to explain to the officers the general plan of the battle, in so far as our immediate front was concerned, stating that the movement forward would be by echelon, beginning with the right of Longstreet's Corps and extending to the left as each brigade came into action; and that, owing to our situation, the Alabama Brigade at the proper time would move by the left flank rapidly, so as to give Barksdale's Mississippi Brigade [13th, 17th, 18th and 21st Mississippi], which would be on our immediate right, room to move forward in proper line.

Thus matters stood until about 4 p.m. when the thunder of cannon up on the right announced the beginning of the action. As Longstreet's brigades came into action the roar of the cannon was accompanied by the rattle of musketry, mingled with the yells of our boys as they moved forward on the run, and the scene was grand and terrific. As the fire and the clamor approached the Alabama Brigade Barksdale threw forward his Mississippians in an unbroken line in the most magnificent charge I witnessed during the war, and led by the gallant Barksdale, who seemed to be fifty yards in front of his brave boys. The scene was grand beyond description.

The order was then given our brigade to move rapidly by the left flank, and the movement was made at full speed until space was cleared sufficient for the Mississippians, and then with right face the brigade moved forward to the assault. Amid showers of grape and canister and dense musketry the first line of the enemy in front gave way precipitately, and then the reserve and supporting line of the enemy was struck, and in turn broke, leaving in our hands several batteries of artillery and many of the killed and wounded.

But no stop was made even for re-formation. On swept the line swiftly, joined by [Brigadier-General Edward Aylesworth] Perry's Florida

Brigade and [Brigadier-General Ambrose Ransom] Wright's Georgia Brigade, across Seminary Ridge and the pike and down the gradual slope toward the heights occupied by another line of the enemy, a distance of at least a third of a mile.

By the time the small brushy drain at the foot of the enemy's position was reached the brigades of Barksdale, Wilcox, Perry, and Wright were in marked confusion, mixed up indiscriminately, officers apart from their men, men without officers, but all pushing forward notwithstanding. Upon striking the third line of the enemy on Cemetery Ridge, and while some of the officers were using their utmost endeavors to get the men in order, couriers were hurried back to the division commander to send forward quickly the two brigades in reserve belonging to [Major-General Richard Heron] Anderson's Division, and the battle went on furiously while awaiting their arrival. The enemy began concentrating heavy masses in our front and on both flanks; but still our ground was held awaiting reënforcements for another assault. The air was thick with missiles of every character, the roar of artillery practically drowning the shrill hiss of the Minies [the bullet named for its French designer, Claude-Etienne Minié]. In spite of every obstacle, the confused and practically disorganized mass of Confederates pressed on up the incline, only to be again forced to sullenly drop back, until at last, becoming nearly surrounded and no reënforcements coming to their aid, the retreat was sounded and the Confederates withdrew, many being captured and the others barely escaping and subjected for a distance to a destructive fire from the enemy.

So ended the second day's fight on this part of the line. The Alabama Brigade lost about one-half its strength in casualties and captures, and retired practically to its original position of the previous morning, where it spent the night.

John Bigelow [9th Massachusetts Light Artillery], *The Peach Orchard, Gettysburg, July 2, 1863: Explained by Official Reports and Maps* (Minneapolis, 1910)

About 3 o'clock p.m. heavy Infantry and Artillery fire was heard on the extreme right and left of our lines and soon . . . "Assembly" was blown; drivers mounted and within five minutes we were off at a lively trot, following our leader to the left, where the firing was getting to be the heaviest.

We were halted, in close order, near the Trostle House. A spirited military spectacle lay before us; General Sickles was standing beneath a tree close by, staff officers and orderlies coming and going in all directions; at the famous "Peach Orchard" angle on rising ground, along the Emmetsburg Road, about 500 yards in our front, white smoke was curling up from the rapid and crashing volleys of [Brigadier-General Charles Kinnaird] Graham's 3rd Corps Infantry . . . as they tried to repel the furious assaults of Longstreet with Kershaw's and Barksdale's Brigades; while the enemy's shells were flying over or breaking around us.

Our halt was of short duration. We . . . started at full gallop for the crest of the ridge, 400 yards distant, extending from the Peach Orchard towards Little Round Top, nearly at right angles to the Emmetsburg Road.

We dropped our guns "in Battery" about 200 yards back of the "Peach Orchard" angle, under a heavy fire from sharpshooters and two Confederate batteries. One man was killed and several wounded before we could fire a single gun, but, the wind being light, we soon covered ourselves in a cloud of powder smoke, for our six Light Twelve [12-pounder bronze Napoleon gun-howitzers] guns were rapidly served, as we engaged the enemy's batteries 1,400 yards away down the Emmetsburg Road, whose attention we were receiving. Our position was in the open and exposed. Besides the sharpshooting . . . we immediately turned an effective fire on a large body of Confederate Infantry, Semmes' Brigade, whom we saw forming around the [George] Rose building, 600 yards in our front. As a swell of ground interfered with the new range of the left section, it was quickly moved around to the right flank of the Battery where the view was unobstructed. Our case shot and shell broke beautifully. One struck beneath the horse of the officer, who had apparently ridden out to give the order to advance—and brought down both horse and rider, causing sufficient delay to enable us, apparently, to break up their formation . . .

Hardly had the enemy around the Rose buildings disappeared, before Kershaw's battle line, extending from the Rose buildings to the Peach Orchard, just on our right, leaped a stone wall along the Emmetsburg Road and in two lines, started across an open field in our front for a skirt of woods on our left, some 400 yards away . . . While the battery had thus been engaged, Hood had swung around beyond the Rose buildings and the contest was raging hot and fierce amid the boulders of Devils Den and the Round Tops on our left; while, with desperate fighting, the pendulum of battle had swung backward and forward four or five times through the Peach Orchard, 200 yards on our right, resulting in the capture of General Graham by the Confederates and the destruction or driving away of his infantry and artillery, much of the latter, owing to loss of horses, having been dragged off by hand.

Colonel [Freeman] McGilvery rode up, at this time, told me that "all of Sickles' men had withdrawn and I was alone on the field, without supports of any kind; limber up and get out." I replied that, "if I attempted to do so, the sharpshooters, on my left front, would shoot us all down." I must "retire by prolonge and firing," in order "to keep them off." He assented and rode away. (A prolonge is a rope, one end of which can be attached to the limber and the other to the gun trail. It enables the latter to be dragged along on the ground, and firing can be continued, although the gun is moving . . .)

Glancing towards the Peach Orchard on my right, I saw that the Confederates (Barksdale's Brigade) had come through and were forming a line 200 yards distant, extending back, parallel with the Emmetsburg Road, as far as I could see, and I must therefore move almost parallel with and in front of their line, in order to reach the exit of the stone wall at Trostle's house 400 yards away. No friendly supports, of any kind, were in sight; but Johnnie Rebs in great numbers. Bullets were coming into our midst from many directions and a Confederate battery added to our difficulties. Still, prolonges were fixed and we withdrew—the left section keeping Kershaw's skirmishers back with canister, and the other two sections bowling solid shot towards Barksdale's men . . .

When we reached the angle of the stone wall at Trostle's house, a swell of ground, 50 yards on our right front, covered us from Barksdale's approaching line and we began to limber up, hoping to get out and back to our lines before they closed in on us; but McGilvery again rode up, told me that back of me for nearly 1,500 yards, between Round Top and the left of the 2nd Corps, the lines were open; there were no reserves, and said, I must hold my position at all hazards until he could find some infantry, or could collect and place some batteries in position to cover the gap . . . Further, we were shut in by the angle of a stone wall, along one line of which, the left, Kershaw's sharpshooters were following us; while on its other line, in front and on our right, Barksdale's Brigade was advancing; nearly half our men and horses were lying killed and wounded at our first position, or on the field, between that and where we then were, for we had been steadily engaged since 4:30 p.m. (it was then 6 o'clock), and but a few rounds of ammunition were left in our chests. However, the orders were given to unlimber, take the ammunition from the chests, place it near the guns for rapid firing and load the guns to the muzzle. They were hardly executed before the enemy appeared breast high above the swell of ground 50 yards in front, already referred to, and firing, on both sides, began . . .

Just before they closed in, the left section, Lieut. [Richard S.] Milton, could not be used, owing to some stone boulders, and was ordered to the rear. One piece went through the gateway of the stone wall, was upset, righted amid a shower of bullets and, Lieut. Milton assisting, was dragged to the rear, the other piece was driven directly over the stone wall and the stones lie today exactly as they were knocked by the wheels then, with a six or eight-inch tree grown up in front, as guardian of the spot.

I rode to the stone wall, hoping to stop some of Milton's cannoneers and have them make a better opening, through which I might rush one or more of the remaining four guns, which were still firing. I sat on my horse calling the men, when my bugler, on my right, drew his horse back on his haunches, as he saw six sharpshooters on our left taking deliberate aim at us. I stopped two, and my horse two more of their bullets. My orderly was near by, and dismounting he raised me from the ground.

I then saw the Confederates swarming in on our right flank, some standing on the limber chests and firing at the gunners, who were still

serving their pieces; the horses were all down; overhead the air was alive with missiles from batteries, which the enemy had now placed on the Emmetsburg Road, and, glancing anxiously to the rear, I saw the longed for batteries just coming into position on high ground, 500 yards away. I then gave orders for the small remnant of the four gun detachments to fall back. My battery had delayed the enemy 30 precious minutes, from 6 to 6:30 o'clock p.m., and its sacrifice had not been in vain.

William Lochren, "The First Minnesota at Gettysburg" (January 14, 1890), *Glimpses of the Nation's Struggle: Papers Read Before the Minnesota Commandery of the Military Order of the Loyal Legion of the United States, 1889-1892*, ed. Edward D. Neill (St. Paul, 1893)

Just then Hancock, with a single aide, rode up at full speed, and . . . vainly endeavored to rally Sickles's retreating forces . . . Quickly leaving the fugitives, Hancock spurred to where we stood, calling out as he reached us, "What regiment is this?" "First Minnesota," replied [Colonel William J.] Colvill. "Charge those lines!" commanded Hancock. Every man realized in an instant what that order meant . . . and in a moment, responding to Colvill's rapid orders, the regiment, in perfect line, with arms at "right shoulder, shift," was sweeping down the slope directly upon the enemy's centre. No hesitation, no stopping to fire, though the men fell fast at every stride before the concentrated fire of the whole Confederate force . . . as soon as the movement was observed. Silently . . . "double-quick" had changed to utmost speed . . .

"Charge!" shouted Colvill as we neared the first line, and with levelled bayonets, at full speed, we rushed upon it, fortunately, as it was slightly disordered in crossing a dry brook. The men were never made who will stand against levelled bayonets coming with such momentum and evident desperation. The first line broke in our front as we reached it, and rushed back through the second line, stopping the whole advance. We then poured in our first fire, and availing ourselves of such shelter as the low bank of the dry brook afforded, held the entire force at bay for a considerable time . . .

W.H. Bullard [Co. C, 70th New York] to Daniel Sickles, September 13, 1897, Daniel E. Sickles Papers, New-York Historical Society

I noticed a commotion near Gen. Sickles and saw him taken from his horse. I hastened to him thinking I could be of service in some way, the aids on his staff gave way for me . . . I immediately found the wound to be a compound fracture of the leg and put on a Turnkey [torniquet], stopped the flow of blood. I shall never forget how white the Gen. was. I gave him something from my Canteen which seemed to revive him. I then placed him on the stretcher and was about to start for the Ambulances which were placed behind large rocks, when the Gen. says before you start Major won't you be kind enough to light a cigar for me. I took one from his Cigar Case which I found in his Inside pocket. I remember them, they were small ones. I bit the end off put it in my mouth lighted it then placed it in the Gen. mouth. He says Ah thank You I also remember the look of astonishment on the faces of the Officers Gen Sickles noticed it I think for he said it is all right I did not stop to think of the difference in rank, my only thought was to help him, and to get him to the Surgeons as soon as possible. I started with him along the line we had to go quite a distance to get to the ambulance . . . as we were hastening along the lines the men and officers noticed we had Gen Sickles and the word passed along the line that he was mortally wounded Gen Sickles heard them and he raised himself up and said No No not so bad as that I am allright and will be with you in a short time . . . You must hold your position and win this battle . . .

Albertus McCreary, "Gettysburg: A Boy's Experience of the Battle," *McClure's Magazine* 33 (July 1909)

We were within the Confederate lines and knew nothing of the state of affairs outside, and were considerably alarmed by the reports given us by the Confederate soldiers. They told us of all sorts of disasters to the Union army. They said their men had taken Harrisburg, Philadelphia, Baltimore, and were nearing Washington, and that it was all up with us. Although we were confined to the house for the next two days, we only took to the cellar at intervals, when there was heavy cannonading. The vibrations could be felt, and the atmosphere was so full of smoke that we could taste saltpeter. One of our party was a deaf and dumb man, who, though he could not hear the firing, plainly felt the vibrations and could tell when the firing was heaviest as well as we. He would spell out on his fingers, "That was a heavy one." The whizzing of the shells overhead and the sharp snap of bullets through the trees in the yard kept us well keyed up.

Our house stood on the corner of Baltimore and High streets, and we did not dare to look out of the windows on the Baltimore Street side. Sharpshooters from Cemetery Hill were watching all the houses for Confederate sharpshooters and picking off every person they saw, since from that distance they could not distinguish citizen from soldier. On the High Street side we could stay out on the porch during the heavy artillery firing.

Along this street from east to west of the town was stretched a line of Confederate infantry in reserve. From time to time they were moved away, and others took their place. I remember how poorly clad they were. Most of them were ragged and dirty, and they had very little to eat. I saw one man with a loaf of moldy bread and a canteen of molasses. He would break off a piece of bread, pour molasses over it, and eat it with what seemed great relish. I asked him if that was all he had to eat. He answered, "Yes, and glad to get it, too." I had many talks with these men as they lay along the pavement and on the cellar doors. They were a sorry lot, poorly equipped and poorly fed. I saw one man passing the house on horseback, without shoes, and with spurs strapped to his bare heels. The officers seemed to be much better cared for.

Diagonally across from us, in the second story of our neighbor's house, a Confederate general had his headquarters. I could see him seated at the window receiving the officers with despatches. If I remember rightly, it was General Ewell.

One day, while I was having a talk with the soldiers, I heard cheering down the street. It seemed to be caused by the passing along High Street, toward our house, of a small body of officers on horseback. As they drew near, the men along our pavement stood and cheered also. One of the men told me it was General Lee and his staff. I had a good look at him as he passed. He looked very much the soldier, sitting very erect in his saddle, with his short-cropped beard and his Confederate gray. The whole staff were a fine-looking set of men at least, they seemed so to my youthful eyes; and it is needless to say that I gazed at them with keen curiosity. They rode up as far as a slight elevation in the street, stopped, took their glasses, and surveyed Cemetery Hill, where they could see the position of their enemy.

John Day Smith, *The History of the Nineteenth Regiment of Maine Volunteer Infantry, 1862-1865* (Minneapolis, 1909)

It was a very sad night to most of the boys of the Regiment. When the roll was called, many a brave boy for the first time failed to respond to his name. The answers made by the living for their dead or wounded comrades were pathetic. As the names of the missing would be called, such answers as these would be returned: 'John was killed before we fired a shot.' 'I saw Frank throw up his arms and fall just after we fired the first volley.' 'Jim was shot through the head.' 'Charley was killed while we were charging across the plain this side of the brick house.' 'I saw Joe lying on the ground, his face covered with blood, but he was not dead.' 'George was killed by a piece of shell, while we were firing.' 'Ed is lying dead some distance this side of the Emmitsburg road.' Strong men sobbed . . .

The sun set on July 2nd at twenty-three minutes past seven, almanac time . . . There was not much sleep that night. The cries of the wounded men, lying between the lines, suffering with pain and burning with fever were most pitiful. The writer vividly remembers responding to a cry for water a few rods in advance of where the Regiment was lying . . . The poor fellow calling for help was a Confederate soldier. He was a fine looking boy, of some seventeen years, and stated that he belonged to one of the Georgia regiments of Wright's Brigade. He was shot through one of his lungs and was bleeding internally. The boy stated that he was the only child of a widowed mother and that he had run away from home, to enlist in the Southern army. His pallid face, blue eyes and quivering lips appealed for sympathy and encouragement. He said that his mother was a Christian woman, but that he was not a Christian. Kneeling by his side, and at the earnest request of this young soldier, the writer, poorly prepared for the sacred duty, tried to pray with and comfort this dying boy. At the first dawn of day upon the following morning this Confederate boy was found in just the position the writer had placed him the evening before—his eyes glazed in death, looking up into the morning sky, yet not seeing nor caring then. The poor mother waiting at the lonely hearthstone never knew what had become of her only child. She no doubt lived in the belief, as well she might, that her prayers had followed and influenced the life and character of her boy. Other mothers, heartbroken, all over the country, waited in vain for the coming of the boy who never returned. Such is war.

EAST CEMETERY HILL & CULP'S HILL

While Lee intended for his main blow on July 2nd to be leveled by James Longstreet against the Union left, he was also determined to press the Union defenders posted on the east face of Cemetery Hill and Culp's Hill—if only to keep them too busy to help the rest of the Army of the Potomac as it was being pummeled by Longstreet. But just as a great deal went awry with Longstreet's attack, so it did with the demonstrations Richard Ewell's corps was directed to make against East Cemetery Hill and Culp's Hill; and yet, they, too, came agonizingly close to bowling over the Army of the Potomac.

Ewell's first problem was organizational. All three of his divisions—under Robert Rodes, Jubal Early, and "Allegheny" Ed Johnson—had been bloodied on July 1st, and Ewell took his time getting them in place for an attack. Rodes's division was spaced across the streets of the town of Gettysburg, and the difficulties in the way of coordinating their movements meant that they never actually got into action at all on July 2nd. When Johnson's artillery battalion, commanded by "Little Latimer"—nineteen-year-old Major Joseph White Latimer—deployed

in midafternoon on Benner's Ridge to bombard the Union guns on Cemetery Hill, the concentrated batteries of the 11th Corps on the hill replied with a devastating blanket of fire that disabled Johnson's guns and mortally wounded Latimer.

Nevertheless, after the sound of Longstreet's attack reached Ewell's ears late that afternoon, Early's and Johnson's divisions went forward with a relentlessness that almost swept over both hills. Harry Hays's impetuous Louisiana brigade (the notorious "Louisiana Tigers") and Robert Hoke's North Carolina brigade (under the temporary command of Isaac Avery) slammed into a string of 11th Corps units holding the base of East Cemetery Hill and broke them apart, then swarmed up the side of the hill. They overran the four Federal batteries of Bruce Ricketts (1st Pennsylvania Light Artillery), Gilbert Reynolds (Battery L, 1st New York Light Artillery), James Stewart (Battery B, 4th U.S. Artillery), and Michael Wiedrich (Battery I, 1st New York Light Artillery), and looked as if they might just keep on going across the top of the Cemetery Hill plateau and into the backs of the 2nd Corps. Only a quick order from Winfield Scott Hancock sent Colonel Samuel Sprigg Carroll's "western" brigade of Ohioans, Indianans, and West Virginians sprinting across Cemetery Hill to drive the rebels back down the slope.

The same, or even worse, might have happened on Culp's Hill. As Longstreet's great attack on the other side of the battlefield reached its climax, General Meade decided to reinforce the 2nd Corps, holding the tail of Cemetery Ridge and the back door to Cemetery Hill, by pulling Henry Warner Slocum's 12th Corps off Culp's Hill to prop up Hancock and the Second Corps. Slocum left only one brigade of New Yorkers under George Sears "Old Pappy" Greene behind, and under almost any other circumstances, they could never have held off "Allegheny" Johnson's Confederate division as it advanced to the attack in the fading light of July 2nd. But "Old Pappy" Greene shrewdly spaced his men out to cover the ground and ordered them to construct crude log breastworks along the two peaks of Culp's Hill. Along with the fragments of the 1st Corps brigades who had survived their pounding the day before, Greene was able to hold off Johnson's attackers until exhaustion and the return of the 12th Corps finally forced the Confederates to break off the assault.

Even so, Ewell's divisions came perilously close to accomplishing what Longstreet had also nearly accomplished on July 2nd, and in Ewell's case, the day ended with George H. Steuart's brigade of Confederates actually clinging to control of the south peak of Culp's Hill. The question for the Army of the Potomac now became insistent: Was it realistic to think they could survive yet one more day's battering? Would it be wiser to do as George Meade had originally planned, and fall back to Pipe Creek while there was still something that could retreat down the Baltimore Pike in good order? That evening, Meade called a council of war at his headquarters at Lydia Leister's small, whitewashed cottage on the Taneytown Road, and put the matter to his corps commanders. To varying degrees, they advised Meade to stand and fight, and Meade agreed.

The very fact that Meade called a council in the first place spun off yet another great controversy that would linger around him, since rumors surfaced almost at once that Meade had decided upon a fallback to Pipe Creek and wanted his generals' endorsement for retreating. Meade vigorously contested the accusations, and even circulated a request that his corps commanders testify that he had never promoted the idea of retreat. But Meade's political and family identity, both as a Democrat and the brother-in-law of a Confederate governor, fueled suspicion, and made his other argument with Dan Sickles even more protracted.

It is possible that Meade was considering a retreat to Pipe Creek simply as a contingency, but even a contingency raised eyebrows. In the end, the council-of-war controversy reveals less about Meade than it does about the political mistrust that existed in the upper ranks of the Army of the Potomac.

A Gallant Captain of the Civil War: Being the Record of the Extraordinary Adventures of Frederick Otto Baron von Fritsch [68th New York], ed. Joseph Tyler Butts (New York, 1902)

Of course we watched the right closely, and about four o'clock I announced that the Confederates were preparing to fire . . . half past six, then it seemed that the Confederate batteries were silenced, but we saw large columns approaching us. In splendid order they came marching through the cornfield, and impetuously they charged Colonel [Leopold] von Gilsa's Brigade, screaming: "We are the Louisiana Tigers!" Our men fired in good time, and their bullets told, but on came the enemy—more and more of them, climbing the wall and forcing the Brigade up the hill behind the batteries. Now our batteries began to fire grape and canister, but some brave fellows came up to one of the batteries and demanded surrender; the battery men, assisted by General [Adelbert] Ames, two officers and myself, cut them down. With hand-spikes and rammers the cannoniers struck at their heads, and my good sword behaved well again. All who had reached the battery were killed, then the guns were reloaded and rapidly fired, and we stood surrounded by dense smoke. General [Carl] Schurz had sent a Brigade to reinforce us, and hearing them advance, I joined and charged with them down the hill. They drove the Confederates back over the wall and then we lay down as our cannons were firing very close over our heads.

William R. Kiefer, *History of the One Hundred and Fifty-third Regiment Pennsylvania Volunteers* (Easton, PA, 1909)

The position occupied by us that morning was . . . at the right, or east, of the cemetery, facing the town . . . About 6 o'clock heavy firing on our left informed us that the contest had commenced, half an hour later our whole line was engaged . . . Time and again did they attempt to mass their columns for the final assault, when as often they were dispersed. The intentions of

the enemy to outflank us becoming momentarily more apparent, a change of front became necessary, and was accomplished with but trifling losses on our side. Nor was the movement made a minute too soon, for hardly had we occupied our new position than the enemy was seen advancing upon it in solid phalanx . . . It was no longer a battle. It was a hand-to-hand conflict, carried on with the valor and vindictiveness of desperation. The arms of ordinary warfare were no longer used. Clubs, knives, stones, fists—anything calculated to inflict pain or death was now resorted to. Now advancing, then retreating, this sort of conflict continued for fully three-quarters of an hour. At one time defeat seemed inevitable. Closely pressed by the enemy we were compelled to retire on our first line of defense, but even here the enemy followed us, while the more daring were already within our lines, and were now resolutely advancing towards our pieces. The foremost had already reached a piece, when throwing himself over the muzzle of the cannon, he called out to the by-standing gunners, 'I take command of this gun!' '*Du sollst sie haben*' [you can have her] was the curt reply of the sturdy German, who, at that very moment, was in the act of firing.

John Richards Boyle, *Soldiers True: The Story of the One Hundred and Eleventh Regiment Pennsylvania Veteran Volunteers* (New York, 1903)

[Jubal] Early, from Ewell's center, advanced against the north front of Cemetery Hill. The brigades of Hays and [Robert Frederick] Hoke (the latter under Colonel [Isaac] Avery), with Gordon in reserve, made the attack. Hays's command comprised four regiments known as the "Louisiana Tigers," all being from that State, and Hoke's was from North Carolina. They marched to the foot of the hill by a sunken and concealed road known as Long Lane, which was sheltered by a grove of locust trees, and silently and in the darkness formed line in its protection. The Hill was defended by Von Gilsa's brigade of the Eleventh Corps in support of Ricketts's and Wiedrich's batteries. It was also commanded by [Captain Greenlief Thurlow] Stevens's Fifth Maine Battery from a spur of Culp's Hill. With a yell the line of Hays and Hoke emerged from the shadows, and rushed the hillside on a run. In a few moments Von Gilsa's brigade was overwhelmed. The guns of the batteries could not be sufficiently depressed to meet the charge and it looked as if the position were gone. But Stevens's battery from the right had a flanking range and poured in double canister in an enfilading fire. It failed to halt the advancing line, which reached the guns of Ricketts and Wiedrich, which were defended with great bravery. One of Ricketts's men, however, quailed and said, "Captain, I am awful sick. May I go to the rear?" Ricketts leveled his revolver at him and shouted, "You stand at your post, or I'll make you sicker;" and the soldier came to his senses and did good work. So hot was the defense of those guns that the enemy subsequently dubbed them "Battery Hell." The Thirty-third Massachusetts struck the left flank of the charging foe, and Hancock sent Carroll's brigade, of his Third Division, and one of the most stubborn hand-to-hand encounters of the war took place around these batteries. Bayonets, clubbed muskets, gun rammers, handspikes, and stones were used in the mad riot of the struggle as the broken lines wrestled in intermingled confusion. But the enemy was overpowered. His expected supports failed to appear, and his defeated fragments reeled down the hill and sought shelter in the darkness. The Louisiana Tigers were practically annihilated. They lost twelve hundred out of seventeen hundred men that were brought into action. Colonel Avery, commanding the North Carolina brigade, was mortally wounded.

Randolph H. McKim, *A Soldier's Recollections: Leaves from the Diary of a Young Confederate* (New York, 1911)

Greatly did officers and men marvel as morning, noon, and afternoon passed in inaction on our part, not on the enemy's, for, as we well knew, he was plying axe and pick and shovel in fortifying a position which was already sufficiently formidable. Meanwhile one of our staff conducted religious services, first in the Tenth Virginia, then in the Second Maryland Regiment, the men gladly joining in the solemn services, which they knew would be for many of their number the last they should ever engage in on earth. At length, after the conclusion of that tremendous artillery duel which for two hours shook the earth, the infantry began to move. It was past six p.m. before our brigade was ordered forward—nearly twenty-four hours after we had gotten into position. We were to storm the eastern face of Culp's Hill, a rough and rugged eminence on the southeast of the town, which formed the key to the enemy's right centre. Passing first through a small skirt of woods, we advanced rapidly in line of battle across a corn field which lay between us and the base of the hill, the enemy opening upon us briskly as soon as we were unmasked. Rock creek, waistdeep in some places, was waded, and now the whole line, except the First North Carolina, held in reserve on our left flank, pressed up the steep acclivity through the darkness, and was soon hotly engaged with the enemy. After the conflict had been going on for some time, I ventured to urge the brigadier-general commanding to send forward the First North Carolina to reinforce their struggling comrades. Receiving orders to that effect, I led the regiment up the hill, guided only by the flashes of the muskets, until I reached a position abreast of our line of fire on the right. In front, a hundred yards or so, I saw another line of fire, but owing to the thick foliage could not determine whether the musket flashes were up or down the hill. Finding that bullets were whistling over our heads, I concluded the force in our front must be the enemy, and seeing, as I thought, an admirable chance of turning their flank, I urged Colonel [Hamilton Allen] Brown to move rapidly forward and fire. When we reached what I supposed the proper position, I shouted, "Fire on them, boys; fire on them!" At that moment Major [William] Parsley, the gallant officer in command of the Third North Carolina, rushed up and shouted, "They are our own men." Owing to the din of battle the command to fire had not been heard except by those nearest to me, and I believe no injury resulted from my mistake. I mention it only to assume the responsibility for the order. Soon after this the works were gallantly charged and taken about 9.30 p.m., after a hard conflict of two hours, in which the Second Maryland and the Third North Carolina were the chief sufferers. Among those who fell severely wounded was Col. James R. Herbert, of the Second Maryland. The losses in the two regiments named were heavy, but the men were eager to press on to the crest of the hill. This, owing to the darkness and the lateness of the hour, it was resolved not to do.

William Kepler, *History of the Three Months' and Three Years' Service from April 16th, 1861, to June 22d, 1864, of the Fourth Regiment Ohio Volunteer Infantry in the War for the Union* (Cleveland, 1886)

As night was lowering its sable curtains over the bloody scene word was received that part of the Eleventh Corps, being taken in front and flank, was compelled to fall back from their support of two batteries on Cemetery Hill. "Attention! Right Face—Double Quick—March!" was instantly obeyed, with [Colonel Samuel Sprigg] Carroll at the head of the Fourteenth Indiana in the lead, the Seventh West Virginia next; a squad of anxious general officers was soon passed, while we hurried by gravestones struck by the spiteful minie ball—toward the cannon's vivid flash and thundering roar; Baltimore Turnpike was crossed, the position of the rebels we hurried by determined only by their fire; hastening toward them, now by the left flank, the Fourth [Ohio] on the right flank of the brigade, through tanglements of retreating men, caissons and horses, up and along a slope, where maddened gunners of captured batteries raved and swore, or cried in very madness, vowing death to meet rather than give up their guns, striking the rebels with fist, rammer, ammunition and stones; greeting, echoing and re-echoing our cheer upon cheer, saying "It's Carroll's brigade, there'll be no more running; give 'em hell, boys." Bayonets and butts of guns at once joined the efforts of the heroic gunners, then infantry and gunner in a general melee, with flanks of regiments overlapping and every-man-in-as-you-can sort of way, drove the enemy from unhitching horses and spiking guns, down over the hill, under the cross-fire of Stevens' battery on our right, and captured a number of prisoners. Weiderick's and Ricketts's batteries were recaptured. Company G of our Seventh West Virginia made sad havoc with their old rebel neighbors. We soon took position by a stone wall, a short distance from the guns toward our right and front, sent out skirmishers and brought in several prisoners; to our right, on Culp's Hill, the terrible racket of musketry continued until near 11 o'clock, by which time the enemy seemed to have withdrawn from our front; having stationed our pickets, those that could endeavored to sleep in spite of the rumbling sounds to our rear, which caused us to fear that our army was falling back, producing much dissatisfaction until it was known that it was the determination of our commanders to fight it out there and then. Aside from this fear the brigade was in the happiest mood, for it knew that it had turned defeat into victory, saved the key to the entire position, thereby averting disaster in compelling us to fall back in confusion and disheartened, in case the enemy had held the hill and turned our guns upon us.

Jesse H. Jones [60th New York], "The Breastworks at Culp's Hill," *Battles and Leaders of the Civil War*, eds. R.U. Johnson & C.C. Buel (New York, 1888), Vol. 3

At 6 o'clock in the evening General Meade, finding himself hard pressed on the left, and deeming an attack on the right wing improbable at so late an hour, called for the Twelfth Corps. Our brigade was detailed to remain and hold the lines of the corps. Word was brought from the officer in charge of our pickets that the enemy was advancing in heavy force in line of battle, and, with all possible celerity, such dispositions as the case admitted of were made. The brigade was strung out into a thin line of separate men as far along the breastworks as it would reach. The intention was to place the men an arm's-length apart, but, by the time the left of the brigade had fairly undoubled files, the enemy was too near to allow of further arrangements being made.

In a short time the woods were all flecked with the flashes from the muskets of our skirmishers. Down in the hollow there, at the foot of the slope, you could catch a glimpse now and then, by the blaze of the powder, of our brave boys as they sprang from tree to tree, and sent back defiance to the advancing foe. With desperation they clung to each covering. For half an hour they obstructed the enemy's approach.

The men restrained their nervous fingers; the hostile guns flamed out against us not fifteen yards in front. Our men from the front were tumbling over the breastwork, and for a breathless moment those behind the breastwork waited. Then out into the night like chain-lightning leaped the zigzag line of fire. Now was the value of breastworks apparent, for, protected by these, few of our men were hit, and feeling a sense of security, we worked with corresponding energy. Without breastworks our line would have been swept away in an instant by the hailstorm of bullets and the flood of men. The enemy worked still farther around to our right, entered the breastwork beyond our line, and crumpled up and drove back, a short distance, our extreme right regiment. They advanced a little way, but were checked by the fire of a couple of small regiments borrowed for the emergency from [Brigadier] General [James S.] Wadsworth, and placed in echelon . . .

The left of our brigade was only about eighty rods from the Baltimore turnpike, while the right was somewhat nearer. There were no supports. All the force that there was to stay the onset was that one thin line. Had the breastworks not been built, and had there been only the thin line of our unprotected brigade, that line must have been swept away like leaves before the wind, by the oncoming of so heavy a mass of troops, and the pike would have been reached by the enemy. Once on the pike, the Confederate commander would have been full in the rear of one-third of our army, firmly planted on the middle of the chord of the area upon which that portion was posted. What the effect must have been it is not needful to describe. The least disaster would have sufficed to force us from the field.

During the night our commanders brought back the remainder of the corps, and, stumbling upon the enemy's pickets, found out what had taken place, something of which until that moment they had been entirely unaware.

Martin L. Olmsted [78th New York], "On the Right at Gettysburg," *National Tribune* (December 17, 1908)

The battle on the right at Culp's Hill has been . . . referred to . . . as the midnight battle . . . The sun was well down in the west, when from the distant hills, edged on their summits with timber . . . regiments of infantry began to appear, and, moving forward, formed in line of battle . . . Watching these as they came into line thru a field glass, and counting battle flags and intervals in the front line, I calculated that there were eight regiments, and of probably from 400 to 500 muskets in each. In rear of these, forming the front line of battle, were two smaller lines of infantry, formed some two or three hundred yards in rear as supporting columns. On their left flank, as a curtain, were two or more regiments moving by the left flank in files of four [in column] . . . I became . . . interested . . . in watching a dashing officer riding a milk-white horse and who appeared to be a field officer, assigning the different commands to their respective positions . . . but it seems to me that something like two hours must have elapsed before the column was fully completed.

Then an officer and staff rode along the front line, and must have made some remarks to the men, as I distinctly saw a flutter of battle flags and hats waving in the air, but they were too far away to be heard. Then the whole mass moved out with arms at right shoulder-shift, their movement in perfect alignment, but with what appeared to me as at a slow, measured tread, evidently intending not to exhaust itself in covering the intervening space. In front of the oncoming lines I took particular notice of two lines of men deployed as skirmishers well out to the front, and about 100 yards distant from each other, the first line vaulting over the intervening fences with which the valley in front was divided into fields and meadows, while the second line leveled these obstructions as they came to them, thus removing and clearing the way for the oncoming lines of battle. The last I saw of my white horse friend, the enemy, he had dismounted, and was leading the advancing line on foot and the horse was being led to the rear . . .

As soon as the advance skirmish line came within reach of us we opened a brisk fire upon it, and the two lines of deployed men were soon battered into one blazing line of musketry . . .

The oncoming line of Confederate infantry halted from time to time, waiting for its advance, to clear the way, while we in the heavy timber made every tree and rock a veritable battlefield, and probably during the whole war a more stubborn skirmish fight was never waged. Our movements were directed by the bugle calls of the Major of the 60th N.Y., which rang clear and distinct above the rage of conflict. The smoke of battle gathering under the dense foliage of the trees, together with the dusk of evening, soon brought out to view the flashes of the musketry, and so near us came the solid line of battle at one time that its tramp, tramp, and the sharp, short commands of its officers became clearly audible.

The main lines of the enemy entering the wood at right angles with our line of defense swung its left around so as to become parallel with ours and come at us with a rush, extending from the foot of the hill and overlapping us, turned our right . . . So determined were the enemy's rushes that in places they reached the works and sought to climb over, and in several places their dead fell within our line on our side of the work . . . How long the attack continued there in the darkness and blackness of night one can form no estimate.

Three distinct assaults were repulsed, each with disaster to the onrushing enemy, and the fighting continued until apparently both the attack and defense had exhausted their ammunition . . . As the night wore on [those] still in line fell into fitful slumber, many leaning against the works. During the night ammunition was brought to us in gunny sacks, and doled out, each man receiving 20 rounds.

"General George H. Steuart's Brigade at the Battle of Gettysburg," *Southern Historical Society Papers* 2 (July 1876)

General Edward Johnson's division (composed of a Louisiana, [John Marshall] Jones', George H. Steuart's and the Stonewall brigades) arrived and formed line of battle the night of July 1st, 1863, on the left of the army. The Stonewall [Brigade] was the extreme left, next ours (Steuart's), and the two other brigades on our right. About 6 p.m. of July 2d, we received orders to advance. We soon met the enemy's skirmishers, pressed them rapidly back, crossed Rock creek, in some places waist deep, pushed up the eastern part of Culp's Hill under a heavy fire of musketry, and were ordered to lie down scarcely thirty yards from the enemy's breastworks. An angle in the enemy's works, not 100 yards to our right, exposed us to a severe flank fire. While lying down, we could distinctly see the Federals rise and fire at us from the works in front. Indeed, they fought so stubbornly, that orders passed up the line that we were firing into our own men, and we began to think that it was Longstreet coming up from the other side. After lying in this position probably fifteen minutes, we were ordered to charge, and as we climbed over the breastworks we distinctly remember seeing dead or wounded Yankees within the works . . .

(Five soldiers who participated in this part of the battle, recently visited Gettysburg and carefully examined the ground. We found the works we captured were on the east and several hundred yards from the summit of Culp's Hill.)

We reformed behind the works, almost at right angles to our original line of advance . . . July 3d Steuart's brigade (composed of the First and Third North Carolina, Second Maryland, Tenth, Twenty-third and

Thirty-seventh Virginia regiments) separated from our line of battle on our right, with rear and flank exposed, with no artillery support, fought for five hours a largely superior force . . . The enemy's artillery played on us from front, rear and flank . . . Only one other brigade came to our assistance, but took no part in the assault. Our brigade was then moved to the left, and our line was reformed. A writer, speaking of the men at this moment, says: "The compressed lip, the stern brow, the glittering eye, told that those before me would fight to the last." When the final order to charge was received, the General remarked, "it is a slaughter pen." A gallant captain replied, "it can't be helped, it is ordered," placed himself at the head of his company, and was killed instantly, less than fifty yards from the foe. The task was impossible for the little brigade, but it obeyed orders. The loss was fearful, our company losing sixty-two (62) out of ninety-odd in the two days' fighting. The men were rallied behind some large boulders of rock (the position they had just charged from), and were forced to retire, from the losses incurred in their charge against, and not before any charge of the enemy, to Rock Creek, several hundred yards to the rear, where, posted as a heavy skirmish line, they continued the contest till night.

Carl Schurz, "The Battle of Gettysburg," *McClure's Magazine* 29 (July 1907)

To look after the wounded of my command, I visited the places where the surgeons were at work . . . At Gettysburg the wounded—many thousands of them—were carried to the farmsteads behind our lines. The houses, the barns, the sheds, and the open barnyards were crowded with moaning and wailing human beings, and still an unceasing procession of stretchers and ambulances was coming in. A heavy rain set in during the day—the usual rain after a battle—and large numbers had to remain unprotected in the open, there being no room left under roof. I saw long rows of men lying under the eaves of the buildings, the water pouring down upon their bodies in streams. Most of the operating tables were placed in the open, where the light was best, some of them partially protected against the rain by tarpaulins or blankets stretched upon poles. There stood the surgeons, their sleeves rolled up to the elbows, their bare arms as well as their linen aprons smeared with blood, their knives not seldom held between their teeth while they were helping a patient on or off the table, or had their hands otherwise occupied; around them pools of blood and amputated arms or legs in heaps, sometimes more than man-high. Antiseptic methods were still unknown at that time. As a wounded man was lifted on the table, often shrieking with pain as the attendants handled him, the surgeon quickly examined the wound and resolved upon cutting off the injured limb. Some ether was administered, and the body put in position in a moment. The surgeon snatched his knife from between his teeth, where it had been while his hands were busy, wiped it rapidly once or twice across his blood-stained apron, and the cutting began. The operation accomplished, the surgeon would look around with a deep sigh, and then—"next!"

And so it went on, hour after hour, while the number of expectant patients seemed hardly to diminish. Now and then one of the wounded, men would call attention to the fact that his neighbor lying on the ground had given up the ghost while waiting for his turn, and the dead body was then quietly removed. Or a surgeon, having been long at work, would put down his knife, exclaiming that his hand had grown unsteady, and that this was too much for human endurance, hysterical tears not seldom streaming down his face. Many of the wounded men suffered with silent fortitude, fierce determination in the knitting of their brows and the steady gaze of their bloodshot eyes. Some would even force themselves to a grim jest about their situation or about the "skedaddling" of the rebels. But there were, too, heart-rending groans and shrill cries of pain piercing the air, and despairing exclamations, "Oh, Lord! Oh, Lord!" or "Let me die!" or softer murmurings in which the words "mother" or "father," or "home" were often heard. I saw many of my command among the sufferers, whose faces I well remembered, and who greeted me with a look or even a painful smile of recognition, and usually with the question what I thought of their chances of life, or whether I could do anything for them, or sometimes, also, whether I thought the enemy were well beaten. I was sadly conscious that many of the words of cheer and encouragement I gave them were mere hollow sound, but they might be at least some solace for the moment.

Thomas W. Hyde, *Following the Greek Cross, Or, Memories of the Sixth Army Corps* (Boston, 1894)

My active little horse, forgetting his seventy or eighty mile ride, took me up the steep northwest side of Little Round Top, to where Hazlett's guns were still firing, though their commander was dead and the rocks seemed to be covered with corpses in light blue Zouave uniform. I afterwards learned that they were the 140th New York. On looking back I could see no enemy firing except by Devil's Den and in the valley, and I was told by an officer ensconced behind a boulder that I had better get out of that if I did not want to be picked off, as the bullets were flattening themselves against the rocks all about. So quickly over the hill I went; and found what was left of the regular brigade under Colonel [James Durrell] Greene [17th U.S. Infantry], and they looked like a small regiment. Speaking to one or two friends I rode back to General Sedgwick and was glad to rest, for the fighting was over on the left for that day. Several of our brigades had been sent as reinforcements to different points, so our command was small. Gloomy reports kept coming in, and near dark Major [Charles Albert] Whittier, the general's confidential aide, told me we were going to march back twenty miles that night, and that the general was going to the headquarters to a council of war. Later, we gladly learned we were to stay where we were. With a blanket and something to eat, and after a soothing pipe, with our saddles for pillows and overcoats for bed and blankets, we were soon sleeping the dreamless sleep of youth and fatigue.

"Minutes of council, July 2, 1863," *The War of the Rebellion: A Compilation of the Official Records of the Union and Confederate Armies* (Washington, DC, 1889), Series 1, Vol. 27 (pt 1)

QUESTIONS ASKED

1. Under existing circumstances, is it advisable for this army to remain in its present position, or to retire to another nearer its base of supplies?

2. It being determined to remain in present position, shall the army attack or wait the attack of the enemy?
3. If we wait attack, how long?

REPLIES

Gibbon:

1. Correct position of the army, but would not retreat.
2. In no condition to attack, in his opinion.
3. Until he moves; until enemy moves.

Williams:

1. Stay.
2. Wait attack.
3. One day.

Birney:

Same as General Williams.

Sykes:

Same as General Williams.

Newton:

1. Correct position of the army, but would not retreat.
2. By all means not attack.
3. If we wait, it will give them a chance to cut our line.

Howard:

1. Remain.
2. Wait attack until 4 p.m. to-morrow.
3. If don't attack, attack them.

Hancock:

1. Rectify position without moving so as to give up field.
2. Not attack unless our communications are cut.
3. Can't wait long; can't be idle.

Sedgwick:

Remain, and wait attack at least one day.

Slocum:

Stay and fight it out.

[MEMORANDUM]

Slocum:

Stay and fight it out.

Newton:

Thinks it is a bad position.

Hancock:

Puzzled about practicability of retiring; thinks by holding on [illegible] to mass forces and attack.

Howard:

Favor of not retiring.

Birney:

Don't know; Third Corps used up, and not in good condition to fight.

Sedgwick:

Doubtful [illegible].

Effective strength about 9,000, 12,500, 9,000, 6,000, 8,500, 6,000, 7,000; total, 58,000.

Minutes of council, held Thursday p.m., July 2.

D[aniel] B[utterfield], M.G., C. of S.

Henry Warner Slocum to L.H. Morgan (January 2, 1864), *In Memoriam: Henry Warner Slocum, 1826-1894* (Albany, NY, 1904)

On the evening of July second a council was called, and each corps commander was asked his opinion as to the propriety of falling back towards Washington that night. The majority opposed it, and after the vote was taken Meade declared that "Gettysburg was no place to risk a battle;" and there is no doubt but for the decision of his corps commanders, the army on the third of July would have been in full retreat. The 4th of July, 1863, instead of being a day of rejoicing throughout the North, would have been the darkest day ever known to our country. This piece of history can be verified by the records of that council . . . You may think this a hard charge to bring against a soldier, but I believe I am fully justified in making it. There are circumstances which I will make known to you when we meet which will convince you that I have not done him injustice. As long as this war continues . . . I shall ask for no court, enter into no controversy, write no letters. But when the danger has passed from us many facts will come to light, giving to the public a better knowledge of the real history of this war than can be obtained through the medium of such reports as that written by General Meade.

Morton Wilkinson [U.S. Senator from Minnesota], "Army of the Potomac" (March 2, 1864), *Congressional Globe*, 38th Congress, 1st session

I am told, and I believe it can be proven, that before the fight commenced at Gettysburg . . . the order went forth from the commander of that army to retreat; and but for the single fact that one of the corps commanders had got into a fight before the dispatch reached him, the whole army would undoubtedly have been retreating, broken, and ineffectual before the powerful forces of General Lee . . . I wish to say, with regard to General Meade, that I believe he is a patriotic man. I believe he is as pure a gentleman as there is in the country. I believe he has the honor of his country at heart. I believe he means and wishes to do his duty; but he has none of that "blundering audacity" of Grant, which will enable him to win battles and to crown his army with glory.

John Sedgwick to Seth Williams (March 10, 1864), *The War of the Rebellion: A Compilation of the Official Records of the Union and Confederate Armies* (Washington, DC, 1889), Series 1, Vol. 27 (pt 1)

My attention has been called to several articles which have recently appeared in the papers, insinuating or charging the general commanding the Army of the Potomac with ordering or favoring a retreat of the army on the evening of July 2, at Gettysburg.

I took no minutes of the council of corps commanders held on the evening of that day, but my present recollection is that three questions, *viz.* of attacking the enemy, of sustaining an attack, or taking up a new position, were submitted. The council was unanimous with, I think, one exception—to sustain the attack in our then present position.

At no time in my presence did the general commanding insist or advise a withdrawal of the army, for such advice would have great weight with me, and I know the matter did not engage my serious attention.

I am positive that the general commanding could not have insisted, much less have given the order, to withdraw the army from its position . . .

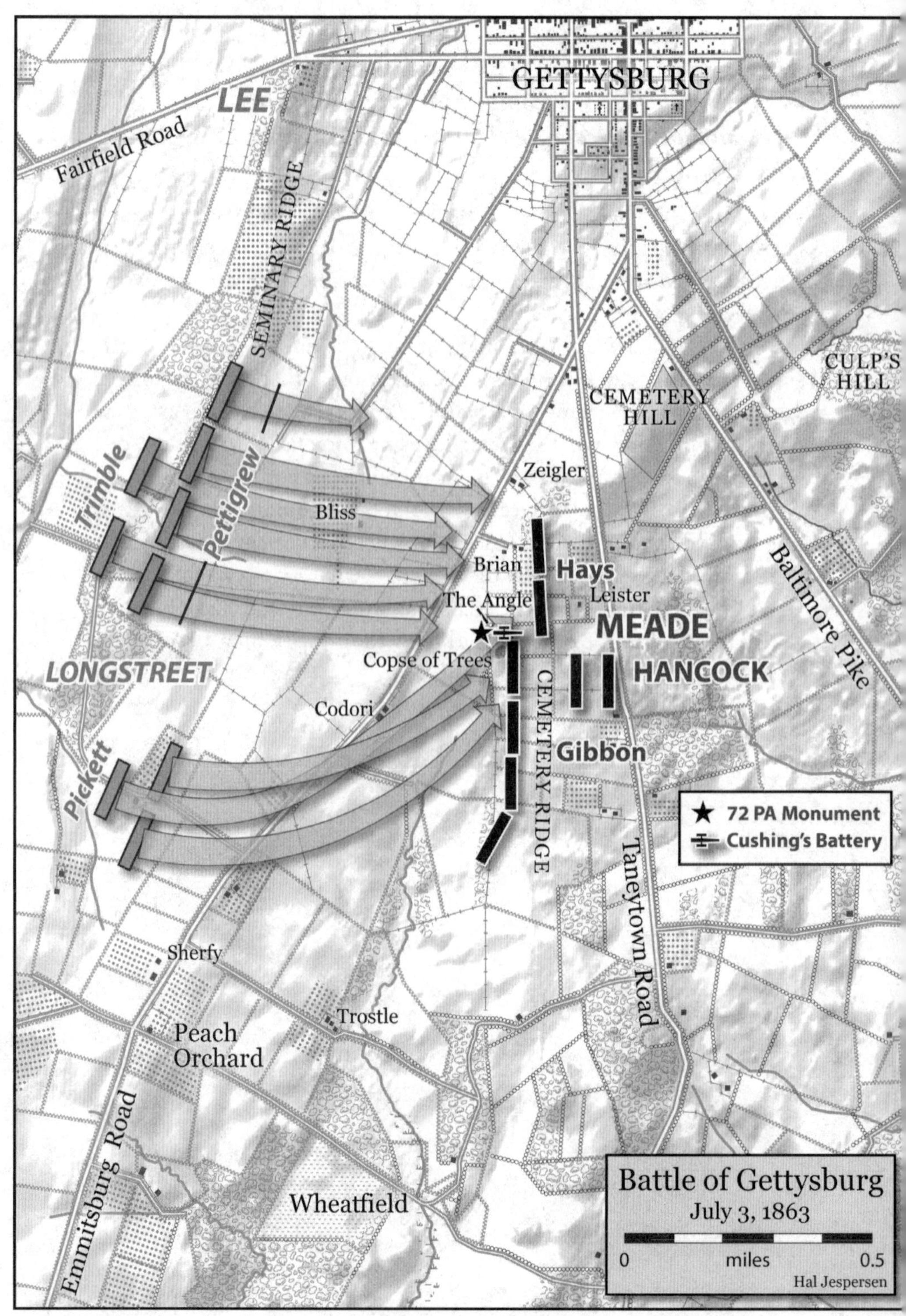

GETTYSBURG
LEE
Fairfield Road
SEMINARY RIDGE
CULP'S HILL
CEMETERY HILL
Trimble
Pettigrew
Zeigler
Bliss
Brian
Hays
Leister
The Angle
MEADE
Baltimore Pike
Copse of Trees
LONGSTREET
HANCOCK
Codori
CEMETERY RIDGE
Pickett
Gibbon
72 PA Monument
Cushing's Battery
Taneytown Road
Sherfy
Trostle
Peach Orchard
Emmitsburg Road
Wheatfield
Battle of Gettysburg
July 3, 1863
0
miles
0.5
Hal Jespersen

THE THIRD DAY

After two days of battering, the best that the Army of the Potomac could give as an account of itself was that it had survived. On July 1st, two of its seven infantry corps—John Reynolds's 1st Corps and Oliver Otis Howard's 11th Corps—had suffered the loss of half their numbers as casualties, and their resilience was down to nearly zero. July 2nd had done even more damage to the 3rd Corps and 5th Corps, as well as one of Winfield Scott Hancock's 2nd Corps' three divisions. For all practical purposes, George Meade could count only on the 12th Corps (which he needed to hold Culp's Hill), the 6th Corps under John Sedgwick, which formed his reserve, and the last two divisions of the 2nd Corps that guarded the back door to Cemetery Hill, on Cemetery Ridge.

At least Meade still held that ridgeline, stretching down to Little Round Top, and his artillery still bristled hub-to-hub from Cemetery Hill. But one more strike like the ones Lee had launched on July 1st and 2nd, and the whole position might cave in and the Army of the Potomac might easily find itself in a hasty and disorganized retreat down the Baltimore Pike toward Maryland. The Confederates knew it, too. One captured Union officer found his rebel captors "very sanguine of their ability to dislodge the Army of the Potomac from its position" and thought "the capture of Washington and Baltimore was considered a thing almost accomplished." After all, Lee had a completely fresh division left from Longstreet's corps to direct at the weakened Federals—three entire brigades of Virginia veterans under James Kemper, Richard Garnett, and Lewis Armistead, and commanded as a division by George E. Pickett—for the knockdown blow.

Which was, in fact, exactly what Lee planned to do on July 3rd. Pickett's division, which had only arrived overnight from Chambersburg, together with six brigades from Powell Hill's corps, which had sat out the fighting on July 2nd, would land the blow. Overall supervision would come from Longstreet, and together they would strike the nape of the Army of the Potomac's neck, just behind Cemetery Hill, where the remainder of Hancock's 2nd Corps stood. The path of the Confederate attack would be smoothed by a coordinated artillery bombardment that would silence the Federal guns on Cemetery Hill, while the Federal infantry over on Culp's Hill would be pinned into place by a renewed attack from Richard Ewell's Confederates. On top of it all, J.E.B. Stuart's long-missing cavalry brigades had at last rejoined Lee overnight and would be available to cause mayhem among the retreating Federals, once Longstreet's blow had crushed the last Federal resistance behind Cemetery Hill.

It should have succeeded. Full-scale, finishing assaults of this sort had ended battles in the Crimean War and the North Italian War in the 1850s, and there was no reason why Longstreet's attack should not have done likewise, with so much in its favor. But once again, lack of effective coordination hamstrung the Confederates. First, Ewell's diversionary attack on Culp's Hill misfired. On the south peak of Culp's Hill, Union and Confederate units had become intermixed overnight, and the next morning a determined push by the 12th Corps drove them off for good. Then, Longstreet did not have Pickett's division ready to jump off from Seminary Ridge until later in the morning, and even then, he did not like the prospect of launching Pickett and his borrowed brigades from Powell Hill across the open mile of farmland that stretched between Seminary Ridge and the Union defenders on Cemetery Ridge. In the weeks (and eventually the years) after the battle, Longstreet would insist that he had counseled Lee not to make the attack, but instead to work the Army of Northern Virginia around the Union left flank and force the Army of the Potomac to abandon Gettysburg. Even when Lee refused to listen, Longstreet still directed Edward Porter Alexander (who would supervise the preliminary artillery bombardment) to advise him if Alexander thought that the bombardment had been ineffective and that the attack should be canceled. Longstreet believed he was simply being prudent. Others would regard it as undermining Lee, and Longstreet's repeated defenses of his dissent would become yet another in the string of postwar Gettysburg controversies.

To the Union defenders of Cemetery Ridge, the great attack—which would become known afterward as "Pickett's Charge," even though Pickett's Virginians were only part of the fifteen-thousand-or-so Confederates who actually made the assault—looked a good deal more overpowering. At one o'clock, the Confederate artillery opened its bombardment, concentrating on Cemetery Hill, but also plastering the 2nd Corps infantry units that held the ridgeline to the rear of the hill. At the front of the 2nd Corps lines were the divisions of John Gibbon and Alex Hays, and holding a small woodlot and a low farm wall were the four regiments that made up Alexander Webb's Philadelphia Brigade (the 69th, 71st, 72nd, and 106th Pennsylvania). In the town, civilians like Michael Jacobs still trembled in their cellars, and farmers as far away as Lancaster could wonder why they heard thunder on a clear day.

Sometime before three o'clock, the Confederate artillery fire slackened and stopped, and the big blocks of rebel infantry stepped out from the woods on Seminary Ridge, dressed their alignments on each other, and surged forward. The sight was one of the most memorable moments of the war, and John Cook (in the 80th New York) compared the formations of Confederate infantry, moving over the ground in perfect order, to "the shadow of a cloud seen from a distance as it sweeps across a sunny field."

It would not stay that way for long. Federal artillerymen who had survived the bombardment trained their guns on the advancing rebels and began tearing holes in their ranks. The Emmittsburg Road ran across the Confederates' front, and its plank fences provided an obstacle to be climbed over, which confused the Confederates' marching order and slowed its momentum. In the last hundred yards or so, they were met by Federal infantry fire from the 2nd Corps until, at the moment of contact, the rebel attackers were little more than wild mobs, following their regimental flags. But they were still dangerous mobs. Pickett's lead brigades pushed Alexander Webb's Philadelphians back from the stone wall they were defending, while Pickett's third brigade, under Lewis Armistead, surged over the remaining guns of Lieutenant Alonzo Hereford Cushing's Battery A, 4th U.S. Artillery. Just on their left flank, still more Confederates were lapping up to a small, whitewashed farmhouse on the edge of Cemetery Hill, and for a moment, it all looked as though the end of the Army of the Potomac had come.

But then, in the smoke and screams and thunder, Pickett's great charge faltered, and in a moment collapsed. Lewis Armistead went down with a fatal wound, Alexander Webb's last regiment, the 72nd Pennsylvania, counterattacked Armistead's Virginians, and the surviving rebels began making their best path back to Seminary Ridge. There, Robert E. Lee rallied Pickett's decimated regiments, never betraying the slightest anger or disappointment in them. In the estimate of a British military observer, Lieutenant-Colonel Arthur Fremantle, of the Coldstream Guards, Lee's behavior was "perfectly sublime."

To the east, J.E.B. Stuart's cavalry engaged in a sword-swinging back-and-forth encounter with Federal cavalry across the farm property of John Rummel, a skirmish that would be remembered chiefly for the role played by Michigan cavalrymen commanded by a boy-general who would earn a different kind of fame on a very different battlefield thirteen years later in dusty Montana: George Armstrong Custer. That night, Lee made the inevitable decision to retreat. The great attack had failed; his army had no strength left to continue the campaign; it was time to return to Virginia and find some way to recover.

Many of Pickett's men would not be returning, chief of whom was

Lewis Armistead. In a cruel irony, Armistead had led his Virginia brigade directly against Federals in the Second Corps commanded by a man who had once been one of his friends in the old army, Winfield Scott Hancock. The next day, Armistead died in an improvised hospital on the George Spangler farm. Hancock almost joined him during the fighting on July 3rd, sustaining a painful wound to the groin which would put an end to his active service a year later. In 1880, Hancock would be the Democratic candidate for the presidency of the United States, only to lose to another Civil War veteran, James Abram Garfield.

Charles F. Morse, *The Twelfth Corps at Gettysburg, July 1st, 2d and 3d, 1863: A Paper Read Before the Military Historical Society of Boston* (Boston, 1917)

The situation on the left had been so absorbing that apparently but little was known of the occurrences on the right, until the fighting was all over. It was probably between nine and ten o'clock when the 1st Division began its march to its old position on the right, the 3d Brigade being in the advance. It was a clear night, with a full moon, but the march was slow, as much of it was across country, and it was perhaps, between ten and eleven o'clock when the advance of the division crossed the Baltimore pike . . . A small squad of men was sent forward, which returned in a few minutes with a single rebel prisoner. The regiment was then formed in line, facing the woods beyond the swale, and a full company was sent out, which went across the swale and returned soon after with twenty-three more prisoners, who were gathered up not far from Spangler's Spring; they all had canteens, and appeared to be straggling about looking for water. Thus far there had been nothing to indicate how much of a force there was in the woods beyond the swale . . . After proceeding perhaps one hundred and fifty yards, it became evident that we were approaching a considerable body of men, but as it had been intimated that some of our own people might be in the woods, Captain [Thomas B.] Fox quietly halted his company and sent two of his men forward to make inquiry. They went on in an ordinary, careless way some twenty yards, and, when in close contact with this unknown force, called out the usual formula on such occasions, "What regiment, boys?" The answer came, "23d Virginia," followed by the exclamation, "Why, they're Yanks," and a slight scuffle, after which one of these men came hustling back; the other remained with his captors. No shot was fired and no aggressive movement was made on the part of the enemy. It still seemed possible that this was not an organized force in our front, and, to settle this question beyond a doubt, Captain Fox ordered his company forward without concealment. There was an almost immediate challenge, to which Captain Fox responded, "Surrender! Come into our lines." The answer to this was, sharp and clear, "Battalion, ready, fire!" and the fire came from quite a long, scattering line, but did little damage, as Captain Fox's company was on a much lower level and the bullets went over their heads; two men only were wounded . . .

At the first streak of dawn the pickets on both sides of the swale began firing, and, as the range was very short, the men had to protect themselves behind rocks and trees. At about the same time, which is named in official reports as 3.30 to 4.30, the artillery of the corps began firing from its position, west of the Baltimore pike, at the breastworks occupied by the enemy at ranges of six hundred to seven hundred yards. This firing was maintained for about fifteen minutes. When it ceased, the 1st Brigade, 1st Division, pressed forward into the woods in their front and began the attack. At the same time with this advance, the enemy began a furious attack on the 2d Division, particularly on Greene's line, charging almost to his breastworks. The fire which they met was so severe and their losses so heavy that they could make no impression

on this well-defended line, but, though repeatedly repulsed, they came again and again to the attack.

At about six a.m., when Greene's Brigade had exhausted its ammunition, [Brigadier-General Thomas L.] Kane's Brigade took its place and Greene's men went to the rear to clean their guns and get a fresh supply of cartridges. About eight a.m. the enemy massed their troops and made a determined attack . . . Two of Johnson's brigades were formed in a column by regiments and made a last, desperate attack on Greene's and Kane's brigades, the latter at that time being on Greene's right; but, though they pushed fairly into our lines, where, according to [Brigadier-General John White] Geary's report, the dead of the 1st Maryland Battalion, which was in the advance, mingled with our own, they were repulsed. In this last charge many of [Brigadier-General James Alexander] Walker's "Stonewall" Brigade threw down their arms and rushed forward with white flags to surrender. Major B[enjamin] W. Leigh, Johnson's adjutant general, rode forward to prevent this surrender, but was shot down when very near our lines. After the last repulse our troops rushed forward with cheers and reoccupied the breastworks they had vacated the evening before, and the defeated enemy retired to Rock Creek.

Charles F. Morse to Robert M. Morse (July 17, 1863), Charles F. Morse Papers, 1861-1943, Massachusetts Historical Society

It was a sad thing calling the rolls and looking at the vacant places of so many officers. Our only consolation was the proud satisfaction that we had done our duty nobly [in] as brave an action as ever a regiment went into. Five color bearers were shot down one after another[,] three were killed, two badly wounded, but the old tattered flag never touched the ground.

The third man who seized it, jumped on to a rock in advance of the regiment, and waved it triumphantly in the air, but the brave action cost him his life. He fell dead [along]side of the others.

I could fill a whole letter recounting similar actions of individuals. I never saw men behave so splendidly. Without one exception they stood their ground and did their work without flinching; it was awful and yet grand to see men expose their lives and lose them, as they did. I will write again very soon . . .

James Longstreet, "Lee in Pennsylvania," *Annals of the War Written by Leading Participants North and South* (Philadelphia, 1879)

I did not see General Lee that night. On the next morning he came to see me, and fearing that he was still in his disposition to attack, I tried to anticipate him by saying: "General, I have had my scouts out all night, and I find that you still have an excellent opportunity to move around to the right of Meade's army and manoeuvre him into attacking us." He replied, pointing with his fist at Cemetery Hill: "The enemy is there, and I am going to strike him." I felt then that it was my duty to express my convictions; I said: "General, I have been a soldier all my life. I have been with soldiers engaged in fights by couples, by squads, companies, regiments, divisions and armies, and should know as well as anyone what soldiers can do. It is my opinion that no 15,000 men ever arrayed for battle can take that position," pointing to Cemetery Hill. General Lee in reply to this ordered me to prepare Pickett's division for the attack. I should not have been so urgent had I not foreseen the hopelessness of the proposed assault. I felt that I must say a word against the sacrifice of my men; and then I felt that my record was such that General Lee would or could not misconstrue my motives. I said no more, however, but turned away. The most of the morning was consumed in waiting for Pickett's men and getting into position. The plan of assault was as follows: Our artillery was to be massed in a wood from which Pickett was to charge, and it was to pour a continuous fire upon the cemetery. Under cover of this fire, and supported by it, Pickett was to charge.

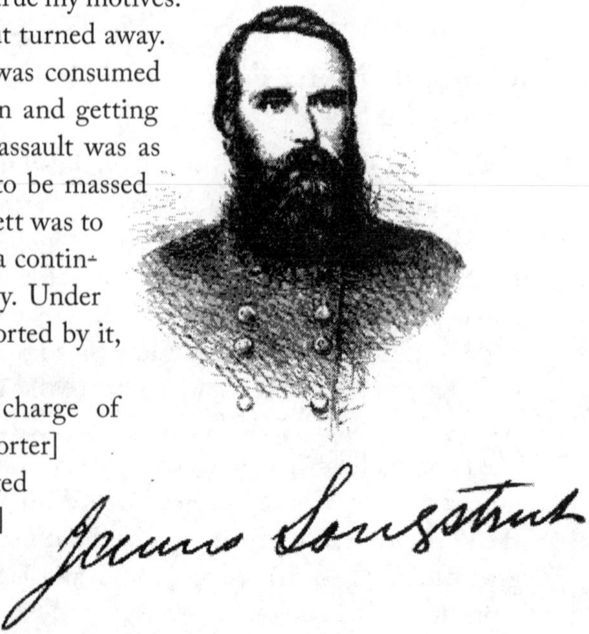

Our artillery was in charge of General E[dward] P[orter] Alexander, a brave and gifted officer. Colonel [James B.] Walton was my chief of artillery, but Alexander being at the head of the column, and being first in position, and being besides an officer of unusual promptness, sagacity and intelligence, was given charge of the artillery. The arrangements were completed about one o'clock. General Alexander had arranged that a battery of seven 11-pound howitzers, with fresh horses and full caissons, were to charge with Pickett, at the head of his line, but General [William Nelson] Pendleton, from whom the guns had been borrowed, recalled them just before the charge was made, and thus deranged this wise plan. Never was I so depressed as upon that day. I felt that my men were to be sacrificed, and that I should have to order them to make a hopeless charge. I had instructed General Alexander, being unwillingly to trust myself with the entire responsibility, to carefully observe the effect of the fire upon the enemy, and when it began to tell to notify Pickett to begin the assault. I was so much impressed with the hopelessness of the charge that I wrote the following note to General Alexander:

> *If the artillery fire does not have the effect to drive off the enemy or greatly demoralize him, so as to make our efforts pretty certain, I would prefer that you should not advise General Pickett to make the charge. I shall rely a great deal on your judgment to determine the matter, and shall expect you to let Pickett know when the moment offers.*

To my note the General replied as follows:

> *I will only be able to judge the effect of our fire upon the enemy by his return fire, for his infantry is but little exposed to view, and the smoke will obscure the whole field. If, as I infer from your note, there is an alternative to this attack, it should be carefully considered before opening our fire, for it will take all of the artillery ammunition we have left to test this one thoroughly, and if the result is unfavorable, we will have none left for another effort, and even if this is entirely successful it can only be so at a very bloody cost.*

I still desired to save my men and felt that if the artillery did not produce the desired effect I would be justified in holding Pickett off. I wrote this note to Colonel Walton at exactly 1:30 p.m.:

> *Let the batteries open. Order great precision in firing. If the batteries at the peach orchard cannot be used against the point we intend attacking, let them open on the enemy at Rocky Hill* [Little Round Top].

The cannonading which opened along both lines was grand. In a few moments a courier brought a note to General Pickett (who was standing near me) from Alexander, which, after reading, he handed to me. It was as follows:

> *If you are coming at all you must come at once, or I cannot give you proper support; but the enemy's fire has not slackened at all; at least eighteen guns are still firing from the Cemetery itself.*

After I had read the note Pickett said to me: "General, shall I advance?" My feelings had so overcome me that I would not speak for fear of betraying my want of confidence to him. I bowed affirmation and turned to mount my horse. Pickett immediately said: "I shall lead my division forward, sir." I spurred my horse to the wood where Alexander was stationed with artillery. When I reached him he told me of the disappearance of the seven guns which were to have led the charge with Pickett, and that his ammunition was so low that he could not properly support the charge. I at once ordered him to stop Pickett until the ammunition had been replenished. He informed me that he had no ammunition with which to replenish. I then saw that there was no help for it, and that Pickett must advance under his orders. He swept past our artillery in splendid style, and the men marched steadily and compactly down the slope.

Edward Porter Alexander, "The Great Charge and Artillery Fighting at Gettysburg," *Battles & Leaders of the Civil War*, eds. R.U. Johnson & C.C. Buel (New York, 1888), Vol. 3

Early in the morning General Lee came around, and I was then told that we were to assault Cemetery Hill, which lay rather to our left. This necessitated a good many changes of our positions, which the enemy did not altogether approve of, and they took occasional shots at us, though we shifted about, as inoffensively as possible, and carefully avoided getting into bunches. But we stood it all meekly, and by 10 o'clock, [Major James] Dearing having come up, we had seventy-five guns in what was virtually one battery, so disposed as to fire on Cemetery Hill and the batteries south of it, which would have a fire on our advancing infantry. Pickett's division had arrived, and his men were resting and eating. Along Seminary Ridge, a short distance to our left, were sixty-three guns of A.P. Hill's corps, under Colonel R[euben] L[indsay] Walker. As their distance was a little too great for effective howitzer fire, General Pendleton offered me the use of nine howitzers belonging to that corps. I accepted them, intending to take them into the charge with Pickett; so I put them in a hollow behind a bit of wood, with no orders but to wait there until I sent for them. About 11, some of Hill's skirmishers and the enemy's began fighting over a barn between the lines, and gradually his artillery and the enemy's took part, until over a hundred guns were engaged, and a tremendous roar was kept up for quite a time. But it gradually died out, and the whole field became as silent as a churchyard until 1 o'clock. The enemy, aware of the strength of his position, simply sat still and waited for us. It had been arranged that when the infantry column was ready, General Longstreet should order two guns fired by the Washington Artillery.* On that signal all our guns were to open on Cemetery Hill and the ridge extending toward Round Top, which was covered with batteries. I was to observe the fire and give Pickett the order to charge. I accordingly took position, about 12, at the most favorable point, just on the left of the line of guns and with one

* In the *United Service Magazine* for August 1885, Lieutenant-Colonel William Miller Owen, of the Washington Artillery, says:

"Returning to the position of the Washington Artillery, we all quietly awaited the order to open the ball. At 1: 30 p.m. a courier dashed up in great haste, holding a little slip of paper, torn evidently from a memorandum-book, on which, written in pencil and addressed to Colonel Walton, was the following: *Headquarters, July 3d, 1863. Colonel: Let the batteries open. Order great care and precision in firing- If the batteries at the Peach Orchard cannot be used against the point we intend attacking, let them open on the enemy on the rocky hill. Most respectfully, J. Longstreet, Lieutenant General Commanding.*

The order to fire the signal-gun was immediately communicated to Major [Benjamin] Eshleman, commanding the Washington Artillery, and the report of the first gun rang out upon the still summer air. There was a moment's delay with the second gun, a friction-primer having failed to explode. It was but a little space of time, but a hundred thousand men were listening. Finally a puff of smoke was seen at the Peach Orchard, then came a roar and a flash, and 138 pieces of Confederate artillery opened upon the enemy's position, and the deadly work began with the noise of the heaviest thunder."

of Pickett's couriers with me. Soon after I received the following note from Longstreet:

> *Colonel: If the artillery fire does not have the effect to drive off the enemy or greatly demoralize him, so as to make our efforts pretty certain, I would prefer that you should not advise General Pickett to make the charge. I shall rely a great deal on your good judgment to determine the matter, and shall expect you to let General Pickett know when the moment offers.*

This note rather startled me. If that assault was to be made on General Lee's judgment it was all right, but I did not want it made on mine. I wrote back to General Longstreet to the following effect:

> *General: I will only be able to judge of the effect of our fire on the enemy by his return fire, for his infantry is but little exposed to view and the smoke will obscure the whole field. If, as I infer from your note, there is any alternative to this attack, it should be carefully considered before opening our fire, for it will take all the artillery ammunition we have left to test this one thoroughly, and, if the result is unfavorable, we will have none left for another effort. And even if this is entirely successful, it can only be so at a very bloody cost.*

To this presently came the following reply:

> *Colonel: The intention is to advance the infantry if the artillery has the desired effect of driving the enemy's off, or having other effect such as to warrant us in making the attack. When the moment arrives advise General Pickett, and of course advance such artillery as you can use in aiding the attack.*

I hardly knew whether this left me discretion or not, but at any rate it seemed decided that the artillery must open. I felt that if we went that far we could not draw back, but the infantry must go too. General A.R. Wright, of Hill's corps, was with me looking at the position when these notes were received, and we discussed them together. Wright said, "It is not so hard to go there as it looks; I was nearly there with my brigade yesterday. The trouble is to stay there. The whole Yankee army is there in a bunch."

I was influenced by this, and somewhat by a sort of camp rumor which I had heard that morning, that General Lee had said that he was going to send every man he had upon that hill. At any rate, I assumed that the question of supports had been well considered, and that whatever was possible would be done. But before replying I rode to see Pickett, who was with his division a short distance in the rear. I did not tell him my object, but only tried to guess how he felt about the charge. He seemed very sanguine, and thought himself in luck to have the chance. Then I felt that I could not make any delay or let the attack suffer by any indecision on my part.

And, that General Longstreet might know my intention, I wrote him only this:

> *General: When our artillery fire is at its best, I shall order Pickett to charge.*

Then, getting a little more anxious, I decided to send for the nine howitzers and take them ahead of Pickett up nearly to musket range, instead of following close behind him as at first intended; so I sent a courier to bring them up in front of the infantry, but under cover of the wood. The courier could not find them. He was sent again, and only returned after our fire was opened, saying they were gone. I afterward learned that General Pendleton had sent for a part of them, and the others had moved to a neighboring hollow to get out of the line of the enemy's fire at one of Hill's batteries during the artillery duel they had had an hour before.

At exactly 1 o'clock by my watch the two signal-guns were heard in quick succession. In another minute every gun was at work. The enemy were not slow in coming back at us, and the grand roar of nearly the whole artillery of both armies burst in on the silence, almost as suddenly as the full notes of an organ would fill a church.

The artillery of Ewell's corps, however, took only a small part, I believe, in this, as they were too far away on the other side of the town. Some of them might have done good service from positions between Hill and Ewell, enfilading the batteries fighting us. The opportunity to do that was the single advantage in our having the exterior line, to compensate for all its disadvantages. But our line was so extended that all of it was not well studied, and the officers of the different corps had no opportunity to examine each other's ground for chances to cooperate.

The enemy's position seemed to have broken out with guns everywhere, and from Round Top to Cemetery Hill was blazing like a volcano. The air seemed full of missiles from every direction. The severity of the fire may be illustrated by the casualties in my own battalion under Major [Francis Kinloch] Huger.

Under my predecessor, General S[tephen] D[ill] Lee, the battalion had made a reputation at the Second Manassas and also at Sharpsburg. At the latter battle it had a peculiarly hard time fighting infantry and superior metal nearly all day, and losing about eighty-five men and sixty horses. Sharpsburg they called "artillery hell." At Gettysburg the losses in the same command, including the infantry that volunteered to help serve the guns, were 144 men and 116 horses, nearly all by artillery fire. Some parts of the Federal artillery suffered in the same proportion under our fire. I heard of one battery losing 27 out of 36 horses in 10 minutes.

Before the cannonade opened I had made up my mind to give Pickett the order to advance within fifteen or twenty minutes after it began. But when I looked at the full development of the enemy's batteries, and knew that his infantry was generally protected from our fire by stone walls . . . it seemed madness to launch infantry into that fire, with nearly three-quarters of a mile to go at midday under a July sun. I let the 15 minutes pass, and 20, and 25, hoping vainly for something to turn up.

Then I wrote to Pickett:

> *If you are coming at all you must come at once, or I cannot give you proper support; but the enemy's fire has not slackened at all; at least eighteen guns are still firing from the cemetery itself.*

Five minutes after sending that message, the enemy's fire suddenly began to slacken, and the guns in the cemetery limbered up and vacated the position.

We Confederates often did such things as that to save our ammunition for use against infantry, but I had never before seen the Federals withdraw their guns simply to save them up for the infantry fight. So I said, "If he does not run fresh batteries in there in five minutes, this is our fight." I looked anxiously with my glass, and the five minutes passed without a sign of life on the deserted position, still swept by our fire, and littered with dead men and horses and fragments of disabled carriages.

Then I wrote Pickett, urgently:

> *For God's sake, come quick. The eighteen guns are gone; come quick, or my ammunition won't let me support you properly.*

I afterward heard from others what took place with my first note to Pickett. Pickett took it to Longstreet, Longstreet read it, and said nothing. Pickett said, "General, shall I advance?" Longstreet, knowing it had to be, but unwilling to give the word, turned his face away. Pickett saluted and said, "I am going to move forward, sir," galloped off to his division and immediately put it in motion.

Longstreet, leaving his staff, came out alone to where I was. It was then about 1:40 p.m. I explained the situation, feeling then more hopeful, but afraid our artillery ammunition might not hold out for all we would want. Longstreet said, "Stop Pickett immediately and replenish your ammunition." I explained that it would take too long, and the enemy would recover from the effect our fire was then having, and we had, moreover, very little to replenish with. Longstreet said, "I don't want to make this attack. I would stop it now but that General Lee ordered it and expects it to go on. I don't see how it can succeed."

I listened, but did not dare offer a word. The battle was lost if we stopped. Ammunition was far too low to try anything else, for we had been fighting three days. There was a chance, and it was not my part to interfere. While Longstreet was still speaking, Pickett's division swept out of the wood and showed the full length of its gray ranks and shining bayonets, as grand a sight as ever a man looked on. Joining it on the left, Pettigrew stretched farther than I could see. General Dick Garnett, just out of the sick ambulance, and buttoned up in an old blue overcoat, riding at the head of his brigade passed us and saluted Longstreet. Garnett was a warm personal friend, and we had not met before for months. We had served on the plains together before the war. I rode with him a short distance, and then we wished each other luck and a good-bye, which was our last.

Then I rode down the line of guns, selecting such as had enough ammunition to follow Pickett's advance, and starting them after him as fast as possible. I got, I think, fifteen or eighteen in all, in a little while, and went with them. Meanwhile, the infantry had no sooner debouched on the plain than all the enemy's line, which had been nearly silent, broke out again with all its batteries. The eighteen guns were back in the cemetery, and a storm of shell began bursting over and among our infantry. All of our guns—silent as the infantry passed between them—reopened over their heads when the lines had got a couple of hundred yards away, but the enemy's artillery let us alone and fired only at the infantry. No one could have looked at that advance without feeling proud of it.

But, as our supporting guns advanced, we passed many poor, mangled victims left in its trampled wake. A terrific infantry fire was now opened upon Pickett, and a considerable force of the enemy moved out to attack the right flank of his line. We halted, unlimbered, and opened fire upon it.

Pickett's men never halted, but opened fire at close range, swarmed over the fences and among the enemy's guns—were swallowed up in smoke, and that was the last of them. The conflict hardly seemed to last five minutes before they were melted away, and only disorganized stragglers pursued by a moderate fire were coming back. Just then, [Cadmus Marcellus] Wilcox's brigade passed by us, moving to Pickett's support. There was no longer anything to support, and with the keenest pity at the useless waste of life, I saw them advance. The men, as they passed us, looked bewildered, as if they wondered what they were expected to do, or why they were there. However, they were soon halted and moved back. They suffered some losses, and we had a few casualties from canister sent at them at rather long range.

From the position of our guns the sight of this conflict was grand and thrilling, and we watched it as men with a life-and-death interest in the result. If it should be favorable to us, the war was nearly over; if against us, we each had the risks of many battles yet to go through. And the event culminated with fearful rapidity. Listening to the rolling crashes of musketry, it was hard to realize that they were made up of single reports, and that each musket-shot represented nearly a minute of a man's life in that storm of lead and iron. It seemed as if 100,000 men were engaged, and that human life was being poured out like water. As soon as it appeared that the assault had failed, we ceased firing in order to save ammunition in case the enemy should advance. But we held our ground as boldly as possible, though we were entirely without support, and very low in ammunition. The enemy gave us an occasional shot for a while and then, to our great relief, let us rest. About that time General Lee, entirely alone, rode up and remained with me for a long time. He then probably first appreciated the full extent of the disaster as the disorganized stragglers made their way back past us . . . It was certainly a momentous thing to him to see that superb attack end in such a bloody repulse. But, whatever his emotions, there was no trace of them in his calm and self-possessed bearing. I thought at the time his coming there very imprudent, and the absence of all his staff-officers and couriers strange. It could only have happened by his express intention. I have since thought it possible that he came, thinking the enemy might follow in pursuit of Pickett, personally to rally stragglers about our guns and make a desperate defense . . .

Samuel Roberts [Co. A, 72nd Pennsylvania], "The 72d Pa.—The Trying March from Falmouth to Gettysburg," *National Tribune* (September 1, 1887)

The morning of the 3d of July passed without anything of a disturbing character, so far as our regiment was concerned. The 106th Pa., except two companies which were on the skirmish line, had been ordered to support Ricketts's battery on Cemetery Hill. The angle occupied by the [Philadelphia] brigade was formed by two stone walls not over 30 inches in height, the west wall facing the Emmittsburg road, 60 yards in length, the north wall running at right angles with the west wall, also 60 yards long. North from the latter a ridge and wall extended to the rear of the west wall. A clump of saplings, not over 30 paces in depth, stood out in relief from the ridge and afforded a most excellent target for the concentrated fire of the enemy's artillery. The left of the west wall was occupied by the 69th Pa., two companies of the 71st being on its right, and the remaining eight companies to the right and rear, behind the wall running north. The 72d Pa. was to the left and rear of the 69th. [Lieut. Alonzo Hereford] Cushing's battery occupied the space embraced in the angle.

The morning hours passed with a quiet that was prophetic of A COMING STORM. Now and then could be heard the crack of a rifle or the distant boom of a gun. Gen. Webb had placed Capt. [Edward B.] Whitacar, of the 72[d] Pa., in command of 40 men, with instructions to cover the rear of the brigade and not to allow anyone to pass to the rear unless wounded. The men were lying upon the ground, some screening themselves from the scorching rays of the sun with shelter tents, wondering what would be the next move. The writer, who was sitting on one end of a rail fence which rested upon the ground, was passively listening to some jesting remarks about some girls in Philadelphia, made by a Sergeant, who was sitting upon the other end of the rails.

It was 1 o'clock when the whiz of a shell, which struck the Sergeant in the breast, was followed by A STREAM OF FIRE from 125 guns on Seminary Ridge, directed at the small clump of trees in the rear of the 69th . . . The fire of the enemy was . . . terrible on account of its duration, lasting two hours. Cushing's battery having been disabled and the larger part of the men killed or wounded, Capt. Cushing advanced toward Gen. Webb, his pants torn by a piece of shell that had wounded him, and in the most nonchalant manner said:

"General, if I had some more men I could work my guns."

Webb replied: "Some of the men here will work your guns."

Men from the 71st Pa., who were near the guns, handled them until after the enemy had crossed the Emmittsburg road.

In the meantime Gen. Webb ordered Adj't [Charles Henry] Banes of his staff to bring up two batteries. He immediately arose from the ground, went to the rear about 100 paces, untied his horse from a sapling, mounted, and under a cloud of bursting shells succeeded in bringing up [Capt. Andrew] Cowan's 1st N.Y. battery. The men of our regiment moved to the right and left to give passage to the battery, which unlimbered a few paces in our front, and was immediately in action and did most excellent service.

About 3 o'clock p.m. we noticed lines of infantry emerging from the woods on Seminary Ridge, preparing for an assault. Our skirmishers, who were some distance in front of the Emmittsburg road, looking to the rear, believed that our main line HAD BEEN DRIVEN BACK or destroyed under the terrible fire of the enemy's artillery; therefore it is not surprising that the enemy labored under the same impression, and advanced with the assurance of success. Our artillery having ceased firing, another false impression was made upon the enemy, who believed they had silenced our guns.

On moved this living tide of Southern chivalry—Pickett's Division of

Virginians in the center, supported on his right by Wilcox and on his left by Pettigrew. The line of Pickett was left-oblique.

Our skirmishers fell back, having to cross two fences that lined the Emmittsburg road. In doing so many were killed or wounded. Our batteries, hitherto silent, were making terrible havoc in the advancing line; but undismayed, Pickett's men pressed forward to the clump of trees, which was the objective of the enemy's artillery. Two brigades to the left and one to the right of [Nicholas] Codori's house crossed the two fences on the Emmittsburg road. Their alignment was disturbed not only by the impediment offered by the fences, but by the terrible fire from the Second Division of the Second Corps.

Pettigrew's Division had moved forward on the left of Pickett, and many of his men had advanced within a few paces of the 12th N.J. of the Second Brigade, [Brigadier-General Alexander] Hays's Division, on our right. The head of the line, wedge-shaped, approached the stone wall, firing as it advanced. The 69th and 71st Pa. replied, loading and firing at will. The artillery had ceased firing. Cushing had fallen, shot through the face. The two companies of the 71st on the right of the 69th had been forced to change position to the rear, over the open spaces on the right of the 69th. Armistead led his men, and the stone wall was passed. The 72d Pa., which was to the left and rear of the 69th, moved by a right-flank right-oblique toward the north stone wall. Coming to a front under fire, about 60 paces from the front wall, upward of 70 of our men fell, killed or wounded.

Rapid firing at close range now took place. Armistead had fallen a few paces to the right and rear of the right company of the 69th. The Confederates who had crossed the wall with him fell back behind it, and used it as a breastwork, with their colors placed on the wall.

[William] Finecy, our Color-Sergeant, had fallen, pierced by several balls. [Francis P.] O'Donnell, [Frederick L.] Mannes, [John W.] Brown, [John] Steptoe and [Adon Gibbs] Wills, of the Color-Guard, each in succession was compelled to RELINQUISH THE COLORS after being severely wounded—Wills and Steptoe mortally. The staff had been severed by a ball a few inches below the joining of the colors.

The order was now given to charge. [Thomas] Murphy, the last of the Color-Guard—afterward shot through the breast at the Wilderness—seized the colors by the remnant of the staff, and swinging his

hat around his head and whirling around, joined the regiment in a dash toward the wall.

In a few minutes the fight was ended. Capt. [Alexander] McCuen captured a stand of colors. Two others were taken, torn from their shafts, and retained by the captors. From the time the regiment moved by the flank until it reached the stone wall, out of 360 men 192 fell killed or wounded. Col. [DeWitt Clinton] Baxter had been wounded the previous day. Capts. Jas. Griffiths and Andrew McBride, and Lieut. Sutton Jones were killed. Capts. [John] Lockhart, [Henry A.] Cook and [Richard L.R.] Shreeve, and Lieuts. [Robert] Stewart, [Frederick] Boland and [Bethuel M.] Healing [or Heulings] were severely wounded . . .

Henry Eyster Jacobs, *Lincoln's Gettysburg World-Message* (Philadelphia, 1919)

At precisely 1.07 p.m. the signal gun sounded; then came a second; and then a terrific crash. For over an hour, from north, northwest and southwest, the Confederate batteries concentrated their fire on the Federal left center. The Federal guns joined in "the diapason of the cannonade." Such a symphony never had been heard before. My father [Rev'd Michael Jacobs] quoted Rev. 10:4, "Seven thunders uttered their voices." It was not one confused uproar; but each gun had its individuality, and the explosions were distinguishable. There was first the discharge of the gun; then the scream of the shell rushing through the air, and then the report as it burst, carrying destruction and death in its pathway, breaking down walls or tearing horrid trenches in the ground. The two sides were also capable of recognition. An elderly lady sitting near us kept count of each shot with the words, "Ours," "theirs," "ours," "theirs." A great gun at the cemetery led the weird chorus. When it would rest to cool, the question was involuntary, "Silenced?"; and then again the tense strain would be relieved as its deep, gruff voice would once more wake the echoes.

But after awhile the Federal guns begin to slacken. We fear the worst. But, no. They are at it once more. But the intervals become longer. The chorus fades out. Slowly, more slowly, still more slowly. At last all have ceased. But the silence that ensues is portentous. There seems to be such art in it as to justify the inference that an important move is about to be executed.

My father, hastening to the garret, turns his glass on the Confederate right. He sees, on Seminary Ridge, a long line of men forming, supported by another; and, at last, their onward march, in magnificent array, toward the Federal line. He watches its steady advance until it is hidden by intervening buildings. Then comes the sound of artillery and the crash of smaller arms. The din is resumed, but the tone is not so loud. It is not long until, through the wrecked cornfield, stragglers are seen almost stealthily returning, a single battleflag, a few hundred men, several mounted officers. I was called to share the sight.

This was the famous charge of Pickett . . .

Charles D. Page, *History of the Fourteenth Regiment, Connecticut Vol. Infantry* (Meriden: Horton Printing, 1906)

Major [William B.] Hincks gives the experience of the regiment: "At about one o'clock there burst upon us most unexpectedly the heaviest cannonade I had ever witnessed . . . We advanced with one impulse for a few paces and lay down just behind the First Delaware men, who had taken our places at the wall. By the good providence of God, the enemy's guns were pointed so that the shot mainly cleared us and went over the crest of the hill into the valley beyond . . . The wall, being built on a ledge of rock, took those shot that fell short and bounded off instead of burying themselves in the ground beneath us and then exploding, tearing in pieces those lying above, as I knew them to do in the grove further to our right. I mention these things to account for the singularly little damage we sustained from its terrific fire . . . The smoke . . . so very thick was it that the sun seemed blotted out. One of the guns was directly behind me and at every discharge, the concussion would throw gravel over me and I could not only see and smell the thick cloud of burning powder, but could taste it also . . ."

Carlton McCarthy, *Detailed Minutiae of Soldier Life in the Army of Northern Virginia, 1861-1865* (Richmond, 1882)

At Gettysburg, when the artillery fire was at its height, a brawny fellow, who seemed happy at the prospect for a hot time, broke out singing:

> *Backward, roll backward, O Time in thy flight:*
> *Make me a child again, just for this fight!*

Another fellow near him replied, "Yes; and a *gal* child at that."

John D.S. Cook [80th New York], "Personal Reminiscences of Gettysburg" (December 12, 1903), *War Talks in Kansas: A Series of Papers Read Before the Kansas Commandery of the Military Order of the Loyal Legion of the United States* (Kansas City, MO, 1906)

General Lee had determined to break our army in two by an attack upon the left center, and massed nearly all his artillery in front of our position to clear the ground for this attack. Between twelve and one o'clock nearly or quite two hundred guns opened their fire upon us and from that time until about four a continuous storm of missiles of every kind poured in upon and over our heads, and the "shriek of shot, the scream of shell," and the sounds of exploding missiles seemed incessant. We hugged the ground behind the low pile of rails which partly concealed us, and awaited our destiny with such composure as we could muster. Again and again a shot struck one of these rails and knocked it around to kill or cripple men lying behind it. Again and again pieces of exploded shells would hit someone in the line with disabling or fatal effect. There was no getting away. To retreat would have been disgrace, and even had we wished it, a retreat would have to be made under the guns of the enemy and almost as dangerous as to remain where we were. Our artillery replied for a while, it seemed to us ineffectually, and the reply fire gradually slackened and nearly ceased.

I recall two incidents of that bombardment. A short distance behind and to my left lay a soldier with head towards the front. The peculiar swish of a solid round shot passed. The ball struck the ground almost at his head and rebounded, carrying with it his cap twenty feet into the air. As it rebounded he gave a curiously awkward "flop" and whirled almost end for end. It was so queer and so awkward that the men near him laughed heartily at what seemed a ridiculous attempt to dodge a shot after it had struck. But he lay perfectly still and some of us went up to investigate. He was found apparently uninjured, but quite dead. I have often heard it said that a man can be killed by the wind of a cannon-ball, but never witnessed it but this once, and even in this case the man may have been killed by the violence with which he was flung around.

The other incident was less tragic. While the storm was at its height General [John] Gibbon, of the Second Corps, in full uniform, with folded arms and in cool dignity walked up and down in front of the line, apparently indifferent to the rain of shot and shell that hurtled around him . . . He wished by an example of indifference to the danger to relieve the mental tension of the soldiers, a tension that might easily degenerate into a panic. I thought as I saw him that the force of his example might be lost and it even prove disheartening if, as seemed probable, he should be struck down while teaching us to despise the danger. Fortunately for him and perhaps for the men, nothing of the kind happened and he paraded slowly back and forth along the line several times, uninjured and admired.

About four o'clock this fire slackened and almost ceased. Then its purpose was disclosed. In front of our position appeared a long line of infantry covered in front by a lighter line of skirmishers advancing in admirable order directly toward us. Of course we began to fire upon them and their skirmishers returned the fire. No one who saw them could help admiring the steadiness with which they came on, like the shadow of a cloud seen from a distance as it sweeps across a sunny field.

As it approached the line slightly changed direction by what is known in ancient tactics as "advancing the right shoulder." This brought its course a little to the right of where we stood. Colonel [Theodore] Gates gave an order to march by the right flank, and the two regiments moved along the front of the Second Corps towards the point of danger, firing as they went.

One reckless fellow rested the muzzle of his gun on my left shoulder and banged away. The report, not six inches from my ear, made me jump, and as I turned to blow up the offender I was overwhelmed by the laughter of the men at the start it had given me. It was more funny for them than for myself.

As our troops rose up to meet them their artillery again opened fire to cover their advance, and the rain of cannon-shot, the fire of the advancing line, the rush of the enemy to break through, and the eager efforts of our men to stop them made a scene of indescribable excitement. Suddenly I felt a blow on the outside of my leg, a little below the hip. For the moment I thought the leg was broken. I stopped, stepped aside, and let down my trousers to see how I was hit. It was a glancing shot, which gave a severe bruise, but had not broken the skin, and I turned and followed the command. By this time the enemy, or what was left of them, had reached our men, and the struggle was hand-to-hand.

A curious thing about this fighting was, that although all the men were armed with bayonets, no one seemed to be using them. Those nearest clubbed their muskets and beat each other over the head, while those not so close kept loading and firing as fast as they could.

A few minutes ended the fray. The charge had failed and the foe turned to retreat. But as the ground over which they had come was swept by our fire, most of those near our line sank to the ground and gave up the attempt to get away.

Our men shouted to them to come in and promised not to hurt them, and at the word hundreds rose up and came into our lines, dropping their arms and crouching to avoid the fire of their own artillery, which was pouring upon our position. I recall one instance. A short distance in front was a clump of bushes among which appeared a white cloth. At first I thought it a rag caught in the brush, but it soon appeared that someone was waving it as a signal. Our boys shouted, "Come in, Johnnie; come in, we won't hurt you," and from behind the bush nearly or quite a dozen men arose and came hurrying and dodging into our line. A line of skirmishers was thrown out to the front, and most of those who had not got away were thus enclosed and captured.

The fire upon us soon died away and we had leisure to look about us. The ground near and in front of us was almost literally covered with killed and wounded.

Just in front of us and not twenty yards away lay a group of Confederate officers, four or five in number, all dead but one, and he stretched across the body of another, gasping his last breath. As soon as he was dead some of our men went to see who they were. The one across whose body the other had died wore the uniform of a colonel, and one of the men found upon him a map of Virginia with a diary of the marches his command had made, and gave it to our colonel. His sword and scabbard were shot to pieces, but one of our sergeants detached his belt and gave it to me, and I occasionally wore it during my service and still have it. It has a curiously formed buckle, showing when clasped the arms of Old Virginia, with the motto "*Sic semper tyrannis*," afterwards made so fatally notorious by [John] Wilkes Booth.*

Soon afterward we detected a Confederate officer trying to get away. He was wounded and could hardly get along. Our men called to him to halt, and he looked back and saw several muskets pointed at him. The view was not encouraging and he surrendered. He was shot in the hip, and our colonel directed me take him to a hospital, and at the same time see if my own injury needed attention. I found a field hospital about a quarter of a mile to the rear, where I turned over the prisoner with injunctions to the attendants to see that he did not get away. The doctor examined my leg, which was badly swollen and discolored, but as I could get about on it,

---

* Since writing these "Reminiscences" I visited Washington on October 1, 1903, for the first time since the war. I there met Hon. John W. Daniel, of Virginia, and in conversation with him about the battle mentioned the fact that I had this belt, which had belonged to Colonel James Gregory Hodges, 14th Virginia Volunteers, and would be glad to give it to some surviving member of his family. Senator Daniel took great interest in the matter, and upon inquiry ascertained that the widow of Colonel Hodges still survived, and put me in communication with her. I have had the satisfaction of being able to send her this relic of her husband and of receiving a greatly prized letter from her in acknowledgment of its return.

and he had nothing there suitable to relieve a contusion, I did not think it worthwhile to bother with it and returned to the regiment.

My return led me past the house where General Meade had established headquarters. He rode up with his staff as I came along. I heard him inquiring about the report that General Longstreet had been killed, and told him I had just come from the front with a captured officer of Pickett's division and that the report was current that General Longstreet had been killed under one of our guns at the head of the charge. He doubted whether the report could be true, and remarked that, "Any army must be in a desperate condition when a corps commander led a charge like that." His instinct was right. The charge was led by a general officer, who fell at our guns and died in a few minutes. Before he died he gave his name as General Armistead. Some of the men near him thought he said "Longstreet" and the report quickly spread that the famous corps commander had fallen. It was this mistaken report which I had heard and repeated to General Meade, who readily showed its improbability.

Franklin Sawyer, *A Military History of the 8th Regiment Ohio Volunteer Infantry, Its Battles, Marches and Army Movements* (Cleveland, 1881)

Nothing more terrific than this storm of artillery can be imagined. The missiles of both armies passed over our heads. . The roar of the guns was deafening, the air was soon clouded with smoke, and the shriek and startling crack of exploding shell above, around, and in our midst; the blowing up of our caissons in our rear; the driving through the air of fence-rails, posts, and limbs of trees; the groans of dying men, the neighing of frantic and wounded horses, created a scene of absolute horror. Our line of skirmishers was kept out to watch any advance; but the rest of the men kept well down in the cut of the road. Here for nearly two hours we sat stock still, and not a word was uttered. Only two of the men were killed during the cannonade, and they were literally cut in two. Capt. [James E.] GREGG, who was then serving on Col. [Samuel Sprigg] CARROLL's Staff as Inspector, had come down just before the fire opened to see how we were getting along, and not being able to return, sat down on a rail with the writer, facing towards the enemy. Presently a solid shot tore through a pile of rails in our front, passed under our seat between us, and bounded away to our rear. The ricochet of round shot in our vicinity was quite frequent as well as the fragments of shells that exploded in the air.

Finally the artillery ceased firing, and all knew that an assault was the next movement. Soon we saw the long line of rebel infantry emerge from the woods along the rebel front, that had hitherto concealed them.

These troops were the division of PICKET, followed by that of PETIGREW. They moved up splendidly, deploying into column as they crossed the long, sloping interval between the Second Corps and their base. At first it looked as if their line of march would sweep our position, but as they advanced their direction lay considerably to our left, but soon a strong line, with flags, directed its march immediately upon us.

I formed . . . a single line, and as the rebels came within short range of our skirmish line, charged them. Some fell, some run back, most of them, however, threw down their arms and were made prisoners. In this maneuver among the killed was Lieut. [Elijah] HAYDEN, Co. H. We changed our front, and taking position by a fence, facing the left flank of the advancing column of rebels, the men were ordered to fire into their flank at will. Hardly a musket had been fired at this time. The front of the column was nearly up the slope, and within a few yards of the line of the Second Corps' front and its batteries, when suddenly a terrific fire from every available gun, from the Cemetery to Round Top Mountain, burst upon them. The distinct, graceful lines of the rebels underwent an instantaneous transformation. They were at once enveloped in a dense cloud of smoke and dust. Arms, heads, blankets, guns and knapsacks were thrown and tossed into the clear air. Their track, as they advanced, was strewn with dead and wounded. A moan went up from the field,

distinctly to be heard amid the storm of battle, but on they went, too much enveloped in smoke and dust now to permit us to distinguish their lines or movements, for the mass appeared more like a cloud of moving smoke and dust than a column of troops. Still it advanced amid the now deafening roar of artillery and storm of battle.

Suddenly the column gave way, the sloping landscape appeared covered, all at once, with the scattered and retreating foe. A withering sheet of missiles swept after them, and they were torn and tossed and prostrated as they ran. It seemed as if not one would escape. Of the mounted officers who rode so grandly in the advance not one was to be seen on the field, all had gone down. The Eighth advanced and cut off three regiments, or remnants of regiments, as they passed us, taking their colors, and capturing many prisoners. The colors captured were those of the Thirty-fourth North Carolina, Thirty-eighth Virginia, and one that was taken from the captor, Sergt. [Daniel] Miller, Co. G, by a staff officer, the number of the regiment not being remembered.

The battle was now over. The field was covered with the slain and wounded, and everywhere were to be seen white handkerchiefs held up asking for quarter. The rebel loss had been terrible, the victory to the Union army complete.

Joseph Ripley Chandler Ward, *History of the One Hundred and Sixth Regiment, Pennsylvania Volunteers* (Philadelphia, 1906)

Meanwhile the enemy had advanced to the fence occupied by the Sixty-Ninth and left of the Seventy-First [Pennsylvania], and, passing to the right of the latter, had taken it in flank and captured or forced back the right of the Sixty-Ninth and two connecting companies of the Seventy-First. General Armistead, with hat on sword, leaps the fence followed by six color bearers with their flags and about one hundred and fifty to two hundred men. At this juncture General Webb calls on his reserve (the Seventy-Second and the detachment of the One Hundred and Sixth) and leads them forward in person to close the gap in the line through which Armistead and his followers are pouring. Glorious leader! His handsome, manly form towered for a moment a central figure between the two lines, as with sword in one hand and hat in the other his order

of "forward to the wall!" rang out cheerily and strong above the noise of battle. If he should fall, Gettysburg is lost. Wounded, he still keeps his feet. His indomitable spirit is communicated to and inspires the men of the Seventy-Second and One Hundred and Sixth. They sweep forward to the fence over Armistead's prostrate body—treading underfoot the rebel standards, whose bearers have fallen beside their leader—the thousands who have reached the fence throw down their arms, and Gettysburg is won!

Frederick Fuger, "Cushing's Battery at Gettysburg," *Journal of the Military Service Institution of the United States* 40 (November-December 1907)

The morning of July 3, 1863, was quiet until about 8 o'clock a.m., when the enemy suddenly opened fire upon our position, exploding three limbers of our battery [Battery A, 4th U.S. Artillery] . . .

General [Henry Jackson] Hunt, Lieutenant Cushing and myself were standing about four yards in rear of No. 3 limber when this explosion took place. General Hunt marked out to me at that time on a piece of paper the direction I should take to get to the ammunition train, but on the explosion we immediately scattered and the general disappeared. The first limber was struck, which caused the second and third limbers' explosion. To our surprise not a single man or horse was injured, although three men were in the rear of each limber getting ready for firing. Drivers being dismounted, the horses ran away, but were stopped by some of our infantry; the wheel horses had their tails singed.

When the Confederates saw this explosion they immediately jumped up and gave an immense yell; we, however, replied to their fire and within a few minutes after an explosion took place in their line, when our men jumped up and returned the compliment.

The firing lasted about thirty minutes, and up to 11 o'clock a.m., we engaged the enemy's artillery three or four times, lasting a few minutes each time; no casualties.

From 11 a.m. to 1 p.m. there was a perfect lull, each party apparently waiting to see what the other was about to do, and at what point the attack was to be made.

About 1 o'clock p.m., the enemy opened upon us with about 150 guns; the Union artillery responded with about 100 guns, occupying a front of about one mile.

Of this bombardment I can only say it was the most terrific cannonade I ever witnessed, in fact, the most terrible the new world has ever seen, and the most prolonged. The earth shook beneath our very feet, and the hills and woods seemed to reel like a drunken man. For one hour and a half this terrific firing was continued, during which time the shrieking of shells, the fragments of rocks flying through the air . . . the splash of bursting shells and shrapnel, and the fierce neighing of wounded artillery-horses, made a picture terribly grand and sublime. About 2.30 p.m. the order "cease firing" was given; this was followed by cessation of the enemy's fire.

In this engagement all our ammunition was expended excepting canister. Shortly after the artillery firing ceased, the Confederate infantry advanced slowly but surely, namely, General Pickett's Division, three brigades, Garnett's, Kemper's and Armistead's.

I will have to say that when our artillery ceased firing Gen. Alex[ander] S[tewart] Webb came up to where Cushing was standing and said to him, "Cushing, it is my opinion that the Confederate infantry will now advance and attack our position." Cushing then said, "I had better run my guns right up to the stone fence and bring all my canister alongside of each piece." General Webb replied, "All right, do so."

Lieutenant Cushing ordered me to run the guns by hand to the stone fence, which was done at once, leaving room enough for Nos. 1 and 2 to work. All the canister was piled up in rear of No. 2; in doing this we were obliged to take a closer interval, say about nine yards, owing to some obstructions toward our left, and on our right were two stone fences at right angles with each other (now called "The Bloody Angle"). As said before, the Confederate infantry advanced, marching in close order with measured steps, as though on parade; it moved forward deliberately, solidly.

When the enemy was within about 400 yards Battery A opened with single charges of canister. At that time Cushing was wounded in the right shoulder, and within a few seconds after that he was wounded in the testicles—a very severe and painful wound.

He called me and told me to stand by him so that I could impart his orders to the battery; he became very ill and suffered frightfully. I wanted him to go to the rear. "No," he said, "I stay right here and fight it out or die in the attempt." When the enemy got within 200 yards double and treble charges of canister were used; those charges opened immense gaps in the Confederate lines. Lieutenant [Joseph] Milne, who commanded the right half battery, was killed when the enemy was within 200 yards of the battery. When the enemy came within about 100 yards from the battery Lieutenant Cushing was shot through the mouth and instantly killed.

When I saw him fall forward I caught him with my arms, ordered two men to take his body to the rear; that placed me in command of the battery and I shouted to my men to obey my command and fire treble charges of canister; but still the Confederates came on. Owing to the dense smoke

I could not see very far to the front, but to my utter astonishment I saw General Armistead leap over the stone fence with quite a number of his men (landing right in the midst of our battery), but my devoted cannoneers and drivers stood their ground, fighting hand-to-hand with pistols, sabers, handspikes and rammers, and with the arrival of the Philadelphia Brigade, commanded by the gallant General Webb, the enemy collapsed and Pickett's charge was defeated.

I want to say here that we had about twenty-eight handspikes, which were all brought up to the guns; those handspikes are the finest weapons for close contact.

General Armistead fell, mortally wounded, where I stood, about seven yards from where Lieutenant Cushing, his young and gallant adversary, was killed.

From my observation I am sure that none of those men who came over the stone fence with General Armistead ever escaped; they were either killed, wounded or captured.

I have been informed by several of my men (their names I cannot now recall) a short time after all was over, that they counted nearly 600 dead Confederates in front of our battery.

The loss in Battery A was very great. Out of ninety horses we lost eighty-three killed; not a sound wheel was left, nine ammunition chests blown up, two officers killed, one officer wounded, seven enlisted men killed, thirty-eight enlisted men wounded.

Arthur James Fremantle, "The Battle of Gettysburg and the Campaign in Pennsylvania. Extract from the Diary of an English Officer Present With the Confederate Army," *Blackwood's Edinburgh Magazine* 94 (September 1863)

When I got close up to General Longstreet . . . I remarked to the General that *"I wouldn't have missed this for anything."* Longstreet was seated at the top of a snake fence at the edge of the wood, and looking perfectly calm and imperturbed. He replied, laughing, *"The devil you wouldn't! I would like to have missed it very much; we've attacked and been repulsed: look there!"*

For the first time I then had a view of the open space between the two positions, and saw it covered with Confederates slowly and sulkily returning towards us in small broken parties, under a heavy fire of artillery . . . The General told me that Pickett's division had succeeded in carrying the enemy's position and capturing his guns, but after remaining there twenty minutes, it had been forced to retire, on the retreat of Heth and Pettigrew on its left. No person could have been more calm or self-possessed than General Longstreet under these trying circumstances, aggravated as they now were by the movements of the enemy, who began to show a strong disposition to advance . . . I remember seeing a General (Pettigrew, I think it was) come up to him, and report that "he was unable to bring his men up again." Longstreet turned upon him and replied with some sarcasm, "Very well; never mind, then, General; just let them remain where they are: the enemy's going to advance, and will spare you the trouble." . . .

If Longstreet's conduct was admirable, that of General Lee was perfectly sublime. He was engaged in rallying and in encouraging the broken troops, and was riding about a little in front of the wood, quite alone—the whole of his Staff being engaged in a similar manner further to the rear. His face, which is always placid and cheerful, did not show signs of the slightest disappointment, care, or annoyance; and he was addressing to every soldier he met a few words of encouragement, such as, "All this will come right in the end: we'll talk it over afterwards; but, in the mean time, all good men must rally. We want all good and true men just now," &c. He spoke to all the wounded men that passed him, and the slightly wounded he exhorted "to bind up their hurts and take up a musket" in this emergency. Very few failed to answer his appeal, and I saw many badly wounded men take off their hats and cheer him.

He said to me, "This has been a sad day for us, Colonel—a sad day; but we can't expect always to gain victories." . . .

Notwithstanding the misfortune which had so suddenly befallen him, General Lee seemed to observe everything, however trivial. When a mounted officer began licking his horse for shying at the bursting of a shell, he called out, "Don't whip him, Captain; don't whip him. I've got just such another foolish horse myself, and whipping does no good." . . .

I saw General [Cadmus Marcellus] Willcox (an officer who wears a short round jacket and a battered straw hat) come up to him, and explain, almost crying, the state of his brigade. General Lee immediately shook hands with him and said, cheerfully, "Never mind, General, *all this has been* MY *fault*—it is *I* that have lost this fight, and you must help me out of it in the best way you can." In this manner I saw General Lee encourage and reanimate his somewhat dispirited troops, and magnanimously take upon his own shoulders the whole weight of the repulse. It was impossible to look at him or to listen to him without feeling the strongest admiration.

James Harvey Kidd, *Personal Recollections of a Cavalryman with Custer's Michigan Cavalry Brigade in the Civil War* (Ionia, MI, 1908)

The troopers were dismounted, standing "in place rest" in front of their horses, when suddenly there burst upon the air the sound of that terrific cannonading that preceded Pickett's charge. The earth quaked. The tremendous volume of sound volleyed and rolled across the intervening hills like reverberating thunder in a storm.

It was then between one and two o'clock . . . General Custer directed Colonel [Russell Alexander] Alger to advance and engage the enemy. The Fifth Michigan, its flanks protected by a portion of the Sixth Michigan on the left, by [Colonel John Baillie] McIntosh's brigade on the right, moved briskly forward towards the wooded screen behind which the enemy was known to be concealed . . .

As the Fifth Michigan advanced from field to field and fence to fence, a line of gray came out from behind the [John] Rummel buildings and the woods beyond. A stubborn and spirited contest ensued. The opposing batteries filled the air with shot and shrieking shell. Amazing marksmanship was shown by [Lieutenant Alexander C.M.] Pennington's battery [Battery

M, 2nd U.S. Artillery], and such accurate artillery firing was never seen on any other field. Alger's men with their eight-shotted [Spencer] carbines forced their adversaries slowly but surely back, the gray line fighting well and superior in numbers, but unable to withstand the storm of bullets. It made a final stand behind the strong line of fences, in front of Rummel's and a few hundred yards out from the foot of the slope wherein, concealed by the woods, Stuart's reserves were posted . . .

Repeating rifles are not only effective but wasteful weapons as well, and Colonel Alger, finding that his ammunition had given out, felt compelled to retire his regiment and seek his horses. Seeing this, the enemy sprang forward with a yell. The Union line was seen to yield . . . On from field to field, the line of gray followed in exultant pursuit . . . Shells dropped and exploded among the skirmishers, while thicker and faster they fell around the position of the reserves. Pennington replied with astonishing effect, for every shot hit the mark, and the opposing artillerists were unable to silence a single union gun. But still they came, until it seemed that nothing could stop their victorious career . . .

Just then, a column of mounted men was seen advancing from the right and rear of the union line. Squadron succeeded squadron until an entire regiment came into view, with sabers gleaming and colors gaily fluttering in the breeze. It was the Seventh Michigan . . . As the regiment moved forward, and cleared the battery, Custer drew his saber, placed himself in front and shouted: "Come on you Wolverines!" . . . Custer led the charge half way across the plain, then turned to the left; but the gallant regiment swept on under its own leaders, riding down and capturing many prisoners.

There was no check to the charge. The squadrons kept on in good form. Every man yelled at the top of his voice until the regiment had gone, perhaps, five or six hundred yards straight towards the Confederate batteries, when the head of column was deflected to the left, making a quarter turn, and the regiment was hurled headlong against a post-and-rail fence that ran obliquely in front of the Rummel buildings. This proved for the time an impassable barrier. The squadrons coming up successively at a charge, rushed pell-mell on each other and were thrown into a state of indescribable confusion, though the rear troops, without order or orders, formed left and right front into line along the fence, and pluckily began firing across it into the faces of the Confederates who, when they saw the impetuous onset of the Seventh thus abruptly checked, rallied and began to collect in swarms upon the opposite side.

Some of the officers leaped from their saddles and called upon the men to assist in making an opening . . . The task was a difficult and hazardous one, the posts and rails being so firmly united that it could be accomplished only by lifting the posts, which were deeply set, and removing several lengths at once . . . Through the passage-way thus effected, the Seventh moved forward, the center squadron leading, and resumed the charge. The Confederates once more fell back before it. The charge was continued across a plowed field to the front and right, up to and past Rummel's, to a point within 200 or 300 yards of the Confederate battery. There another fence was encountered, the last one in the way of reaching the battery, the guns of which were pouring canister into the charging column as fast as they could fire . . .

The scattered portions of the Seventh began to fall back through the opening in the fence . . . Alger who, when his ammunition gave out, hastened to his horses, had succeeded in mounting one battalion, commanded by Major L[uther] S[teven] Trowbridge, and when the Ninth and Thirteenth Virginia struck the flank of the Seventh Michigan, he ordered that officer to charge and meet this new danger. Trowbridge and his men dashed forward with a cheer, and the enemy in their turn were put to flight. Past the Rummel buildings, through the fields, almost to the fence where the most advanced of the Seventh Michigan had halted, Trowbridge kept on. But he, too, was obliged to retire before the destructive fire of the Confederate cannon . . .

Then, as it seemed, the two belligerent forces paused to get their second breath . . . But the wily Confederate had kept his two choicest brigades in reserve for the supreme moment, intending then to throw them into the contest and sweep the field with one grand, resistless charge . . . A body of mounted men began to emerge from the woods on the left of the Confederate line, northeast of the Rummel buildings, and form column to the right as they debouched into the open field. Squadron after squadron, regiment after regiment, orderly as if on parade, came into view, and successively took their places.

Then Pennington opened with all his guns. Six rifled pieces, as fast as they could fire, rained shot and shell into that fated column. The effect was deadly. Great gaps were torn in that mass of mounted men, but the rents were quickly closed . . . There were two brigades—eight regiments—under their own favorite leaders. In the van, floated a stand of colors. It was the battle-flag of Wade Hampton, who with Fitzhugh Lee was leading the assaulting column. In superb form, with sabers glistening, they advanced. The men on foot gave way to let them pass. It was an inspiring and an imposing spectacle, that brought a thrill to the hearts of the spectators on the opposite slope. Pennington double-shotted his guns with canister, and the head of the column staggered under each murderous discharge. But still it advanced, led on by an imperturbable spirit, that no storm of war could cow.

On and on, nearer and nearer, came the assaulting column, charging straight for [Alanson Merwin] Randol's battery [Batteries E & G, 1st U.S. Artillery]. The storm of canister caused them to waver a little, but that was all . . . Then [Brigadier-General David McMurtrie] Gregg rode over to the First Michigan, and directed [Colonel Charles H.] Town to charge. Custer dashed up with similar instructions, and as Town ordered sabers to be drawn, placed himself by his side, in front of the leading squadron.

With ranks well closed, with guidons flying and bugles sounding, the grand old regiment of veterans, led by Town and Custer, moved forward to meet that host, outnumbering it three to one. First at a trot, then the command to charge rang out, and with gleaming saber and flashing pistol, Town and his heroes were hurled right in the teeth of Hampton and Fitzhugh Lee. Alger, who with the Fifth had been waiting for the right moment, charged in on the right flank of the column as it passed, as did some of McIntosh's squadrons, on the left. One troop of the Seventh, led by Lieutenant Dan Littlefield, also joined in the charge.

Then it was steel to steel. For minutes—and for minutes that seemed like years—the gray column stood and staggered before the blow; then yielded and fled. Alger and McIntosh had pierced its flanks, but Town's impetuous charge in front went through it like a wedge, splitting it in twain, and scattering the confederate horsemen in disorderly rout back to the woods from whence they came.

During the last melee, the brazen lips of the cannon were dumb. It was a hand-to-hand encounter between the Michigan men and the flower of the southern cavaliers, led by their favorite commanders.

Stuart retreated to his stronghold, leaving the Union forces in possession of the field . . .

Almira Hancock, *Reminiscences of Winfield Scott Hancock* (New York, 1887)

[Before the war] a never-to-be-forgotten evening was the one spent at our home by the officers who were to start upon their overland trip to the South . . . Before leaving, the General [Albert Sidney Johnston] said to his wife [Eliza Croghan Griffin Johnston], "Come, sing me one or two of the old songs you used to sing, [Sidney Nelson's] 'Mary of Argyle,' and [Frederick N. Crouch's] 'Kathleen Mavourneen.'" She complied reluctantly in the presence of such an audience, saying, with deep emotion, that she felt as though her music days were over . . . The most crushed of the party was Major Armistead, who, with tears, which were contagious, streaming down his face, and hands upon Mr. Hancock's shoulders, while looking him steadily in the eye, said, "Hancock, good-by; you can never know what this has cost me, and I hope God will strike me dead if I am ever induced to leave my native soil, should worse come to worst." Turning to me, he placed a small satchel in my hand, requesting that it should not be opened except in the event of his death, in which case the souvenirs it contained, with the exception of a little prayer-book, intended for me, and which I still possess, should be sent to his family. On the fly-leaf of this book is the following: "Lewis A. Armistead. Trust in God and fear nothing." . . . I, as well as my husband, believed that he courted the death that finally came to him at Gettysburg . . . Three out of the six from whom we parted on that evening in Los Angeles were killed in front of General Hancock's troops, and others wounded.

THE RETREAT

Robert E. Lee recognized almost at once after the failure of the great attack on July 3rd that it was no longer possible to continue his invasion of Pennsylvania. The Army of Northern Virginia had sustained too many casualties in the battle, had consumed too much ammunition that it had no easy way of replenishing, and had suffered too great a shock to its morale. That night, he summoned Brigadier-General John Imboden, who commanded one of the three Confederate cavalry brigades which had stayed with Lee's army during the campaign, and put him in charge of organizing a withdrawal. The retreat would move westward, back over South Mountain, and finally to Williamsport, where the Confederates would recross the Potomac into Virginia. Jeb Stuart's other cavalry units would have the task of screening the retreat from prying Federal pursuers.

It would not be easy work, since the rebels would have the extra burden

of moving all their wounded and their Yankee prisoners, and the weather turned heavy and rain-swollen. Federal cavalry harassed the retreating rebel infantry at Monterey Pass and struck Lee's seventeen-mile-long wagon train at Greencastle; on July 6th, Stuart's cavalry would have to fight delaying actions at Hagerstown and Boonsboro. And when the Confederates finally reached Williamsport on July 7th, they found that the incessant rains had made the Potomac River unfordable. In a reminiscence of the retreat written two decades later for *The Century Illustrated Magazine*'s "Battle and Leaders of the Civil War" series, Imboden described the agonies suffered by Lee's army, emotionally and physically, as a descent into despair. Nevertheless, the rains finally slowed, and on the evening of July 13th, Lee and the Army of Northern Virginia were able to cross the Potomac.

Recriminations for the defeat began among the Confederates almost at once, with George Pickett blaming the failure of the July 3rd attack on Lee's decision to hold two of Pickett's brigades back in Virginia to guard Richmond. Still more fingers were pointed at Jeb Stuart and Ambrose Powell Hill, and (according to James Longstreet) even Lee was shaken with self-doubt. Their outlook would not be helped by news that would soon arrive of the surrender on July 4th of Vicksburg to Ulysses Grant. From that moment, Southern self-confidence in winning Confederate independence began to ebb away.

In the Army of the Potomac, the end of the battle set off immediate rejoicings, and George Meade issued a congratulatory order to his soldiers "for the glorious result of the recent operations" and urged them "to drive from our soil every vestige of the presence of the invader." But Meade was in no mood to drive them too aggressively. His army had also lost heavily in the battle, and Meade—who had only been in command for a week—was chary of treading too hard on the Confederates' heels. Gettysburg was the first victory Meade's army had earned in many months, and he was not eager to throw it away by egging the rebels into some kind of backlash. He called yet another council of war on the evening of July 4th, and gingerly took up pursuit with his infantry the next day, and did not descend upon the cornered Confederates at Williamsport until July 12th.

Abraham Lincoln saw Gettysburg as a golden opportunity to follow up and destroy Lee's army and the rebellion altogether, and he grew swiftly and increasingly frustrated at Meade's caution. He was especially jarred by Meade's willingness to talk about driving the rebels from "our soil," as though the conquest of the Confederacy itself was not within view. His frustration boiled over on July 14th, when he learned that Lee had seized a brief window of clear weather and the fall of the Potomac's flooding to slip across the river under cover of night and out of Meade's grasp. Meade learned of Lincoln's anger, and at once offered his resignation. Lincoln might have been willing to accept it, too, and when New York City erupted in riots over the new draft laws that were going into force, Lincoln and his cabinet were tempted to wonder if some vast anti-war conspiracy was at work to blunt Union success. But there was no practical way he would cashier the first commander of the Army of the Potomac to win a clear-cut victory. He wrote a sad, critical letter to Meade, but never sent it.

Meade, for his part, never doubted that his caution was fully justified. But that did not stop the eruption of recriminations on the Union side over the battle, which were almost as bitter as those of the Confederates. Acid-pen reporters, like Lorenzo Livingston Crounse, of *The New York Times*, celebrated the achievement of the Army of the Potomac, but lashed most of the civilians of Gettysburg as ungrateful cheats. Dan Sickles, who recovered from the amputation of his leg with extraordinary speed, spent his recuperation in Washington, DC, telling tales to his onetime fellow congressmen about the spinelessness of George Meade. Sure enough, when the Joint Committee on the Conduct of the War held hearings the following March, Meade was the target of hostile questioning from the committee and some embarrassing testimony from his subordinates about the feebleness of the pursuit to Williamsport. (Opinion in the ranks was even more severe: Soldiers sharply criticized Meade for not reaping "the harvest of martial glory" by attacking the cornered rebels and ending the war at one stroke.) And for the rest of his life, Meade would be dogged by whispered accusations that he had deliberately ignored advice—from Lincoln and his own corps commanders—to crush the Confederates at Williamsport.

The town of Gettysburg awoke on the morning after the battle to face an entirely unlooked-for future. As Union troops slowly reoccupied the town on July 4th, civilians came out of hiding, grateful to have been spared, and even some Union soldiers—chief among them an 11th Corps brigade commander, Alexander Schimmelfennig—emerged from cellars and lofts where they had escaped the confused fighting on the first day of the battle. Confederate officer prisoners were granted temporary paroles and mixed and mingled with the town's civilians, and in the case of one

Virginia lieutenant, James Crocker, renewed old acquaintances from his student days at Pennsylvania College.

Above all, there was a stupendous work of cleanup to be done. The battlefield was thickly littered with human and animal corpses (whose decomposition was already making the air almost unbreathable in the summer temperatures) and the detritus of battle: broken wagons, weapons, equipment, uniform pieces. Alexander Gardner, the famous protégé of the photographer Mathew Brady, would arrive to begin recording horrifying images of the torn battlefield, to be followed a week later by Brady himself. A vast military hospital was laid out east of the town—to take advantage of the rail line that ran into Gettysburg from nearby Hanover—and named Camp Letterman for the Army of the Potomac's medical director, Jonathan Letterman. By July 10th, the governor of Pennsylvania, Andrew Curtin, was in Gettysburg, and plans were begun that would convert Gettysburg into something approaching a shrine of the nation.

John Daniel Imboden, "Lee at Gettysburg," *The Galaxy* 11 (April 1871)

When night closed upon the grand scene our army was repulsed. Silence and gloom pervaded our camps. We knew that the day had gone against us, but the extent of the disaster was not known except in high quarters. The carnage of the day was reported to have been frightful, but our army was not in retreat, and we all surmised that with to-morrow's dawn would come a renewal of the struggle; and we knew that if such was the case those who had not been in the fight would have their full share in the honors and the dangers of the next day. All felt and appreciated the momentous consequences of final defeat or victory on that great field. These considerations made that, to us, one of those solemn and awful nights that everyone who fought through our long war sometimes experienced before a great battle.

Few camp fires enlivened the scene. It was a warm summer's night, and the weary soldiers were lying in groups on the luxuriant grass of the meadows we occupied, discussing the events of the day or watching that their horses did not straggle off in browsing around. About eleven o'clock a horseman approached and delivered a message from General Lee, that he wished to see me immediately. I mounted at once, and, accompanied by Lieutenant [George W.] McPhail of my staff, and guided by the courier, rode about two miles toward Gettysburg, where half a dozen small tents on the roadside were pointed out as General Lee's headquarters for the night. He was not there, but I was informed that I would find him with General A.P. Hill half a mile further on. On reaching the place indicated, a flickering, solitary candle, visible through the open front of a common tent, showed where Generals Lee and Hill were seated on camp stools, with a county map spread upon their knees, and engaged in a low and earnest conversation. They ceased speaking as I approached, and after the ordinary salutations General Lee directed me to go to his headquarters and wait for him. He did not return until about one o'clock, when he came riding alone at a slow walk and evidently wrapped in profound thought.

There was not even a sentinel on duty, and no one of his staff was about. The moon was high in the heavens, shedding a flood of soft silvery light, almost as bright as day, upon the scene. When he approached and saw us, he spoke, reined up his horse, and essayed to dismount. The effort to do so betrayed so much physical exhaustion that I stepped forward to assist him, but before I reached him he had alighted. He threw his arm across his saddle to rest himself, and fixing his eyes upon the ground leaned in silence upon his equally weary horse; the two forming a striking group, as motionless as a statue. The moon shone full upon his massive features, and revealed an expression of sadness I had never seen upon that fine countenance before, in any of the vicissitudes of the war through which he had passed. I waited for him to speak until the silence became painful and embarrassing, when to break it, and change the current of his thoughts, I remarked in a sympathetic tone, and in allusion to his great fatigue:

"General, this has been a hard day on you."

This attracted his attention. He looked up and replied mournfully: "Yes, it has been a sad, sad day to us," and immediately relapsed into his thoughtful mood and attitude. Being unwilling again to intrude upon his reflections, I said no more. After a minute or two he suddenly straightened up to his full height, and turning to me with more animation, energy, and excitement of manner than I had ever seen in him before, he addressed me in a voice tremulous with emotion, and said:

"General, I never saw troops behave more magnificently than Pickett's division of Virginians did to-day in their grand charge upon the enemy.

And if they had been supported, as they were to have been—but, for some reason not yet fully explained to me, they were not—we would have held the position they so gloriously won at such a fearful loss of noble lives, and the day would have been ours."

After a moment he added in a tone almost of agony: "Too bad! *Too bad!!* Oh! Too Bad!!!"

I never shall forget, as long as I live, his language, and his manner, and his appearance and expression of mental suffering. Altogether it was a scene that a historical painter might well immortalize had one been fortunately present to witness it.

In a little while he called up a servant from his sleep to take his horse; spoke mournfully, by name, of several of his friends who had fallen during the day; and when a candle had been lighted invited me alone into his tent, where, as soon as we were seated, he remarked:

"We must return to Virginia. As many of our poor wounded as possible must be taken home. I have sent for you because your men are fresh, to guard the trains back to Virginia. The duty will be arduous, responsible, and dangerous, for I am afraid you will be harassed by the enemy's cavalry. I can spare you as much artillery as you require, but no other troops, as I shall need all I have to return to the Potomac by a different route from yours. All the transportation and all the care of the wounded will be intrusted to you. You will recross the mountain by the Chambersburg road, and then proceed to Williamsport by any route you deem best, without halting. There rest and feed your animals, then ford the river, and make no halt till you reach Winchester, where I will again communicate with you."

After a good deal of conversation he sent for his chiefs of staff and ordered them to have everything in readiness for me to take command the next morning, remarking to me that the general instructions he had given would be sent to me next day in writing. As I was about leaving to return to my camp, he came out of his tent and said to me in a low tone: "I will place in your hands tomorrow a sealed package for President Davis, which you will retain in your own possession till you are across the Potomac, when you will detail a trusty commissioned officer to take it to Richmond with all possible despatch, and deliver it immediately to the President. I impress it upon you that whatever happens this package must not fall into the hands of the enemy. If you should unfortunately be captured, destroy it."

On the morning of the 4th my written instructions and the package for Mr. Davis were delivered to me. It was soon apparent that the wagons and ambulances and the wounded could not be ready to move till late in the afternoon. The General sent me four four-gun field batteries, which with my own gave me twenty-two guns to defend the trains.

Shortly after noon the very windows of heaven seemed to have been opened. Rain fell in dashing torrents, and in a little while the whole face of the earth was covered with water. The meadows became small lakes; raging streams ran across the road in every depression of the ground; wagons, ambulances, and artillery carriages filled the roads and fields in all directions. The storm increased in fury every moment. Canvas was no protection against it, and the poor wounded, lying upon the hard, naked boards of the wagon-bodies, were drenched by the cold rain. Horses and mules were blinded and maddened by the storm, and became almost unmanageable. The roar of the winds and waters made it almost impossible to communicate orders. Night was rapidly approaching, and there was danger that in the darkness the "confusion" would become "worse confounded." About four p.m. the head of the column was put in motion and began the ascent of the mountain. After dark I set out to gain the advance. The train was seventeen miles long when drawn out on the road. It was

moving rapidly, and from every wagon issued wails of agony. For four hours I galloped along, passing to the front, and heard more—it was too dark to see—of the horrors of war than I had witnessed from the battle of Bull Run up to that day. In the wagons were men wounded and mutilated in every conceivable way. Some had their legs shattered by a shell or Minie ball; some were shot through their bodies; others had arms torn to shreds; some had received a ball in the face, or a jagged piece of shell had lacerated their heads. Scarcely one in a hundred had received adequate surgical aid. Many had been without food for thirty-six hours. Their ragged, bloody, and dirty clothes, all clotted and hardened with blood, were rasping the tender, inflamed lips of their gaping wounds. Very few of the wagons had even straw in them, and all were without springs. The road was rough and rocky. The jolting was enough to have killed sound, strong men. From nearly every wagon, as the horses trotted on, such cries and shrieks as these greeted the ear:

"O God! why can't I die?"

"My God! will no one have mercy and kill me and end my misery?"

"Oh! stop one minute and take me out and leave me to die on the roadside."

"I am dying! I am dying! My poor wife, my dear children! what will become of you?"

Some were praying; others were uttering the most fearful oaths and execrations that despair could wring from them in their agony. Occasionally a wagon would be passed from which only low, deep moans and sobs could be heard. No help could be rendered to any of the sufferers. On, on; we must move on. The storm continued and the darkness was fearful. There was no time even to fill a canteen with water for a dying man; for, except the drivers and the guards disposed in compact bodies every half mile, all were wounded and helpless in that vast train of misery. The night was awful, and yet in it was our safety, for no enemy would dare attack us when he could not distinguish friend from foe. We knew that when day broke upon us we would be harassed by bands of cavalry hanging on our flanks. Therefore our aim was to go as far as possible under cover of the night, and so we kept on. It was my sad lot to pass the whole distance from the rear to the head of the column, and no language can convey an idea of the horrors of that most horrible of all nights of our long and bloody war.

Daybreak on the morning of the 5th found the head of our column at Greencastle, twelve or fifteen miles from the Potomac at Williamsport, our point of crossing. Here our apprehended troubles from the Union cavalry began. From the fields and cross-roads they attacked us in small bodies, striking the column where there were few or no guards, and creating great confusion.

To add still further to our perplexities, a report was brought that the Federals in large force held Williamsport. This fortunately proved untrue. After a great deal of harassing and desultory fighting along the road, nearly the whole immense train reached Williamsport a little after the middle of the day. The town was taken possession of; all the churches, school-houses, etc., were converted into hospitals, and proving insufficient, many of the private houses were occupied. Straw was obtained on the neighboring farms; the wounded were removed from the wagons and houses; the citizens were all put to cooking and the army surgeons to dressing wounds. The dead were selected from the train—for many had perished on the way—and were decently buried. All this had to be done because the tremendous rains had raised the river more than ten feet above the fording stage, and we could not possibly cross.

Our situation was frightful. We had over 10,000 animals and all the wagons of General Lee's army under our charge, and all the wounded that could be brought from Gettysburg. Our supply of provisions consisted of a few wagon loads of flour and a small lot of cattle. My effective force was only about 2,100 men and twenty-odd field pieces. We did not know where our army was; the river could not be crossed; and small parties of cavalry were still hovering around. The means of ferriage consisted of two small boats and a small wire rope stretched across the river, which owing to the force of the swollen current broke several times during the day. To reduce the space to be defended as much as possible, all the wagons and animals were parked close together on the river bank.

Believing that an attack would soon be made upon us, I ordered the wagoners to be mustered, and, taking three out of every four, organized them into companies, and armed them with the weapons of the wounded men found in the train. By this means I added to my effective force about five hundred men. Slightly wounded officers promptly volunteered their services to command these improvised soldiers; and many of our quartermasters and commissaries did the same thing. We were not seriously molested on the 5th; but next morning about nine o'clock information reached me that a large body of cavalry from Frederick, Maryland, was rapidly advancing to attack us. As we could not retreat further, it was at once frankly made known to the troops that unless we could repel the threatened attack we should all become prisoners, and that the loss of his whole transportation would probably ruin General Lee; for it could not be replaced for many months, if at all, in the then exhausted condition of the Confederate States. So far from repressing the ardor of the troops, this frank announcement of our peril inspired all with the utmost enthusiasm. Men and officers alike, forgetting the sufferings of the past few days, proclaimed their determination to drive back the attacking force or perish in the attempt. All told, we were less than 3,000 men. The advancing force we knew to be more than double ours, consisting, as we had ascertained, of five regular and eight volunteer regiments of cavalry, with eighteen guns, all under the command of Generals [John] Buford and [Judson] Kilpatrick. We had no works of any kind; the country was open and almost level, and there was no advantage of position we could occupy. It must necessarily be a square stand-up fight, face to face. We had twenty-two field guns of various calibre, and one Whitworth. These were disposed in batteries, in semi-circle, about one mile out of the village, on the summit of a very slight rising ground that lies back of the town. Except the artillery, our troops were held out of view of the assailants, and ready to be moved promptly to any menaced point along the whole line of nearly two miles in extent. Knowing that nothing could save us but a bold "bluff" game, orders had been given to the artillery as soon as the advancing forces came within range to open fire along the whole line, and keep it up with the utmost rapidity.

A little after one o'clock they appeared on two roads in our front, and our batteries opened. They soon had their guns in position, and a very lively artillery fight began. We fired with great rapidity, and in less than an hour two of our batteries reported that their ammunition was exhausted. This would have been fatal to us but for the opportune arrival at the critical moment of an ammunition train from Winchester. The wagons were ferried across to our side as soon as possible, and driven on the field in a gallop to supply the silent guns. Not having men to occupy half our line, they were moved up in order of battle, first to one battery, then withdrawn and double-quicked to another, but out of view of our assailants till they could be shown at some other point on our line. By this manoeuvring we made the impression that we had a strong supporting force in rear of all our guns along the entire front. To test this, Generals Buford and Kilpatrick dismounted five regiments and advanced them on foot on our right. We concentrated there all the men we had, wagoners and all, and thus, with the aid of the united fire of all our guns directed at the advancing line, we drove it back, and rushed forward two of our batteries four or five hundred yards further to the front. This boldness prevented another charge, and the fight was continued till near sunset with the artillery. About that time General Fitzhugh Lee sent a message from toward Greencastle, that if we could hold out an hour he would reinforce us with 3,000 men. This intelligence elicited a loud and long-continued cheer along our whole line, which was heard and understood by our adversaries, as we learned from prisoners taken. A few minutes later General J.E.B. Stuart, advancing from Hagerstown, fell unexpectedly upon the rear of their right wing, and in ten minutes they were in rapid retreat by their left flank in the direction of Boonsborough. Night coming on enabled them to escape.

By extraordinary good fortune we had thus saved all of General Lee's trains. A bold charge at any time before sunset would have broken our feeble lines, and we should all have fallen an easy prey to the Federals. This came to be known as "the wagoners' fight" in our army, from the fact that so many of them were armed and did such gallant service in repelling the attack made on our right by the dismounted regiments.

Our defeat that day would have been an irreparable blow to General Lee, in the loss of all his transportation. Every man engaged knew this, and probably in no fight of the war was there a more determined spirit shown than by this handful of cooped-up troops. The next day our army from Gettysburg arrived, and the country is familiar with the manner in which it escaped across the Potomac on the night of the 9th.

It may be interesting to repeat one or two facts to show the peril in which we were until the river could be bridged. About 4,000 prisoners taken at Gettysburg were ferried across the river by the morning of the 9th, and I was ordered to guard them to Staunton. Before we had proceeded two miles I received a note from General Lee to report to him in person immediately. I rode to the river, was ferried over, and galloped out toward

Hagerstown. As I proceeded I became satisfied that a serious demonstration was making along our front, from the heavy artillery fire extending for a long distance along the line. I overtook General Lee riding to the front near Hagerstown. He immediately reined up, and remarked that he believed I was familiar with all the fords of the Potomac above Williamsport, and the roads approaching them. I replied that I knew them perfectly. He then called up some one of his staff to write down my answers to his questions, and required me to name all fords as high up as Cumberland, and describe minutely their character, and the roads and surrounding country on both sides of the river, and directed me to send my brother, Colonel [George William] Imboden, to him to act as a guide with his regiment, if he should be compelled to retreat higher up the river to cross it. His situation was then very precarious. When about parting from him to recross the river and move on with the prisoners, he told me they would probably be rescued before I reached Winchester, my guard was so small, and he expected a force of cavalry would cross at Harper's Ferry to cut us off; and he could not spare to me any additional troops, as he might be hard pressed before he got over the river, which was still very much swollen by the rains. Referring to the high water, he laughingly inquired, "Does it ever quit raining about here? If so, I should like to see a clear day."

These incidents go to show how near Gettysburg came to ending the war in 1863. If we had been successful in that battle, the probabilities are that Baltimore and Washington would at once have fallen into our hands; and at that time there was so large a "peace party" in the North, that the Federal Government would have found it difficult, if not impossible, to carry on the war. General Lee's opinion was that we lost the battle because Pickett was not supported, "as he was to have been." On the other hand, if Generals Buford and Kilpatrick had captured the ten thousand animals and all the transportation of Lee's army at Williamsport, it would have been an irreparable loss, and would probably have led to the fall of Richmond in the autumn of 1863. On such small circumstances do the affairs of nations sometimes turn.

James Longstreet, "Lee's Invasion of Pennsylvania," *The Century Illustrated Magazine* 33 (February 1887)

The armies remained in position, the Confederates on Seminary Ridge extending around Gettysburg, the left also drawn back, the Federals on Cemetery Ridge, until the night of the 4th, when we took up the march in retreat for Virginia.

That night, while we were standing round a little fire by the roadside, General Lee said again the defeat was all his fault. He said to me at another time, "You ought not to have made that last attack." I replied, "I had my orders, and they were of such a nature there was no escape from them." During that winter, while I was in east Tennessee, in a letter I received from him he said, "If I only had taken your counsel even on the 3d, and had moved around the Federal left, how different all might have been."

The only thing Pickett said of his charge was that he was distressed at the loss of his command. He thought he should have had two of his brigades that had been left in Virginia; with them he felt that he would have broken the line . . .

Lee's hope in entering the campaign was that he would be in time to make a successful battle north of the Potomac, with such advantages as to draw off the army at Vicksburg as well as the Federal troops at other points.

I do not think the general effect of the battle was demoralizing, but by a singular coincidence our army at Vicksburg surrendered to Grant on the 4th, while the armies of Lee and Meade were lying in front of each other, each waiting a movement on the part of the other, neither victor, neither vanquished. This surrender, taken in connection with the Gettysburg defeat, was, of course, very discouraging to our superior officers, though I do not know that it was felt as keenly by the rank and file. For myself, I felt that our last hope was gone, and that it was now only a question of time with us.

James Longstreet, *From Manassas to Appomattox: Memoirs of the Civil War in America* (Philadelphia, 1896)

On the forenoon of the 13th, General Lee sent for me, and announced that the river was fordable and the bridge repaired, that the trains would be started at once, and the troops would follow when night could conceal the move . . . It occurred to me that the hurried move during a single night would be troublesome; suggestion was offered that the trains and wounded should move over during the night, and give us easy march the next night, but the waters on the other side were high, and only enough mills running to supply food from day to day, and the weather treacherous, so the general thought it better to hurry on. The march by the Williamsport crossing over the firm, broad turnpike was made without trouble. The route to the bridge was over a new road; at the ends of the bridge were green willow poles to prevent the wheels cutting through the mud, but the soil underneath was wet and soggy under the long season of rain, and before night rain again began to fall.

General Lee, worn by the strain of the past two weeks, asked me to remain at the bridge and look to the work of the night. And such a night is seldom experienced even in the rough life of the soldier. The rain fell in showers, sometimes in blinding sheets, during the entire night; the wagons cut deep in the mud during the early hours, and began to stall going down the hill, and one or two of the batteries were stalled before they reached the bridge. The best standing points were ankle-deep in mud, and the roads half-way to the knee, puddling and getting worse. We could only keep three or four torches alight, and those were dimmed at times when heavy rains came. Then, to crown our troubles, a load of the wounded came down, missed the end of the bridge, and plunged the wagon into the raging torrent. Right at the end of the bridge the water was three feet deep, and the current swift and surging. It did not seem possible that a man could be saved, but every one who could get through the mud and water rushed to their relief, and Providence was there to bring tears of joy to the sufferers. The wagon was righted and on the bridge and rolled off to Virginia's banks. The ground under the poles became so puddled before daylight that they would bend under the wheels and feet of the animals until they could bend no farther, and then would occasionally slip to one side far enough to spring up and catch a horse's foot and throw him broadside in the puddled mud. Under the trials and vexations every one was exhausted of patience, the general and staff were ready for a family quarrel as the only relief for their pent-up trouble, when daylight came, and with it General Lee to relieve and give us opportunity for a little repose.

"The Editor's Table," *Southern Literary Messenger* 37 (September 1863)

The fall of Vicksburg and Port Hudson, the repulse at Gettysburg and the retreat of Lee back to the Rappahannock, the battering down of Fort Sumter and the apprehended fall of Charleston, bad as they are singly, still worse combined, might be regarded with complacency if the spirit of the people were what it should be. But this cannot be affirmed. In all parts of the country there is great depression, and in many States positive disaffection.

To some extent, this is the inevitable result of so many, and so serious disasters. But the root of the prevalent disaffection lies deeper. It cannot be denied that the people have lost confidence in their rulers. Nor can it be truthfully charged that this want of confidence is due to disasters alone. The people do not lack perception, however defective they may be in ratiocination . . . The indications are that no change for the better need be expected . . .

Under this conviction, we find it almost as hard to prophesy success . . . or to proclaim cheerfulness and confidence which are non-existent. There are those who seem to think that in time of popular depression, the utterance of a deliberate lie is an excusable, if not incumbent act of patriotism. Others are so gifted with sanguine faculties, as to see clear skies and fair weather in the midst of tempest and night . . . For ourselves, we think now, as we thought nearly two years ago—that the South will have to fight two governments instead of one, and its strongest opponent, now as heretofore, is at home.

George G. Meade, "General Orders No. 68," *The War of the Rebellion: A Compilation of the Official Records of the Union and Confederate Armies* (Washington, DC, 1889), Series 1, Vol. 27 (pt 3)

July 4, 1863—4.15 p.m.

The commanding general, in behalf of the country, thanks the Army of the Potomac for the glorious result of the recent operations.

An enemy, superior in numbers, and flushed with the pride of a successful invasion, attempted to overcome and destroy this army. Utterly baffled and defeated, he has now withdrawn from the contest. The privations and fatigue the army has endured, and the heroic courage and gallantry it has displayed, will be matters of history, to be ever remembered. Our task is not yet accomplished, and the commanding general looks to the army for greater efforts to drive from our soil every vestige of the presence of the invader.

It is right and proper that we should, on all suitable occasions, return our grateful thanks to the Almighty Disposer of events, that in the goodness of his providence He has thought fit to give victory to the cause of the just.

By command of Major-General Meade . . .

Abraham Lincoln to Henry W. Halleck (July 6, 1863), *Collected Works of Abraham Lincoln*, ed. R.P. Basler (New Brunswick, NJ, 1953), Vol. 6

I left the telegraph office a good deal dissatisfied. You know I did not like the phrase, in Orders, No. 68, I believe, "Drive the invaders from our soil." Since that, I see a dispatch from General [William Henry] French, saying the enemy is crossing his wounded over the river in flats, without saying why he does not stop it, or even intimating a thought that it ought to be stopped. Still later, another dispatch from General Pleasonton, by direction of General Meade, to General French, stating that the main army is halted because it is believed the rebels are concentrating "on the road toward Hagerstown, beyond Fairfield," and is not to move until it is ascertained that the rebels intend to evacuate Cumberland Valley.

These things all appear to me to be connected with a purpose to cover Baltimore and Washington, and to get the enemy across the river again without a further collision, and they do not appear connected with a purpose to prevent his crossing and to destroy him. I do fear the former purpose is acted upon and the latter is rejected.

If you are satisfied the latter purpose is entertained and is judiciously pursued, I am content. If you are not so satisfied, please look to it.

Yours, truly, A. Lincoln

George G. Meade to Margaretta Sergeant Meade, George G. Meade, jnr., *The Life and Letters of George Gordon Meade, Major-General United States Army* (New York, 1913), Vol. 2

[July 8, 1863]

I think we shall have another battle before Lee can cross the river, though from all accounts he is making great efforts to do so. For my part, as I have to follow and fight him, I would rather do it at once and in Maryland than to follow into Virginia . . . I claim no extraordinary merit for this last battle, and would prefer waiting a little while to see what my career is to be before making any pretensions. I did and shall continue to do my duty to the best of my abilities, but knowing as I do that battles are often decided by accidents, and that no man of sense will say in advance what their result will be, I wish to be careful in not bragging before the right time . . . From the time I took command till to-day, now over ten days, I have not changed my clothes, have not had a regular night's rest, and many nights not a wink of sleep, and for several days did not even wash my face and hands, no regular food, and all the time in a great state of mental anxiety. Indeed, I think I have lived as much in this time as in the last thirty years.

[July 10, 1863]

I expect in a few days, if not sooner, again to hazard the fortune of war. I know so well that this is a fortune and that accidents, etc., turn the tide of victory, that, until the question is settled, I cannot but be very anxious. If it should please God again to give success to our efforts, then I could be more tranquil. I also see that my success at Gettysburg has deluded the people and the Government with the idea that I must always be victorious, that Lee is demoralized and disorganized, etc., and other delusions which will not only be dissipated by any reverse that I should meet with, but would react in proportion against me. I have already had a very decided correspondence with General Halleck upon this point, he pushing me on, and I informing him I was advancing as fast as I could.

[July 14, 1863]

I found Lee in a very strong position, intrenched. I hesitated to attack him, without some examination of the mode of approaching him. I called my corps commanders together, and they voted against attacking him. This morning, when I advanced to feel his position and seek for a weak point, I found he had retired in the night and was nearly across the river. I immediately started in pursuit, and my cavalry captured two thousand prisoners, two guns, several flags, and killed General Pettigrew. On reporting these facts to General Halleck, he informed me the President was very much dissatisfied at the escape of Lee. I immediately telegraphed I had done my duty to the best of my ability, and that the expressed dissatisfaction of the President I considered undeserved censure, and asked to be immediately relieved. In reply he said it was not intended to censure me, but only to spur me on to an active pursuit, and that it was not deemed sufficient cause for relieving me. This is exactly what I expected; unless I did impracticable things, fault would be found with me. I have ignored the senseless adulation of the public and press, and I am now just as indifferent to the censure bestowed without just cause.

Diary of Gideon Welles, Secretary of the Navy under Lincoln and Johnson, ed. John T. Morse (Boston, 1911), Vol. 1

July 14, Tuesday

We have accounts of mobs, riots, and disturbances in New York and other places in consequence of the Conscription Act. Our information is very meagre; two or three mails are due; the telegraph is interrupted. There have been powerful rains which have caused great damage to the railroads and interrupted all land communication between this and Baltimore.

There are, I think, indubitable evidences of concert in these riotous movements, beyond the accidental and impulsive outbreak of a mob, or mobs . . . This conjunction is not all accidental, but parts of a great plan. In the midst of all this and as a climax comes word that Lee's army has succeeded in recrossing the Potomac. If there had been an understanding between the mob conspirators, the Rebels, and our own officers, the combination of incidents could not have been more advantageous to the Rebels.

The Cabinet-meeting was not full to-day. Two or three of us were there, when Stanton came in with some haste and asked to see the President alone. The two were absent about three minutes in the library. When they returned, the President's countenance indicated trouble and distress; Stanton was disturbed, disconcerted. [Secretary of the Interior John P.] Usher asked Stanton if he had bad news. He said, "No." Something was said of the report that Lee had crossed the river. Stanton said abruptly and curtly he knew nothing of Lee's crossing. "I do," said the President emphatically, with a look of painful rebuke to Stanton. "If he has not got all of his men across, he soon will."

The President said he did not believe we could take up anything in Cabinet to-day. Probably none of us were in a right frame of mind for deliberation; he was not. He wanted to see General Halleck at once. Stanton left abruptly. I retired slowly. The President hurried and overtook me. We walked together across the lawn to the Departments and stopped and conversed a few moments at the gate. He said, with a voice and countenance which I shall never forget, that he had dreaded yet expected this; that there has seemed to him for a full week a determination that Lee, though we had him in our hands, should escape with his force and plunder. "And that, my God, is the last of this Army of the Potomac! There is bad faith somewhere. Meade has been pressed and urged, but only one of his generals was for an immediate attack, was ready to pounce on Lee; the rest held back. What does it mean, Mr. Welles? Great God! what does it mean?" . . . I can see that the shadows which have crossed my mind have clouded the President's also. On only one or two occasions have I ever seen the President so troubled, so dejected and discouraged.

Two hours later I went to the War Department. The President lay upon a sofa in Stanton's room, completely absorbed, overwhelmed with the news. He was, however, though subdued and sad, calm and resolute. Stanton had asked me to come over and read [Charles A.] Dana's report of the materials found at Vicksburg. The amount is very great, and the force was large. Thirty-one thousand two hundred prisoners have been paroled. Had Meade attacked and captured the army above us, as I verily believe he might have done, the Rebellion would have been ended . . .

July 15, Wednesday

We have the back mails this morning. The papers are filled with accounts of mobs, riots, burnings, and murders in New York. There have been outbreaks to resist the draft in several other places. This is anarchy, the fruit of the seed sown by the Seymours and others. In New York, Gov. Horatio Seymour is striving—probably earnestly now—to extinguish the flames he has contributed to kindle. Unless speedy and decisive measures are taken, the government and country will be imperiled. These concerted outbreaks and schemes to resist the laws must not be submitted to or treated lightly. An example should be made of some of the ringleaders and the mob dispersed. It is reported that the draft is ordered to be stopped. I hope this is untrue. If the mob has the ascendency and controls the action of the government, lawful authority has come to an end . . .

Seward called on me to-day with the draft of a Proclamation for Thanksgiving . . . With Meade's failure to capture or molest Lee in his retreat and with mobs to reject the laws, it was almost a mockery, yet we have much to be thankful for. A wise Providence guards us and will, it is hoped, overrule the weakness and wickedness of men and turn their misdeeds to good . . .

Abraham Lincoln to George G. Meade (July 14, 1863), *Collected Works of Abraham Lincoln*, ed. R.P. Basler (New Brunswick, NJ, 1953), Vol. 6

I have just seen your despatch to Gen. Halleck, asking to be relieved of your command, because of a supposed censure of mine. I am very—very—grateful to you for the magnificent success you gave the cause of the country at Gettysburg; and I am sorry now to be the author of the slightest pain to you. But I was in such deep distress myself that I could not restrain some expression of it. I had been oppressed nearly ever since the battles at Gettysburg, by what appeared to be evidences that yourself, and Gen. [Darius Nash] Couch, and Gen. [William Farrar] Smith, were not seeking a collision with the enemy, but were trying to get him across the river without another battle. What these evidences were, if you please, I hope to tell you at some time, when we shall both feel better. The case, summarily stated is this. You fought and beat the enemy at Gettysburg; and, of course, to say the least, his loss was as great as yours. He retreated; and you did not, as it seemed to me, pressingly pursue him; but a flood in the river detained him, till, by slow degrees, you were again upon him. You had at least twenty thousand veteran troops directly with you, and as many more raw ones within supporting distance, all in addition to those who fought with you at Gettysburg; while it was not possible that he had received a single recruit; and yet you stood and let the flood run down, bridges be built, and the enemy move away at his leisure, without attacking him. And Couch and Smith! The latter left Carlisle in time, upon all ordinary calculation, to have aided you in the last battle at Gettysburg; but he did not arrive. At the end of more than ten days, I believe twelve, under constant urging, he reached Hagerstown from Carlisle, which is not an inch over fifty-five miles, if so much. And Couch's movement was very little different.

Again, my dear general, I do not believe you appreciate the magnitude of the misfortune involved in Lee's escape. He was within your easy grasp, and to have closed upon him would, in connection with our other late successes, have ended the war. As it is, the war will be prolonged indefinitely. If you could not safely attack Lee last monday, how can you possibly do so South of the river, when you can take with you very few more than two thirds of the force you then had in hand? It would be unreasonable to expect, and I do not expect you can now effect much. Your golden opportunity is gone, and I am distressed immeasureably because of it.

I beg you will not consider this a prossecution, or persecution of yourself. As you had learned that I was dissatisfied, I have thought it best to kindly tell you why.

To Gen. Meade, never sent, or signed

"Testimony of General G.K. Warren" (March 9, 1864), *Report of the Joint Committee on the Conduct of the War at the Second Session, Thirty-Eighth Congress* (Washington, DC, 1865)

Question. What was the condition of our army after the final repulse of the enemy; were our men much fatigued and discouraged, or were they in good spirits?

Answer. They were in splendid spirits; they were not fatigued then . . . but we had lost a great many of our most spirited officers . . . General Reynolds was dead, and General Hancock was wounded

and carried to the rear. Many officers of lower rank, but relatively of as much importance as they were, were killed or wounded. We were very much shattered in that respect; and there was a tone amongst most of the prominent officers that we had quite saved the country for the time, and that we had done enough; that we might jeopard all that we had won by trying to do too much.

QUESTION. Do you know of any council of war held after the final repulse of the enemy?

ANSWER. Yes, sir; I think there was a talk that night about what to do.

QUESTION. What was the opinion and decision of that council?

ANSWER. On the morning of the 4th General Meade ordered demonstrations in front of our line, but they were very feebly made; and when the officers met together that evening to report the state of things in their front, there was so little definitely known as to the position and designs of the enemy that after some consultation they determined, I believe, to try and find out something before they did move. I know that was the result. I made the offer that night that if they would give me command of a division by 8 o'clock the next morning, I would tell them whether the enemy was retreating or not. It was not even known whether the enemy was retreating or not. On the morning of the 5th I went out with the 6th corps. General Meade gave orders for a division of the 6th corps to go with me, and for the whole corps to follow if I wanted . . .

On the evening of the 4th of July there was a discussion of the question whether we should move right after the enemy through the mountains, or move towards Frederick; that question was not decided, for the reason that we did not know enough about the enemy; and to have gone off the battle-field before the enemy did would have been giving up the victory to them . . .

On the 6th a large portion of the army moved towards Emmettsburg, and all that was left followed the next day. On July 7th the headquarters were at Frederick. On July 8th headquarters were at Middletown, and nearly all the army was concentrated in the neighborhood of that place and South mountain. On July 9th headquarters were at South Mountain House, and the advance of the army at Boonsboro' and Rohrersville. On July 10th the headquarters were moved to Antietam creek; the left of the line crossed the creek, and the right of the line moved up near Funkstown. On the 11th of July the engineers put a new bridge over the Antietam creek; the left of the line advanced to Fairplay and Jones's Crossroads, while the right remained nearly stationary. In my opinion we should have fought the enemy the next morning, July 12th.

Henry Nichols Blake [11th Massachusetts], *Three Years in the Army of the Potomac* (Boston, 1865)

All knew at noon that Lee had retreated; because the bands, clerks, and other non-combatants, arrived from the rear; and strains of music, intermingled with cheers, resounded along the lines from Wolf Hill to Roundtop. The citizens, who deserted their houses when Lee approached, returned, with their large families of small children, in haycarts and similar vehicles, which were followed by the horses, cattle, and swine which they had wisely taken away with them . . . Although a few of the inhabitants manifested a strong sympathy, and said, "Destroy our property, but drive away the rebels, and we are satisfied," Gen. [Alexander] Hayes . . . asserted in my hearing, that "the people who live on the border, in the vicinity of Gettysburg, are as base traitors as can be found in Virginia." Another officer from the same State remarked to me, "These Dutch farmers care for nothing except their cabbages; and, if they can make money out of Lee's army, they don't care how long they stay here." These tight-fisted miscreants, taking advantage of the necessities of the wounded, obtained a dollar for a loaf of bread or quart of milk; named a price for water and bandages; and, in the absence of most of the ambulances, conveyed them in their miserable wagons from the hospitals to the railroad depot, and demanded the most exorbitant amounts for their services . . .

When all the facts attending this battle are fully understood, the historian will award the highest praise to the courage of the rank and file and the skill of the subordinate officers, and ascribe to Gen. Meade a very small degree of the honor for this decisive triumph . . . During the gigantic struggle, Gen. Meade neither attacked the rebels, nor pursued them when they were completely shattered and had fled in confusion, but acted solely upon the defensive; and his able subordinates and their brave soldiers sowed, while he reaped, the harvest of martial glory which was produced by their successful labors upon the plains of Gettysburg . . .

The correspondents of the press misrepresent the facts nine times in ten when they assert that veterans are anxious to fight; but upon this day the soldiers who bore muskets wished to hear the commands, "Take arms," and "Charge," because they knew then . . . that it would have captured all the cannon, *materiel*, and men from the enemy, and finished the Rebellion . . . The national soldiers, thoroughly equipped and furnished with sufficient ammunition; animated by the glorious triumphs of Gettysburg, the surrender of Vicksburg . . . and the success which crowned the cause in every section of the country; knowing the perilous circumstances of the disorganized mass in their front, and that a battle fought at this point would prevent an almost endless tramp, besides numberless conflicts in the disagreeable wildernesses of Virginia—wished with a united voice to be led to the work of carnage . . .

Deep gloom pervaded the army as soon as it was ascertained that Lee had been allowed to escape destruction . . . Six months after this shameful failure, I heard the shouts of some men, "Who voted against the attack at Williamsport?"

"The drunkard ———!"

"The traitor ———!" and noticed one of these obnoxious corps commanders, who was reeling to and fro upon his horse . . .

The correspondents of the newspapers eagerly questioned the staff-officers to ascertain the details of the battle which they had not witnessed; and by this means I obtained a knowledge of the origin of many untruthful items—that Gen. This saved the day at one point, and Gen. That at another time turned defeat into victory. A large number of skulkers concealed themselves in the forests, or bivouacked near the hospitals, and feigned wounds by binding up their heads and arms in blood-stained bandages, or limped, with the assistance of a crutch, in apparent pain; and details of the provost-guard frequently patrolled the ground to seize these base wretches, and escort them to the front.

The army thieves, who lurked in the rear and waited for the cessation of the conflict before they plundered the slain, grasped with their remorseless hands the valuables, clothing, and rations of the unwary, wounded soldiers . . .

"Address by Maj. Gen. Daniel E. Sickles, U.S.A." (September 19, 1903), *In Memoriam: Henry Warner Slocum, 1826-1894* (Albany, 1904)

Slocum used to say to his intimate friends, "I have in my possession a small scrap of paper three or four inches long" (which he described by holding up two fingers), "about that size," he said, "that would throw a flood of light on the battle of Gettysburg; but it will be time enough bye-and-bye to turn on the light," intimating that the "scrap of paper" would appear after his death.

Lorenzo L. Crounse, "Further Details of the Battle of Gettysburgh," *New York Times* (July 9, 1863)

The history of the great battle cannot now be either fully or truthfully written. The ignominious retreat of the enemy, and the pursuit of our own forces, renders the gathering of facts and lists of casualties very difficult . . . I have a dozen themes, all pressing for mention in this letter, and scarcely time for doing justice to one of them.

One of the most important is the extent of our losses. There are all sorts of wild estimates, some of them too, I am sorry to say, by gentlemen of the medical profession, who ought to know better. I have carefully culled all the reports yet in, and though the fighting was the severest of the war, yet I do not see how the actual casualties can exceed seventeen thousand, and probably will not go above fifteen thousand. Several thousand men are counted among the missing, but they are not prisoners—they are on a grand straggle, and the country from Frederick to Westminster, to Hanover, to Gettysburgh, and back again to Frederick, swarms with loose men away from their commands—luxuriating among the farm-houses as long as their money lasts, and safe from the gobble of provost-guards, of which, by the way, nobody has seen any lately.

The country must not over-estimate the results of the victorious contests of last week. True, people were famishing for a success at the hands of the Army of the Potomac, and having got it, they applaud to the skies. It is already better than Antietam, and it may be a great deal better, but let not false reports be born only to be extinguished in bitter disappointment. And to our captures. Whoever is so sensational as to pen the deliberate falsehoods with reference to the number of prisoners and guns captured, should at once be compelled to wear a straight-jacket. Either thing could be easily verified—the first by going to the Provost-Marshal-General, and the second by going to the chief ordnance officer. I applied at the former's office last evening, and learned that the number of prisoners, including rebels wounded, thus far reported, was nearly eleven thousand. I know now that we captured no artillery whatever, and the enemy none from us.

But there is one thing the country cannot have too much of—sympathy for the fallen—or cannot give too much—aid for the wounded, and unstinted praise for the valorous ones, whose steady and unflinching courage have turned the tide of successive disaster into a sweeping and surging victory—let a nation be truly thankful.

And *apropos* to this, let me make it a matter of undeniable history that the conduct of the majority of the male citizens of Gettysburgh, and the surrounding County of Adams, is such as to stamp them with dishonor and craven-hearted meanness . . . The male citizens mostly ran away, and left the women and children to the mercy of their enemies . . .

In honorable contrast to this sordidness was the conduct of Prof. [Martin Luther] STOEVER and his amiable wife. As many as twelve wounded Union soldiers at once lay upon his dining-room floor, receiving from himself and Mrs. [Elizabeth McConaughy] STOEVER a constant care. His spacious yard was for days a free ordinary, where our men ate their fill, without money and without price not only, but with that hearty and cheerful welcome which so reanimates the weary. In his celler he concealed three Union officers for three days while the town was in possession of the rebels—anxiously determined to save them from arrest and the Libby Prison. His wife fed them stealthily during that time. This generous man encountered Mr. [Samuel] WILKESON while searching for his son's body [Lieut. Bayard Wilkeson], and overcame him wholly with his tender outpouring of sympathy and offers of service. He subsequently sought him out and compelled him to come to his home and take food. The next day, as Mr. WILKESON was passing the Professor's door to an undertaker's, he placed his little son on the watch for him, and as Mr. W. returned he went out and tenderly forced him in, and showed him a room prepared for his use so long as he should stay in Gettysburgh, and then insisted upon his sitting down to a tea table generously and elegantly spread for him and five other strangers.

Squire SAMUEL DONBORROW, living near Two Taverns, five miles east of Gettysburgh, for days fed scores of men and officers, including Gen. [Solomon] Meredith wounded; kept his wife and servants cooking constantly, and provided large amounts of food for the wounded, and for all this he refused compensation. He has a noble son in the army, who he would have thus done by. He came home to see his father, and that father blessed him as they parted, and said, "My son, I wish to save your life if I can; don't expose yourself to needless danger, but reflect credit upon your family—do your duty." And that son, now two years a soldier in the Reserves, does his duty . . .

John Burns, a resident of Gettysburgh, about fifty years of age, took his own shot-gun and joined in the battle on Thursday, in defence of his home. He fought very bravely, as was shown by his receiving five wounds, none of them serious, however.

Carl Schurz, "The Battle of Gettysburg," *McClure's Magazine* 29 (July 1907)

The general feeling in our ranks was that we had won a victory and that we had now to reap its fruits. The instinct of the soldiers demanded a prompt aggressive movement upon the enemy, and I think the instinct of the soldiers was right. The strongest of our army corps, the Fifth, kept in reserve, was substantially intact. Hardly any of the other corps had suffered so much as to be incapable of vigorous action. Their spirits were elated to genuine enthusiasm by the great event of the day. An order for a general advance seemed to be the natural outcome of the moment, and many men in the ranks fairly cried for it. But it did not come. Our skirmishers followed the retreating enemies for a certain distance and then returned with their prisoners without having touched the positions from which the attacking force had emerged. Then two or three batteries of

rebel artillery galloped forth from the belt of timber which screened the enemy's scattered forces. They advanced a short distance, unlimbered, fired a few discharges, limbered up again, and galloped back—probably to make us believe that the enemy, although repulsed, was still on the ground in fighting trim. (I do not remember having seen this fact stated in any of the histories of the battle of Gettysburg, but I observed it with my own eyes, and the impression is still vivid in my memory.)

Soon darkness and deep silence fell upon the battle-field. Officers and men, utterly exhausted by the fatigues and excitements of the past three days, dropped asleep in the ranks. In a moment we of the Eleventh Corps were soundly asleep among the shattered grave-stones. About two o'clock in the morning I was suddenly aroused by a sharp but short rattle of musketry, the sound coming clearly from the plain on the north side of the town. It lasted only a few seconds—then complete stillness again. What could it mean? Only that the enemy was withdrawing his pickets and that some of our outposts had sent a volley after them. This was my own opinion and that of my officers. The next minute we were fast asleep . . .

Of all the losses we had suffered in the first day's bloody battle, that of my old friend [Brigadier-General Alexander] Schimmelfennig went nearest to my heart. He had not only been an officer of exceptional ability, but my military instructor in the old German days, and a dear personal friend. We did not know what had become of him—whether he lay dead on the field, or had been wounded or made a prisoner by the enemy. Some of his officers had last seen him in the thickest of the fight and had observed that when the order to retreat was given, he had left the field in the rear of his command. Further their accounts did not go. Now, when on the early morning after the three days' struggle I entered the town of Gettysburg—what should I see? In the door of one of the houses on the main street, General Schimmelfennig, alive and waving his hat to me. "Hallo!" he shouted. "I knew you would come. I have been preparing for you. You must be hungry. I found some eggs in this house and saved them for you. We shall have them fried in a few minutes. Get off your horse and let us take breakfast together." It was a jolly repast, during which he told us his story. When, during that furious fight of the first day, the order to retreat reached him, he did his best to take his command out of the fire line in as orderly a shape as possible—a very difficult operation under any circumstances—and therefore left the field in the rear of his troops. But when he reached the town, he found the streets crowded with a confused mass of artillery and vehicles of all sorts, and disorganized men. Somehow he was crowded into a blind lane and suddenly ran against a high fence barring his progress, while some rebel infantrymen in hot pursuit were yelling close behind him. To clear the tall fence on horseback was impossible. He therefore dismounted and climbed over it. While he was on the top rail, his pursuers came up to him, and one of them knocked him on the head with the butt of his gun. The blow did not hurt him much, but he let himself drop on the other side of the fence as if he were dead, or at least stunned. Fortunately he wore an ordinary cavalry overcoat over his general's uniform, so that no sign of his rank was visible. The rebel soldiers, thus taking him for a mere private, then passed by him.

After a little while he cautiously raised his head and discovered that he was alone in a little kitchen-garden, and that within a few yards of him there was a small stable or shed that might serve him as a temporary shelter. He crawled into it and found a litter of straw on the ground, as well as some bread crumbs and other offal which seemed to have been intended for pigs. Soon he heard voices all around him, and from the talk he could catch, he concluded that the rebels had taken possession of the town and were making preparations for its defense.

There he lay then in his pig-sty, alone and helpless, surrounded on all sides by enemies who might have discovered him at any moment, but fortunately did not, and unknown to the inhabitants of the house to which the kitchen-garden belonged. He had nothing to eat except the nauseous scraps he found on the ground, and nothing to drink except the few drops that were left in his field flask. And in this condition he lay from the afternoon of the 1st of July until the early morning of the 4th. But worse than hunger and thirst during those two and a half days and three nights was his feverish anxiety concerning the course of the battle. There was an ill-omened silence during the first night and the early forenoon of the second day. Had our army withdrawn? From the noises he heard he could only conclude that the enemy held the town of Gettysburg in force. But the roar of cannon and the rattle of the musketry during the afternoon assured him that our army was present in force, too. Only he could not tell which side had the advantage, or whether there was any advantage achieved by either side. And so it was on the third day, when the battle seemed to rage furiously at different times and at different points, apparently neither advancing nor receding, until late in the afternoon the artillery became silent and a mighty Union cheer filled the air. Then his hope rose that something favorable to us had happened. Still he was disquieted again by the continued presence of the rebel infantry around him, until late in the night he heard something like the passing around of an order among them in a low voice, whereupon they seemed quietly to slink away. Then perfect stillness. At break of day he ventured his head out of the pig-sty, and finding the kitchen-garden completely deserted, he went into the house, the inhabitants of which greeted him first with some apprehension, but then, upon better knowledge of the situation, with great glee. A happy moment it was to me when I could telegraph Mrs. [Sophie] Schimmelfennig, who was with my family at Bethlehem, Pennsylvania, that her husband, who had been reported missing after the first day's battle, had been found, sound and safe!

James Francis Crocker, "Prison Reminiscences: An Address, Read Before Stonewall Camp, Confederate Veterans, Portsmouth, Virginia, February 2^d^, 1904," *Southern Historical Society Papers* 34 (1906)

In the charge of Pickett's Division at the battle of Gettysburg I was wounded and taken prisoner. With some others I was taken to the Twelfth Corps Hospital, situated in the rear of the left battle line of the Federals. I was here treated with much kindness and consideration. Among other officers who showed me kindness was Col. [Augustus Wade] Dwight, of New York. Professor [Martin] Stoever, of Pennsylvania College, at which I graduated in 1850, on a visit to the Hospital met me, accidentally, and we had a talk of the old college days.

I wore in the battle a suit of gray pants and jacket. They were a little shabby. After I had been at the hospital a few days it occurred to me that I ought to make an effort to get a new outfit so as to make a more decent appearance. The ways and means were at command. I wrote to an old friend and former client, then living in Baltimore, for a loan. A few days afterwards two Sisters of Charity came into the hospital and inquired for me. They met me with gracious sympathy and kindness. One of them took me aside, and, unobserved, placed in my hand a package of money, saying it was from a friend, and requested no name be mentioned. They declined to give me any information. I never knew who they were. There was a mystery about them. They could not have come for my sake alone. But this I know, they were angels of mercy.

I made known to the authorities my wish to go to Gettysburg, and while there to avail myself of the opportunity of getting a new suit. The authorities of the hospital, through Col. Dwight, conferred on me a great honor—the honor of personal confidence—absolute confidence. They gave me a free pass to Gettysburg, with the sole condition that I present it at the Provost office there and have it countersigned. I went alone, unattended. The fields and woods were open to me. They somehow knew—I know not how—that I could be trusted; that my honor was more to me than my life.

On my way to town I called by the Eleventh Corps Hospital, to which General Armistead had been taken, to see him. I found that he had died. They showed me his freshly made grave. To my inquiries they gave me full information. They told me that his wound was in the leg; that it ought not to have proved mortal; that his proud spirit chafed under his imprisonment and his restlessness aggravated his wound. Brave Armistead! The bravest of all that field of brave heroes! If there be in human hearts a lyre, in human minds a flame divine, that awakens and kindles at the heroic deeds of man, then his name will be borne in song and story to distant times.

I had my pass countersigned at the Provost office. It gave me the freedom of the city. There were many Federal officers and soldiers in the city. It was a queer, incongruous sight to see a rebel lieutenant in gray mingling in the crowd, and apparently at home. They could see, however, many of the principal citizens of the town cordially accosting, and warmly shaking by the hand, that rebel. I met so many old friends that I soon felt at home. As I was walking along the main street, a prominent physician, Dr. [Charles] Horner, stopped me and renewed the old acquaintanceship. He pointed to a lady standing in a door not far away, and asked me who it was. I gave the name of Miss Kate Arnold, a leading belle of the college days. He said, "She is my wife and she wants to see you." There was a mutually cordial meeting. While standing in a group of old friends I felt a gentle tap on my shoulder from behind. It was my dear old professor of mathematics, [Michael] Jacobs. He whispered to me in the kindest, gentlest way not to talk about the war. I deeply appreciated his kindness and solicitude. But I had not been talking about the war. The war was forgotten as I talked of the olden days.

On another street a gentleman approached me and made himself known. It was Rev. David Swope, a native of Gettysburg, who was of the next class below mine. He manifested genuine pleasure in meeting me. He told me he was living in Kentucky when the war broke out. He recalled a little incident of the college days. He asked me if I remembered in passing a certain house I said to a little red-headed girl with abundant red curls, standing in front of her house, "I'll give you a levy for one of those curls." I told him that I remembered it as if it were yesterday. He said that little girl was now his wife; and that she would be delighted to see me. He took me to a temporary hospital where there were a large number of our wounded. He had taken charge of the hospital, and manifested great interest in them and showed them every tender care and kindness. I fancied that those Kentucky days had added something to the sympathy of his kind, generous nature towards our wounded; and when I took leave of him, I am sure the warm grasp of my hand told him, better than words, of the grateful feelings in my heart.

I must ask indulgence to mention another incident. I met on the college campus a son of Prof. [Henry Louis] Baugher, who was then president of the college, and who was president when I graduated. The son [H.L. Baugher, jnr.] gave me such a cordial invitation to dine with him and his father that I accepted it. They were all very courteous; but I fancied I detected a reserved dignity in old Dr. Baugher. It was very natural for him to be so, and I appreciated it. The old Doctor, while kindhearted, was of a very positive and radical character, which he evinced on all subjects. He was thoroughly conscientious, and was of the stuff of which martyrs are made.

He was thoroughly orthodox in his Lutheran faith; and in politics, without ever hearing a word from him, I venture to say he was in sympathy with, I will not say, Thaddeus Stevens, but with [William Lloyd] Garrison and [Wendell] Phillips. My knowledge of him left me no need to be told that his views and feelings involved in the war were intense. And there he was, breaking bread with a red-handed rebel in his gray uniform, giving aid and comfort to the enemy. Was he not put to it to keep mastery of himself?

Happy for man that he is double-sighted; that there is within him a quality allied to conscience—call it charity—that enables him to choose on which side to look. The venerable Doctor saw before him only his old student, recalled only the old days, and their dear memories. If there was anything between his heart and his country's laws, there was nothing between his heart and his Saviour's sweet charity.

And here I must relate an incident of those old days not wholly irrelevant and inopportune. I graduated in 1850. I had the honor to be the valedictorian of my class. In preparing my address I took notice of the great excitement then prevailing on account of the discussion in Congress of the bill to admit California as a State into the Union. Great sectional feeling was aroused through this long protracted discussion in the Senate. One senator dared use the word "disunion" with a threat. The very word sent a thrill of horror over the land. I recall my own feeling of horror. In my address to my classmates I alluded to this sectional feeling, deprecating it, and exclaimed, "Who knows, unless patriotism should triumph over sectional feeling but what we, classmates, might in some future day meet in hostile battle array."

Dr. Baugher, as president of the college, had revision of our graduating speeches, and he struck this part out of my address. But alas! it was a prophetic conjecture; and members of our class met in after years, not only in battle array, but on the fields over which, in teaching botany, Prof. Jacobs had led us in our study of the wild flowers that adorned those fields.

Frederick Rauscher, *Music on the March, 1862–'65: With the Army of the Potomac. 114th Regt. P.V., Collis' Zouaves* (Philadelphia, 1892)

On the 4th of July, General Birney, who was now in command of the corps—General Sickles having lost a leg near the Peach Orchard—sent for the band to come up to the line of battle, to play in honor of the

National Anniversary. We performed the national airs, including the Star Spangled Banner. At that moment the rebels sent a shell over our line. It flew above our heads, however, and did no damage. This was one of the last shots they fired on this field, probably to have us believe they were still there for a fight.

Abraham T. Brewer [Co. A], *History Sixty-first Regiment Pennsylvania Volunteers, 1861-1865* (Pittsburgh, 1911)

What the eyes beheld passing over that field in the way of death and destruction, Union and Rebel, cannot be described . . . The wounded had nearly all been taken away, but the dead had not been touched. They lay as they fell, in every conceivable position. Sometimes one lay across another as if the top one had stooped to take a dying message and instantly lost his life. The battle wreckage included everything belonging to soldiers afoot or on horseback, such as caps, hats, shoes, coats, guns, cartridge and cap boxes, belts, canteens, haversacks, blankets, tin cups, horses, saddles and swords . . . Nearby we saw where a battery had stood in the midst of a terrific struggle. One gun was dismounted, a caisson had exploded and we noticed one place where three out of four horses belonging to a gun had been killed and lay with their harness on.

Francis Amasa Walker, *History of the Second Army Corps in the Army of the Potomac* (New York, 1886)

[The] field of battle presented a curious sight. Parties were gathering up the arms abandoned by the enemy and sticking the bayonets in the ground, so that there were acres of muskets standing as thick as trees in a nursery.

James Silliman [28th Pennsylvania] to Matilda Silliman (July 9, 1863), in James Silliman Letterbook, Union League of Philadelphia Archives

12th Corps Hospital
2 mile east Gettysburg July 9 1863
Dear Sister

I wrote you a letter since I have been here, the particulars of which I mentioned. My foot is somewhat better, but I am not able to walk on it much it being very painful. I am very tired of being here. We have shipped quite a number of our wounded off. All those who were able to walk to Gettysburg have done so and have taken the cars for there to Baltimore. We have about 300 here yet and they are sent off as fast as they can be. The Dr. [Henry Ernest] Goodman who is in charge of this Hospital wanted me to go to Baltimore but I think I will remain here as long as the Dr. says. By that time I may get well enough to go direct to the Regt without going to a Baltimore Hospital. I dread getting into a Hospital. I have seen enough of one here. I would like very much to get a leave of absence for about 20 days as I am completely worn out. I have not been well since we left Aquia Creek. I am still very weak and am troubled with this dizziness whenever I get up or get out into the sun. I am hard up for a change of clothing, not having had one since we left Leesburg, our wagons not being with us. I got a pair of muslin drawers here yesterday, also a pair of cotton socks. Our wounded are getting along very well, the weather being very favorable for them. We have lost about 25 since the Hospital was established, half of them being Rebs . . . The Sanitary Mission [U.S. Sanitary Commission] are sending in many delicacies, but they are only given to the worst cases and the Doctors and Hospital Bummers. The Christian Mission [U.S. Christian Commission] is also around with their papers

and tracts in one hand and a bottle of whiskey in the other. They are as Dr. Goodman says a perfect bore.

I do not Know what is going on out side this place. We have many rumors all of which we place no reliance in, papers we do not get to see. I should like to see full particulars of the 3 days fight. I have no idea where the enemy are but if they are not in the Gaps in South Mountain [I] think most likely they have made their escape. I do not Know where [Major-General Darius] Couch is. If the enemy have crossed the [Potomac] River I do not think we will follow them, we not having force enough. Our Corps went towards Frederick going over the same road we came. I think they are now in the neighborhood of Antietam. We heard firing yesterday in the direction of Hagerstown. I do not know how I will get my letters, they will all go on to the Regiment. If this Hospital moves this week I will go on to Baltimore and remain there till I get better. If there is any chance of getting a leave of absence for 10 or 15 days I will try and get one.

Your Bro,
Jim

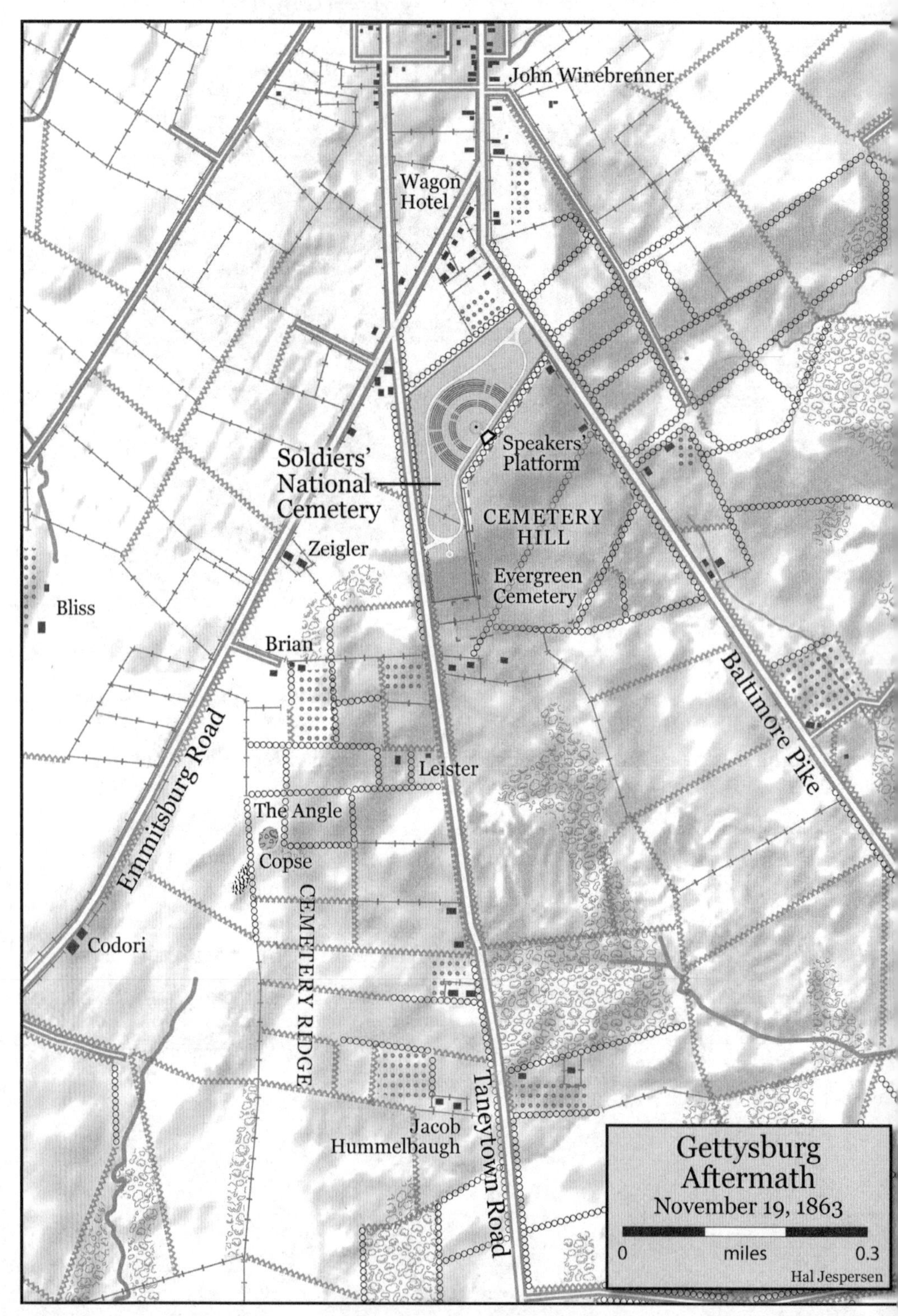
John Winebrenner
Wagon Hotel
Speakers' Platform
Soldiers' National Cemetery
CEMETERY HILL
Zeigler
Evergreen Cemetery
Bliss
Brian
Baltimore Pike
Emmitsburg Road
Leister
The Angle
Copse
CEMETERY RIDGE
Codori
Taneytown Road
Jacob Hummelbaugh
Gettysburg Aftermath
November 19, 1863
0
miles
0.3
Hal Jespersen

THE ADDRESS & REMEMBRANCE

The Battle of Gettysburg ended on July 3rd, but what followed was a continuing series of conflicts over how the battle should be understood, a struggle that continues to this day. The recognition that something momentous had happened at Gettysburg was certainly a common one, starting with Abraham Lincoln, whose off-the-cuff remarks at the White House on July 7th may almost stand as a rough draft of the more famous address he would give four months later. Lincoln understood the Civil War as a challenge to the fundamental idea of self-government by a nation of equal citizens; whenever any portion of those citizens decided they would no longer live by the agreed-upon political rules, then democracy itself would collapse inward. Americans had made this notion the foundation of their government; if Americans, of all people, could not make it work, then the idea of democracy would stand as an embarrassed failure in the gloating view of every monarchy and dictatorship in the world. That the news of Gettysburg (along with the surrender of

NATIONAL MONUMENT,
TO BE ERECTED AT
GETTYSBURG, PA.

Vicksburg) arrived on the weekend of the Fourth of July was for Lincoln a symbol of the connection between the war and the American experiment itself, and a call to redouble every effort to bring the war to a successful conclusion.

The opportunity to describe this connection in a more formal way emerged out of the first post-Gettysburg clash. In 1862, Congress had made provision for the creation of national cemeteries for the fallen soldiers of its armies, and after Governor Curtin's battlefield visit, plans were drawn up by David Wills, a Gettysburg lawyer and Pennsylvania political operative to establish such a cemetery at Gettysburg. He was countered by David McConaughy, another Gettysburg Republican and the president of the association that maintained the Evergreen Cemetery on Cemetery Hill, who planned to convert part of that cemetery "for the burial of our own dead" and create a "National Monument in memory of the battle and the dead." Wills adroitly outmaneuvered McConaughy, arranging for the purchase of seventeen acres on Cemetery Hill, adjacent to the Evergreen Cemetery, signing contracts for landscaping with the noted landscape architect William Saunders, and directing the reburial of over 3,000 Union dead from the battle.

Dedication ceremonies for the Soldiers' National Cemetery were originally scheduled for October, then postponed to November 19th to accommodate both the slow pace of reburials and the availability of the principal speaker, Edward Everett, the former Massachusetts governor and senator. Wills also invited Lincoln to deliver "a few appropriate remarks" as the actual dedication sentences. The 272 words Lincoln spoke there have eclipsed not only Everett's two-and-a-half-hour address, but every other American political utterance since the Declaration and the Constitution. Lincoln's opening phrase—"Fourscore and seven years ago"—seems to have been modeled on a widely admired speech given two years before by Speaker of the House Galusha Grow, whose message anticipated much of what Lincoln would say. Lincoln, however, had the greater gift of utterance, not to say the greater compression of thought into the simplest of words, and it is Lincoln's use of those words at Gettysburg that are the most vividly remembered.

This did not, however, put an end to the conflicts. A monument was erected at the center of the cemetery in 1869, and although the monument was often understood as marking the platform that had been erected six years before for Lincoln and Everett, in fact, considerable debate has ensued about the actual location of the speakers' platform. A more serious and drawn-out debate would emerge about how—and by whom—the battle should be celebrated. Since the Soldiers' National Cemetery was federal property, David McConaughy compensated for his disappointment over the cemetery's location by leading the formation of a Gettysburg Battlefield Memorial Association in 1864 that began buying up significant parcels of the onetime battlefield. The GBMA was entirely a Union-veteran-run affair. Over the following three decades, it sponsored the erection of 320 monuments on the property it had purchased, all of them Union ones, and the speeches and ceremonies that accompanied their dedication celebrated the glories of a Union triumph and the victory of emancipation.

But the celebrations did not stay Union property. In 1869, a town Memorial Day parade excluded "the colored Sabbath school from the line of procession," and starting in 1888, veterans of both the Union and Confederate armies began holding joint reunions on the Gettysburg battlefield, culminating in a gigantic fiftieth-anniversary event in 1913 where the principal speaker was President Woodrow Wilson—the first Southern Democrat to be elected to the presidency since the Civil War.

His message was about the triumph of forgetfulness over memory: "We have found one another again as brothers and comrades in arms, enemies no longer, generous friends rather, our battles long past, the quarrel forgotten, except that we shall not forget the splendid valor, the manly devotion of men then arrayed against one another, now grasping hands and smiling into each other's eyes." In his speech, it was as though slavery and race had never been issues. Twelve years later, in 1925, the Pennsylvania state chapter of the Ku Klux Klan felt free to hold a march and rally at Gettysburg, which "welcomed the horde of white-robed figures."

In 1895, the GBMA turned over title of its properties to the federal government, to be administered by the War Department, which, in turn, would surrender management of the battlefield and the acquisition of still more acreage to the Department of the Interior and the National Park Service. In so doing, the federal government could not resist mounting demands from Southern states to erect monuments of their own, the first being the Virginia state monument in 1917. The monument was positioned on the spot where Lee had watched Pickett's division march to its doom, and was to have praised Virginia's soldiers for fighting in defense of "the faith of their fathers" (an inscription the War Department prevailed upon the Virginians to withdraw, along with any depiction of the Confederate flag). The dedication speaker was a Confederate veteran, Leigh Richmond, who had no hesitation in defending slavery as "the noblest melioration of an inferior race, of which history can note."

And yet, the words that endured at Gettysburg were Lincoln's, and the "proposition" that the battle vindicated was equality. A century after Lincoln, an American vice president (who would shortly become president), Lyndon Baines Johnson, would reassert Lincoln's principle on the same battlefield where Lincoln had spoken. Gettysburg today remains the focus of debate, reinterpretation, and remembrance. It is understood variously as the pivot on which the Civil War turned, as the foremost American example of historic preservation, as the rebirth of American democracy, and as a historical showcase for reenactments, tourism, and even merchandise. There is nothing that shows any abatement in American affections and interest in what is, after all, a wonderfully typical American small town in south-central Pennsylvania.

Abraham Lincoln, "Response to a Serenade" (July 7, 1863), *Collected Works of Abraham Lincoln*, ed. R.P. Basler (New Brunswick, NJ, 1953), Vol. 6

Fellow-citizens: I am very glad indeed to see you tonight, and yet I will not say I thank you for this call, but I do most sincerely thank Almighty God for the occasion on which you have called. How long ago is it? eighty odd years—since on the Fourth of July for the first time in the history of the world a nation by its representatives, assembled and declared as a selfevident truth that "all men are created equal." That was the birthday of the United States of America. Since then the Fourth of July has had several peculiar recognitions. The two most distinguished men in the framing and support of the Declaration were Thomas Jefferson and John Adams—the one having penned it and the other sustained it the most forcibly in debate—the only two of the fifty-five who sustained [signed] it being elected President of the United States. Precisely fifty years after they put their hands to the paper it pleased Almighty God to take both from the stage of action. This was indeed an extraordinary and remarkable event in our history. Another President [James Monroe], five years after, was called from this stage of existence on the same day and month of the year; and now, on this last Fourth of July just passed, when we have a gigantic Rebellion, at the bottom of which is an effort to overthrow the principle that all men were [are?] created equal, we have the surrender of a most powerful position and army on that very day, and not only so, but in a succession of battles in Pennsylvania, near to us, through three days, so rapidly fought that they might be called one great battle on the 1st, 2d and 3d of the month of July; and on the 4th the cohorts of those who opposed the declaration that all men are created equal, "turned tail" and run. Gentlemen, this is a glorious theme, and the occasion for a speech, but I am not prepared to make one worthy of the occasion. I would like to speak in terms of praise due to the many brave officers and soldiers who have fought in the cause of the Union and liberties of the country from the beginning of the war. There are trying occasions, not only in success, but for the want of success. I dislike to mention the name of one single officer lest I might do wrong to those I might forget. Recent events bring up glorious names, and particularly prominent ones, but these I will not mention . . .

Galusha Aaron Grow, "Address to the United States House of Representatives" (July 4, 1861), *Patriotic and Heroic Eloquence: A Book for the Patriot, Statesman and Student*, ed. W.R. Wallace (New York, 1861)

Fourscore years ago fifty-six bold merchants, farmers, lawyers, and mechanics, the representatives of a few feeble colonists, scattered along the Atlantic sea-board, met in convention to found a new empire, based on the inalienable rights of man. Seven years of bloody conflict ensued, and the 4th of July, 1776, is canonized in the hearts of the great and the good as the jubilee of oppressed nationalities; and in the calendar of heroic deeds it marks a new era in the history of the race. Three quarters of a century have passed away, and those few feeble colonists, hemmed in by the ocean in front, the wilderness and the savage in the rear, have spanned a whole continent, with great empires of free States, rearing throughout its

vast wilderness temples of science and of civilization upon the ruins of savage life. Happiness seldom if ever equaled has surrounded the domestic fireside, and prosperity unsurpassed has crowned the national energies; the liberties of the people have been secured at home and abroad, while the national ensign floats honored and respected in every commercial mart of the world.

On the return of this glorious anniversary, after a period but little exceeding that of the allotted lifetime of man, the people's Representatives are convened in the Council Chambers of the Republic, to deliberate upon the means for preserving the Government under whose benign influence these grand results have been achieved.

A rebellion—the most causeless in the history of the race—has developed a conspiracy of longstanding to destroy the Constitution formed by the wisdom of our fathers, and the Union cemented by their blood. This conspiracy, nurtured for long years in secret councils, first develops itself openly in acts of spoliation and plunder of public properly, with the connivance or under the protection of treason enthroned in all the high places of the Government, and at last in armed rebellion for the overthrow of the best Government ever devised by man. Without an effort in the mode prescribed by the organic law for a redress of all grievances, the malcontents appeal only to the arbitrament of the sword, insult the nation's honor, trample upon its flag, and inaugurate a revolution which, if successful, would end in establishing petty jarring confederacies, or despotism and anarchy, upon the ruins of the republic, and the destruction of its liberties . . .

Every race and tongue almost is represented in the grand legion of the Union: their standards proclaim in language more impressive than words, that here indeed is the home of the emigrant and the asylum of the exile. No matter where was his birth-place, or in what clime his infancy was cradled, he devotes his life to the defense of his adopted land, the vindication of its honor, and the protection of its flag, with the same zeal with which he would guard his hearthstone or his fireside. All parties, sects, and conditions of men not corrupted by the institutions of human bondage, forgetting bygone rancors or prejudices, blend in one united phalanx for the integrity of the Union and the perpetuity of the republic . . .

The merchant, the banker, and the tradesman, with an alacrity unparalleled, proffer their all at the altar of their country, while from the counter, the workshop, and the plow, brave hearts and stout arms, leaving their tasks unfinished, rush to the tented field . . .

In view of this grandest demonstration for self-preservation in the history of nationalities, desponding patriotism may be assured that the foundations of our national greatness still stand strong, and that the sentiment which to-day beats responsive in every loyal heart will for the future be realized. No flag alien to the sources of the Mississippi river will ever float permanently over its mouths till its waters are crimsoned in human gore; and not one foot of American soil can ever be wrenched from the jurisdiction of the Constitution of the United States until it is baptized in fire and blood . . .

In God is our trust;
And the star-spangled banner forever shall wave
O'er the land of the free and the home of the brave.

Those who regard it as mere cloth bunting fail to comprehend its symbolical power. Wherever civilization dwells, or the name of Washington is known, it bears in its fold the concentrated power of armies and of navies, and surrounds its votaries with a defense more impregnable than battlement, wall, or tower. Wherever on the earth's surface an American citizen may wander, called by pleasure, business, or caprice, it is a shield secure against outrage and wrong—save on the soil of the land of his birth.

As the guardians of the rights and liberties of the people, it becomes your paramount duty to make it honored at home as it is respected abroad. A government that cannot command the loyalty of its own citizens is unworthy the respect of the world, and a government that will not protect its loyal citizens deserves the contempt of the world.

He who would tear down this grandest temple of constitutional liberty, thus blasting forever the hopes of crushed humanity, because its freemen, in the mode prescribed by the Constitution, select a Chief Magistrate not acceptable to him, is a parricide to his race and should be regarded as a common enemy of mankind.

This Union once destroyed is a shattered vase that no human power can reconstruct in its original symmetry. "Coarse stones when they are broken may be cemented again—precious ones never."

If the republic is to be dismembered and the sun of its liberty must go out in endless night, let it set amid the roar of cannon and the din of battle, when there is no longer an arm to strike or a heart to bleed in its cause; so that coming generations may not reproach the present with being too imbecile to preserve the priceless legacy bequeathed by our fathers, so as to transmit it unimpaired to future times.

Abraham Lincoln, "Address delivered at the dedication of the Cemetery at Gettysburg," *Collected Works of Abraham Lincoln*, ed. R.P. Basler (New Brunswick, NJ, 1953), Vol. 7

Four score and seven years ago our fathers brought forth on this continent, a new nation, conceived in Liberty, and dedicated to the proposition that all men are created equal.

Now we are engaged in a great civil war, testing whether that nation, or any nation so conceived and so dedicated, can long endure. We are met on a great battlefield of that war. We have come to dedicate a portion of that field, as a final resting place for those who here gave their lives that that nation might live. It is altogether fitting and proper that we should do this.

But, in a larger sense, we cannot dedicate—we cannot consecrate—we cannot hallow—this ground. The brave men, living and dead, who struggled here, have consecrated it, far above our poor power to add or detract. The world will little note, nor long remember what we say here, but it can never forget what they did here. It is for us the living, rather, to be dedicated here to the unfinished work which they who fought here have thus far so nobly advanced. It is rather for us to be here dedicated to the great task remaining before us—that from these honored dead we take increased devotion to that cause for which they gave the last full measure of devotion—that we here highly resolve that these dead shall not have died in vain—that this nation, under God, shall have a new birth of freedom—and that government of the people, by the people, for the people, shall not perish from the earth.

November 19. 1863.

ABRAHAM LINCOLN

John Trowbridge, *The South: A Tour of Its Battlefields and Ruined Cities, a Journey Through the Desolated States* (Hartford, CT, 1866)

In the month of August, 1865, I set out to visit some of the scenes of the great conflict through which the country had lately passed . . . From Harrisburg I went, by the way of York and Hanover, to Gettysburg. Having hastily secured a room at a hotel in the Square, (the citizens call it the "Di'mond,") I inquired the way to the battle-ground.

"You are on it now," said the landlord, with proud satisfaction—for it is not every man that lives, much less keeps a tavern, on the field of a world-famous fight. "I tell you the truth," said he; and, in proof of his words (as if the fact were too wonderful to be believed without proof), he showed me a Rebel shell imbedded in the brick wall of a house close by . . .

Gettysburg is the capital of Adams County: a town of about three thousand souls—or fifteen hundred, according to John Burns, who assured me that half the population were Copperheads, and that they had no souls. It is pleasantly situated on the swells of a fine undulating country, drained by the headwaters of the Monocacy. It has no especial natural advantages; owing its existence, probably, to the mere fact that several important roads found it convenient to meet at this point, to which accident also is due its historical renown. The circumstance which made it a burg made it likewise a battle-field.

About the town itself there is nothing very interesting. It consists chiefly of two-story houses of wood and brick, in dull rows, with thresholds but little elevated above the street. Rarely a front yard or blooming garden-plot relieves the dreary monotony. Occasionally there is a three-story house, comfortable, no doubt, and sufficiently expensive, about which the one thing remarkable is the total absence of taste in its construction. In this respect Gettysburg is but a fair sample of a large class of American towns, the builders of which seem never once to have been conscious that there exists such a thing as beauty.

John Burns, known as the "hero of Gettysburg," was almost the first person whose acquaintance I made. He was sitting under the thick shade of an English elm in front of the tavern. The landlord introduced him as "the old man who took his gun and went into the first day's fight." He rose to his feet and received me with sturdy politeness; his evident delight in the celebrity he enjoys twinkling through the veil of a naturally modest demeanor. "John will go with you and show you the different parts of the battle-ground," said the landlord. "Will you, John?"

"Oh, yes, I'll go," said John, quite readily; and we set out . . .

A mile south of the town is Cemetery Hill, the head and front of an important ridge, running two miles farther south to Round Top—the ridge held by General Meade's army during the great battles . . . It was a soft and peaceful summer day. There was scarce a sound to break the stillness, save the shrill note of the locust, and the perpetual click-click of the stone-cutters at work upon the granite headstones of the soldiers' cemetery. There was nothing to indicate to a stranger that so tranquil a spot had ever been a scene of strife. We were walking in the time-hallowed place of the dead, by whose side the martyr-soldiers who fought so bravely and so well on those terrible first days of July, slept as sweetly and securely as they.

"It don't look here as it did after the battle," said John Burns. "Sad work was made with the tombstones. The ground was all covered with dead horses, and broken wagons, and pieces of shells, and battered muskets, and everything of that kind, not to speak of the heaps of dead." But now the tombstones have been replaced, the neat iron fences have been mostly repaired, and scarcely a vestige of the fight remains. Only the burial-places of the slain are there. Thirty-five hundred and sixty slaughtered Union soldiers lie on the field of Gettysburg. This number does not include those whose bodies have been claimed by friends and removed.

The new cemetery, devoted to the patriot slain, and dedicated with fitting ceremonies on the 19th of November, 1863, adjoins the old one [Evergreen Cemetery]. In the centre is the spot reserved for the monument, the cornerstone of which was laid on the 4th of July, 1865. The cemetery is semi-circular, in the form of an amphitheatre, except that the slope is reversed, the monument occupying the highest place. The granite headstones resemble rows of semicircular seats. Side by side, with two feet of ground allotted to each, and with their heads towards the monument, rest the three thousand five hundred and sixty. The name of each, when it could be ascertained, together with the number of the company and regiment in which he served, is lettered on the granite at his head. But the barbarous practice of stripping such of our dead as fell into their hands, in which the Rebels indulged here as elsewhere, rendered it impossible to identify large numbers. The headstones of these are lettered "Unknown." At the time when I visited the cemetery, the sections containing most of the unknown had not yet received their headstones, and their resting-places were indicated by a forest of stakes. I have seen few sadder sights . . .

I looked into one of the trenches, in which work-men were laying foundations for the headstones, and saw the ends of the coffins protruding. It was silent and dark down there. Side by side the soldiers slept, as side by side they fought . . . Eighteen loyal States are represented by the tenants of these graves. New York has the greatest number—upwards of eight hundred; Pennsylvania comes next in order, having upwards of five hundred . . . Sons of Massachusetts fought for Massachusetts on Pennsylvania soil. If they had not fought, or if our armies had been annihilated here, the whole North would have been at the mercy of Lee's victorious legions. As Cemetery Hill was the pivot on which turned the fortunes of the battle . . . Cemetery Hill should be first visited by the tourist of the battle-ground. Here a view of the entire field, and a clear understanding of the military operations of the three days, are best obtained . . . You are in the focus of a half-circle, from all points of which was poured in upon this now silent hill such an artillery fire as has seldom been concentrated upon one point of an open field in any of the great battles upon this planet. From this spot extend your observations as you please.

Guided by the sturdy old man, I proceeded first to Culp's Hill, following a line of breastworks into the woods. Here are seen some of the soldiers' devices, hastily adopted for defence. A rude embankment of stakes and logs and stones, covered with earth, forms the principal work; aside from which you meet with little private breastworks, as it were, consisting of rocks heaped up by the trunk of a tree, or beside a larger rock, or across a cleft in the rocks, where some sharpshooter stood and exercised his skill at his ease.

The woods are of oak chiefly, but with a liberal sprinkling of chestnut, black-walnut, hickory, and other common forest trees . . . Yet here remain more astonishing evidences of fierce fighting than anywhere else about Gettysburg. The trees in certain localities are all scarred, disfigured, and literally dying or dead from their wounds. The marks of balls in some of the trunks are countless. Here are limbs, and yonder are whole tree-tops, cut off by shells. Many of these trees have been hacked for lead, and chips containing bullets have been carried away for relics . . .

Plenty of Rebel knapsacks and haversacks lie rotting upon the ground; and there are Rebel graves nearby in the woods. By these I was inclined to pause longer than John Burns thought it worth the while. I felt a pity for these unhappy men, which he could not understand. To him they were dead Rebels, and nothing more; and he spoke with great disgust of an effort which had been made by certain "Copperheads" of the town to have all the buried Rebels now scattered about in the woods and fields gathered together in a cemetery near that dedicated to our own dead . . .

The next morning, according to agreement, I went to call on the old hero. I found him living in the upper part of a little whitewashed two-story house, on the corner of two streets west of the town. A flight of wooden steps outside took me to his door. He was there to welcome me. John Burns is a stoutish, slightly bent, hale old man, with a light-blue eye, a long, aggressive nose, a firm-set mouth expressive of determination of character, and a choleric temperament. His hair, originally dark-brown, is considerably bleached with age; and his beard, once sandy, covers his face (shaved once or twice a week) with a fine crop of silver stubble. A short, massy kind of man; about five feet four or five inches in height, I should judge . . . On the morning of the first day's fight he sent his wife away, telling her that he would take care of the house. The firing was nearby, over Seminary Ridge. Soon a wounded soldier came into the town and stopped at an old house on the opposite corner. Burns saw the poor fellow lay down his musket, and the inspiration to go into the battle seems then first to have seized him. He went over and demanded the gun.

"What are you going to do with it?" asked the soldier.

"I'm going to shoot some of the damned Rebels!" replied John.

He is not a swearing man, and the strong adjective is to be taken in a strictly literal, not a profane, sense.

Having obtained the gun, he pushed out on the Chambersburg Pike, and was soon in the thick of the skirmish.

"I wore a high-crowned hat and a long-tailed blue; and I was seventy year old."

The sight of so old a man, in such costume, rushing fearlessly forward to get a shot in the very front of the battle, of course attracted attention. He fought with the Seventh Wisconsin Regiment; the Colonel of which ordered him back, and questioned him, and finally, seeing the old man's patriotic determination, gave him a good rifle in place of the musket he had brought with him . . .

The next day I mounted a hard-trotting horse and rode to Round Top. On the way I stopped at the historical peach-orchard, known as [Joseph] Sherfy's, where Sickles's Corps was repulsed, after a terrific conflict, on Thursday, the second day of the battle. The peaches were green on the trees then; but they were ripe now, and the branches were breaking down with them. One of Mr. Sherfy's girls [Anna]—the youngest she told me—was in the orchard. She had in her basket rare-ripes to sell. They were large and juicy and sweet—all the redder, no doubt, for the blood of the brave that had drenched the sod. So calm and impassive is Nature, silently turning all things to use. The carcass of a mule, or the god-like shape of a warrior cut down in the hour of glory—she knows no difference between them, but straightway proceeds to convert both alike into new forms of life and beauty.

Between fields made memorable by hard fighting I rode eastward, and, entering a pleasant wood, ascended Little Round Top. The eastern slope of this rugged knob is covered with timber. The western side is steep, and wild with rocks and bushes. Nearby is the Devil's Den, a dark cavity in the rocks, interesting henceforth on account of the fight that took place here for the possession of these heights . . .

A little farther on is Round Top itself, a craggy tusk of the rock-jawed earth pushed up there towards the azure. It is covered all over with broken ledges, boulders, and fields of stones. Among these the forest-trees have taken root—thrifty Nature making the most of things even here. The serene leafy tops of ancient oaks tower aloft in the bluish-golden air. It is a natural fortress, which our boys strengthened still further by throwing up the loose stones into handy breastworks.

Returning, I rode the whole length of the ridge held by our troops, realizing more and more the importance of that extraordinary position. It is like a shoe, of which Round Top represents the heel, and Cemetery Hill the toe . . . At a point well forward on the foot of this shoe, Meade had his headquarters. I tied my horse at the gate, and entered the little square box of a house which enjoys that historical celebrity. It is scarcely more than a hut, having but two little rooms on the ground-floor, and I know not what narrow, low-roofed chambers above. Two small girls, with brown German faces, were paring wormy apples under

the porch; and a round-shouldered, bareheaded, and barefooted woman [Lydia Leister], also with a German face and a strong German accent, was drawing water at the well. I asked her for drink, which she kindly gave me, and invited me into the house.

The little box was whitewashed outside and in, except the floor and ceilings and inside doors, which were neatly secured. The woman sat down to some mending, and entered freely into conversation. She was a widow, and the mother of six children [James Leister, Jr., Eliza, Amos, Daniel, Hannah, and Matilda]. The two girls cutting wormy apples at the door were the youngest, and the only ones left to her. A son in the army [James] was expected home in a few days . . .

Of the magnitude of a battle fought so desperately during three days, by armies numbering not far from two hundred thousand men, no adequate conception can be formed. One or two facts may help to give a faint idea of it. Mr. [Henry] Culp's meadow, below Cemetery Hill—a lot of near twenty acres—was so thickly strown with Rebel dead, that Mr. Culp declared he "could have walked across it without putting foot upon the ground." Upwards of three hundred Confederates were buried in that fair field in one hole . . . Below Round Top, near five hundred sons of the South lie promiscuously heaped in one huge sepulchre. Of the quantities of iron, of the wagon-loads of arms, knap-sacks, haversacks, and clothing, which strewed the country, no estimate can be made. Government set a guard over these, and for weeks officials were busy in gathering together all the more valuable spoils. The harvest of bullets was left for the citizens to glean. Many of the poorer people did a thriving business picking up these missiles of death, and selling them to dealers; two of whom alone sent to Baltimore fifty tons of lead collected in this way from the battlefield.

"Remarks of Hon. Samuel W. Pennypacker, LL.D., Governor of the Commonwealth, Dedication of the Statue of John Burns of Gettysburg" (July 1, 1903), *Pennsylvania at Gettysburg: Ceremonies at the Dedication of the Monuments*, ed. J.P. Nicholson (Harrisburg, PA, 1904)

As Washington recognized the extraordinary valor of the heroine of Monmouth, so did Lincoln show honor to the hero of Gettysburg. When on the occasion of the dedication of the National Cemetery, Nov. 19, 1863, he visited this field and delivered that immortal address, [John] Burns, along with thousands of others, was introduced to him at night-fall just before he started to an assemblage in the Presbyterian church. The day had been one of splendid pageantry, tho' to the President, moving over the scenes of a sickening carnage, it must have been a day of unspeakable sorrow, but he seems to have forgotten every other consideration in his resolve to do honor to the aged civilian, who defying every peril, had thrown himself upon the altar of his country.

Surrounded and followed by cheering crowds the great-hearted and noble President linked arms with the plain and fearless citizen, and together they walked around Center Square and up Baltimore street, a picturesque contrast, the President towering head and shoulders above the crowd, Burns a fleshy little body vainly attempting to keep step with him, the former having on that morning delivered a speech that will survive until liberty dies, the latter just recovering from wounds, received in a patriotic feat, which has scarcely a parallel—the Chief Magistrate of the Republic and an obscure representative of the common people. And so our national Congress honored him, placing his name by a special act upon the pension roll of the country—that, too, at the very time when the State of Pennsylvania bore him on a similar roll for his services in the war of 1812. And now this grand old Commonwealth, proud of her son, adds to her own laurels by the erection of this monument in commemoration of his superlative heroism.

And we do well, fellow citizens, in rendering here, on the anniversary of his daring feat, this final tribute to the memory of our townsman, who so surprisingly and so justly became one of the most famous characters of the war for the Union. Who can estimate the debt which our nation owes to such a spirit of self-sacrifice and unmeasured devotion, what strength it derives from this species of moral fiber, what independence and security, what majesty and glory accrue to the Republic from a citizenship which in any crisis and at any cost springs to its defense?

Such men, high-minded, self-sacrificing men, "men who know their rights and knowing dare maintain," constitute the life-blood of the State.

The poet sings

> *Ill fares the land, to hastening ills a prey,*
> *Where wealth accumulates and men decay.*

Wealth is accumulating among us at an appalling rate. Let us see to it that men do not decay—for the increase of wealth has seldom failed to result in moral and national decadence. Let us see to it by the spirit of eternal vigilance that America continue[s] to produce a race of men like John Burns, and our rank in the forefront of the great world powers will continue as long as the granite and bronze of this monument, here dedicated to personal heroism and valor.

"Dedication of Monument, 84th Regiment Infantry: Address of Captain Thomas E. Merchant" (September 11, 1889), *Pennsylvania at Gettysburg: Ceremonies at the Dedication of the Monuments*, ed. J.P. Nicholson (Harrisburg, PA, 1904)

It was the greatest of rebellions against the grandest of governments . . . The once soldiers of the Confederacy are entitled, as individuals, to every manly consideration at our hands . . . but their organized bodies have no claim upon us for recognition . . . They have been asking that the war be forgotten, and yet they would keep us daily reminded by the flaunting of the Confederate bars [the Confederate "Stars and Bars" flag].

No monument to treason should have been permitted a place on this or other field, and being here should be returned to the donors, not to be erected elsewhere.

No government is strong enough to glorify treason against itself, nor to encourage it anywhere . . .

There can be no true call for a union of the blue and the gray. Let all don the blue. In place of waiting for the chasm to be closed, flank it and locate upon our side.

"Address of Hon. Charles Devens" [September 17, 1877], *Dedication of the Monument on Boston Common Erected to the Memory of the Men of Boston Who Died in the Civil War* (Boston, 1877)

Nor is this Monument, while it asserts our belief in the fidelity of these men, in any sense unkind or ungenerous towards those with whom they were engaged in deadly strife . . . Whatever we may think of their cause, that as a people they believed in it cannot fairly be questioned. Men do not sacrifice life and property without stint or measure except in the faith that they are right . . . and have a right to have their bravery and sincerity admitted, even if more cannot be conceded. The great conflict . . . has established forever, if the force of arms can establish anything,

that the Republic is one and indivisible, and amid the roar of battle and the clash of arms the institution of slavery, which divided us as a nation, which made of the States two classes diverse and discordant, has passed away . . . As we consider all the woes which must have followed the dismemberment of the Union, as we contemplate the vast gain for peace, freedom, and equality by the emancipation of the subject race from slavery and the dominant race itself from the corrupting influence of this thraldom, who shall say that we have any right to deplore the past except with mitigated grief?

"Address at the Dedication of the Virginia Memorial at Gettysburg, Friday, June 8, 1917, by Leigh Robinson," *Southern Historical Society Papers* 42 (September 1917)

It is my cherished faith that what is true of Lee is true of the cause we served, which pierced with wounds for us is sacred; and crowned with thorns for us is holy. The glowing pieties which laid down lives, laid down fortunes, laid down all save sacred honor, will grow as time grows. The story of our arms is safe. Military schools abroad impart to their pupils for their guidance the valiant passions of our comrades and their captains. Our adversaries are willing to concede the prowess which gives point to their own. There is no need to defend the unassailed—still less the unassailable.

There is a voice which says: All this heroism was "ghastly error;" heroism for a cause which was intrinsically false—false to the rights of man. They who so speak think all too lightly of a cause hallowed by such sacrifice. In memorials, like the present, is felt the refutation of the charge. There are things too high, too deep, too appealing to the genuine grace of sympathy, for memory to be other than a shrine. Better proof could not be offered of the truth of a cause, than the truth to it before our eyes today. There is in constancy to conviction, a dignity it is instinctive to respect . . .

Not by fighting, but by famine, was resistance to be subdued; by war to fireside and field; until, by want of food, strength to resist should be quite vanquished—subjugation by strangulation . . . For this the alleged justification was the ill treatment of the Southern slaves by the Southern masters to whom by Old and New England the slave ancestry had been so industriously sold . . . With some diffidence I will say: If the service of the slave had been compulsory, it was a compulsion which had liberated from degradation . . . Southern slavery will hold up the noblest melioration of an inferior race, of which history can take note—the government of a race incapable of self-government, for a greater benefit to the governed than to the governors.

Lyndon Baines Johnson, "The Vice-President at Gettysburg" (May 30, 1963), *Civil Service Journal* 4 (July-September 1963)

On this hallowed ground, heroic deeds were performed and eloquent words were spoken a century ago.

We, the living, have not forgotten—and the world will never forget—the deeds or the words of Gettysburg. We honor them now as we join on this Memorial Day of 1963 in a prayer for permanent peace of the world and fulfillment of our hopes for universal freedom and justice.

We are called to honor our own words of reverent prayer with resolution in the deeds we must perform to preserve peace and the hope of freedom.

We keep a vigil of peace around the world.

Until the world knows no aggressors, until the arms of tyranny have been laid down, until freedom has risen up in every land, we shall maintain our vigil to make sure our sons who died on foreign fields shall not have died in vain.

As we maintain the vigil of peace, we must remember that justice is a vigil, too—a vigil we must keep in our own streets and schools and among the lives of all our people—so that those who died here on their native soil shall not have died in vain.

One hundred years ago, the slave was freed.

One hundred years later, the Negro remains in bondage to the color of his skin.

The Negro today asks justice.

We do not answer him—we do not answer those who lie beneath this soil—when we reply to the Negro by asking, "Patience."

It is empty to plead that the solution to the dilemmas of the present rests on the hands of the clock. The solution is in our hands. Unless we are willing to yield up our destiny of greatness among the civilizations of history, Americans—white and Negro together—must be about the business of resolving the challenge which confronts us now.

Our nation found its soul in honor on these fields of Gettysburg one hundred years ago. We must not lose that soul in dishonor now on the fields of hate.

To ask for patience from the Negro is to ask him to give more of what he has already given enough. But to fail to ask of him—and of all Americans—perseverance within the processes of a free and responsible society would be to fail to ask what the national interest requires of all its citizens.

The law cannot save those who deny it but neither can the law serve any who do not use it. The history of injustice and inequality is a history of disuse of the law. Law has not failed—and is not failing. We as a nation have failed ourselves by not trusting the law and by not using the law to gain sooner the ends of justice which law alone serves . . .

If it is empty to ask Negro or white for patience, it is not empty—it is merely honest—to ask perseverance. Men may build barricades—and others may hurl themselves against those barricades—but what would happen at the barricades would yield no answers. The answers will only be wrought by our perseverance together. It is deceit to promise more as it would be cowardice to demand less.

In this hour, it is not our respective races which are at stake—it is our nation. Let those who care for their country come forward, North and South, white and Negro, to lead the way through this moment of challenge and decision. The Negro says, "Now." Others say, "Never." The voice of responsible Americans—the voice of those who died here and the great man who spoke here—their voices say, "Together." There is no other way.

Until justice is blind to color, until education is unaware of race, until opportunity is unconcerned with the color of men's skins, emancipation will be a proclamation but not a fact. To the extent that the proclamation of emancipation is not fulfilled in fact, to that extent we shall have fallen short of assuring freedom to the free.

Gettysburg Order of Battle

Listed by corps, then by divisions and commanders within that corps, along with brigade commanders for each brigade within a division, plus artillery

ARMY *of the* POTOMAC

Maj.-Gen. George Gordon Meade

1st CORPS: Maj.-Gen. John F. Reynolds

1. Brig.-Gen. *James Samuel Wadsworth*—Meredith ("Iron Brigade"), Cutler
2. Brig.-Gen. *John Cleveland Robinson*—Paul, Baxter
3. Maj.-Gen. *Abner Doubleday*—Rowley, Stone, Stannard

   Artillery Brigade: Col. *Charles Shiels Wainwright*

2nd CORPS: Maj.-Gen. Winfield Scott Hancock

1. Brig.-Gen. *John Curtis Caldwell*—Cross, Kelly ("Irish Brigade"), Zook, Brooke
2. Brig.-Gen. *John Gibbon*—Harrow, Webb, Hall
3. Brig.-Gen. *Alexander Hays*—Carroll, Smyth, Willard

   Artillery Brigade: Capt. *John Gardner Hazard*

3rd CORPS: Maj.-Gen. Daniel Edgar Sickles

1. Maj.-Gen. *David Bell Birney*—Graham, Ward, de Trobriand
2. Brig.-Gen. *Andrew Atkinson Humphreys*—Carr, Brewster, Burling

   Artillery Brigade: Capt. *George E. Randolph*

5TH CORPS: Maj.-Gen. George Sykes

1. Brig.-Gen. *James Barnes* —Tilton, Sweitzer, Vincent
2. Brig.-Gen. *Romeyn Beck Ayres*—Day, Burbank, Weed
3. "Pa. Reserve Division" Brig.-Gen. *Samuel Wylie Crawford*—McCandless, Fisher

   Artillery Brigade: Capt. *Augustus P. Martin*

6TH CORPS: Maj.-Gen. John Sedgwick

1. Brig.-Gen. *Horatio G. Wright*—Torbert, Bartlett, Russell
2. Brig.-Gen. *Albion Parris Howe*—Grant, Neill
3. Brig.-Gen. *John Newton*—Shaler, Eustis, Wheaton

   Artillery Brigade: Col. *Charles Henry Tompkins*

11TH CORPS: Maj.-Gen. Oliver Otis Howard

1. Brig.-Gen. *Francis Channing Barlow*—Von Gilsa, Ames
2. Brig.-Gen. *Adolf von Steinwehr*—Coster, Smith
3. Maj.-Gen. *Carl Schurz*—Schimmelfennig, Krzyzanowski

   Artillery Brigade: Maj. *Thomas W. Osborn*

12TH CORPS: Maj.-Gen. Henry Warner Slocum

1. Brig.-Gen. *Alpheus Starkey Williams*—McDougall, Lockwood, Ruger
2. "White Star": Brig.-Gen. *John White Geary*—Candy, Kane, Greene

   Artillery Brigade: 1st Lt. *Edward Duchman Muhlenberg*

CAVALRY CORPS: Maj.-Gen. Alfred Pleasonton

1. Brig.-Gen. *John Buford*—Gamble, Devin, Merritt
2. Brig.-Gen. *David McMurtrie Gregg*—McIntosh, Gregg
3. Brig.-Gen. *Hugh Judson Kilpatrick*—Farnsworth, Custer

   Horse Artillery: Capt. *James Madison Robertson,* Capt. *John Caldwell Tidball*

RESERVE ART: Brig.-Gen. Robert Ogden Tyler

1. 1st Regular Art B: Capt. *Dunbar Richard Ransom*
2. 1st Volunteer Art B: Lt.-Col. *Freeman McGilvery*

3. 2nd Volunteer Art B: Capt. *Elijah D. Taft*
4. 3rd Volunteer Art B: Capt. *James F. Huntington*
5. 4th Volunteer Art B: Capt. *Robert H. Fitzhugh*

ARMY *of* NORTHERN VIRGINIA

Gen. Robert Edward Lee

Brig.-Gen. *William Nelson Pendleton* (Reserve Artillery)—Escort: 39th VA Cav Batn. (cos. A & C)

LONGSTREET'S CORPS: Lt.-Gen. James Longstreet

1. Maj.-Gen. *Lafayette McLaws*—Kershaw, Semmes, Barksdale, Wofford
   Artillery: Col. *Henry Coalter Cabell*
2. Maj.-Gen. *George E. Pickett*—Garnett, Armistead, Kemper
   Artillery: Maj. *James Dearing*
3. Maj.-Gen. *John Bell Hood*—G.T. Anderson, Law, Robertson, Benning
   Artillery: Maj. *Mathias Winston Henry*, Maj. *John C. Haskell*
   Reserve Artillery: Col. *James B. Walton*

EWELL'S CORPS: Lt.-Gen. Richard Stoddert Ewell

1. Maj.-Gen. *Jubal A. Early*—Hays ("Louisiana Tigers"), Smith, Avery, Gordon
   Artillery: Lt.-Col. *Hilary Pollard Jones*
2. Maj.-Gen. *Edward "Allegheny Ed" Johnson*—Steuart, Walker ("Stonewall Brigade"), J.M. Jones, Williams
   Artillery: Lt.-Col. *R. Snowden Andrews* (*w.*, June 15), Maj. *Joseph White Latimer*
3. Maj.-Gen. *Robert Emmett Rodes*—Daniel, Doles, Iverson, Ramseur, O'Neal
   Artillery: Lt.-Col. *Thomas Henry Carter*
   Reserve Artillery: Col. *John Thompson Brown*

HILL'S CORPS: Lt.-Gen. Ambrose Powell Hill

1. Maj.-Gen. *Richard Heron Anderson*—Wilcox, Mahone, Wright, Posey, Lang

   Artillery: Lt.-Col. *A.S. Cotts*

2. Maj.-Gen. *Henry Heth*—Pettigrew, Archer, Davis, Brockenbrough

   Artillery: Lt.-Col. *John Jameson Garnett*

3. Maj.-Gen. *William Dorsey Pender*—Lane, Thomas, Scales, Perrin

   Artillery: Maj. *William Thomas Poague*
   Reserve Artillery: Col. *Reuben Lindsay Walker*

STUART'S CAVALRY DIVISION: Maj.-Gen. James Ewell Brown Stuart

Cav. Brigade:

1. Brig.-Gen. *Wade Hampton III*
2. Brig.-Gen. *Beverly Holcombe Robertson*
3. Brig.-Gen. *Fitzhugh Lee*
4. Brig.-Gen. *Albert Gallatin Jenkins*
5. Col. *John Randolph Chambliss*
6. Brig.-Gen. *William Edmondson Jones*
7. Imboden's Command: Brig.-Gen. *John Daniel Imboden*

   Horse Art: Cav. D: Maj. *Robert Franklin Beckham*

INDEX

UNFINISHED RAILROAD
Chambersburg Pike
HERR'S RIDGE
OAK HILL
Forney
McLean
Herr's Tavern
Spangler
MCPHERSON'S RIDGE
OAK RIDGE
Hagy
County Almshouse
Herr
RR CUTS
McPherson
Herbst Woods
Penn. College
Seminary
SEMINARY RIDGE
Willoughby Run
Black Horse Tavern
Fairfield Road
Evergreen Cemetery
Zeigler
Bliss
Brian
Leister
Angle
Copse
Pitzer's Run
Codori
CEMETERY RIDGE
Taneytown Road
Spangler
Klingle
Sherfy
Marsh Creek
Pitzer Schoolhouse
Peach Orchard
Trostle
STONY HILL
Rose
Wheatfield
LITTLE ROUND TOP
DEVIL'S DEN
Emmitsburg Road
Bushman
ROUND TOP
BUSHMAN HILL
Plum Run